Advance Pra

Winning Fantasy Baseball

"Larry is possibly the best fantasy baseball player in the world."

—Nando Di Fino, senior fantasy writer, CBSsports.com

"Larry is almost certainly Earth's greatest fantasy player. His record of success in experts leagues is, at this point, ridiculous. The seasons Larry played at ages 50–54 are the fantasy equivalent of the games Barry Bonds played at ages 35–39. We should be testing him regularly . . . or at least that's what I thought before reading *Winning Fantasy Baseball*. It turns out Larry is just a master tactician. Anyone of any skill level will be a better player after reading this book."

—Andy Behrens, fantasy writer, *Yahoo! Sports*

"Larry should be your E.F. Hutton for fantasy baseball advice; when he talks, you should listen. While other guys are out talking on radio, television, and social media, Larry is reviewing the numbers and putting the moves in place to win experts leagues and competitions year after year after year. Teddy Roosevelt was talking about Larry when he said to speak softly and carry a big stick. He has a totem pole's worth of league titles and the respect of everyone in the fantasy baseball industry."

—Jason Collette, fantasy writer, *RotoWire*

"Larry challenges some of your assumptions about how to be successful in this game. His track record demands your attention, and this book demanded mine. There are many ways to win a league, but to consistently win a league is something else. Larry provides a road map to do so that can take any player to a new level."

—Jason Grey, professional scout for the Tampa Bay Rays, and three-time Tout Wars and two-time LABR champion

"I've played against Larry. I'm glad I read his book. Now I have a chance to beat him."

—Alex Patton, founder of pattonandco.com and
author of six books on fantasy baseball

"It's all about winning, and all Larry Schechter does is win."

—Ron Shandler, columnist for *USA Today*, author of
Baseball Forecaster, and founder of BaseballHQ.com

"With its game smarts wryly explained using real-world examples from Schechter's long and successful experience, this book should become for fantasy baseball players what Doyle Brunson's SuperSystem became for poker players: the indispensable guide to understanding the game and winning. The only drawback was that I didn't get to bed until 3:30 A.M. because I couldn't stop reading it."

—Patrick Davitt, BaseballHQ.com

"This is good stuff. I hadn't thought about mixed auctions the way Schechter does. All I knew was that the pricing structure is not rational. I can't believe how stupid I have been not to see it his way."

—Gene McCaffrey, founder, Wise Guy Baseball

"The part about how position scarcity can be overrated is very clearly articulated—a lot of fantasy blogs try to make that point, but don't make it as clear as Schechter does. This book rocks!"

—Michael Cohen, former writer for *CDM Sports* fantasy baseball
hotsheet and *Fantasy Baseball Index* magazine.

"Outstanding statistical and dollar value analysis. The position scarcity piece was unique and enlightening, almost groundbreaking."

—Dennis LePore, head writer and editor, *The Sandlot Shrink*

"I was impressed by the depth of Schechter's observations, analyses, and recommendations. If you are not enjoying consistent roto success, this book will show you why."

—Mike Lombardo, three-time NL Tout Wars champion

LARRY SCHECHTER

Winning

Fantasy

Baseball

SECRET STRATEGIES OF A
NINE-TIME NATIONAL CHAMPION

EMERALD
BOOK CO.

Published by Emerald Book Company
Austin, TX
www.emeraldbookcompany.com

Distributed by Emerald Book Company

For ordering information or special discounts for bulk purchases, please contact Emerald Book Company at PO Box 91869, Austin, TX 78709, 512.891.6100.

Design, Cover Design, and composition by Greenleaf Book Group LLC
Cover image copyright R. Gino Santa Maria, 2013. Used under license from Shutterstock.com

Cataloging-in-Publication data

Schechter, Larry.
   Winning fantasy baseball : secret strategies of a nine-time national champion /
Larry Schechter.—1st ed.
   p. ; cm.
   Issued also as an ebook.
   ISBN: 978-1-937110-57-4
   1. Fantasy baseball (Game). I. Title.
GV1202.F33 S34 2014
793.93   2013944434

Part of the Tree Neutral® program, which offsets the number of trees
consumed in the production and printing of this book by taking proactive steps,
such as planting trees in direct proportion to the number of trees used:
www.treeneutral.com

TreeNeutral

Printed in the United States of America on acid-free paper

14 15 16 17 18 19   10 9 8 7 6 5 4 3 2 1

First Edition

Contents

Acknowledgments

I would like to thank Michael Cohen, Gene McCaffrey, and Dennis LePore for their early feedback and encouragement when I wasn't sure if I was actually going to write a book. Thanks also to Todd Zola for our many strategy discussions. And to Ron Shandler for writing a terrific foreword.

Additionally, I'd like to thank Tristan Cockroft, Mike Gianella, and Greg Ambrosius, as well as everyone who provided a review or quote for the book cover and website.

Special thanks to my editors and designers and the entire staff at Greenleaf Book Group.

Above all, I appreciate my wife, Joanne, my daughter, Talia, and my son, Jared, for all of their help and support, as well as for putting up with my fantasy baseball obsession.

Finally, thanks to Dan Okrent for inventing this game. Damn, I wish I'd thought of it!

Foreword

by Ron Shandler

For several years during the last decade, I used an advertising slogan for my website that said, simply, "It's All About Winning." The supporting argument was that it didn't matter how accurate your projections were, or how quantitatively rigorous your valuation model was, or what draft strategy you employed. All that mattered was that you won.

Well, that's what Larry Schechter does. He just wins.

He's never played major league baseball. He's not a media insider. He's not a full-time baseball analyst.

But it doesn't matter, because all he does is win.

He's won big money in national high-stakes competitions. He's "owned" the Tout Wars national experts leagues. He started by winning three mixed-league titles in a row. Then after getting "promoted" into the American League–only contest (the league profiled in the *Fantasyland* book and movie), he took home titles in his first three tries.

These are leagues in which the other owners *are* media insiders and full-time baseball analysts. These are the leagues I helped create in 1998 as an exhibition for the most talented professional experts in the industry. Frankly, we are stumped as to Larry's stranglehold on us.

If it happened once, we could write it off as luck. If he pulled off the feat twice, we could still probably discount it. But when you keep winning again and again—six times now, in nine tries—there has to be something more to it.

Several years ago, I decided to research the elements that contribute to consistent success. I polled a dozen of the most prolific fantasy champions over the past few decades and asked them to rank six variables, ranging from the "best in-draft strategy" (which finished first) to "most accurate projections" (which finished last).

Larry was included in that group. When he sent me his rankings, he added this comment:

I would add a variable to your list. One of the big reasons for my success is *taking the time* to be very prepared for an auction/draft, and *taking time* during the year to stay current on news, contextual elements, making roster moves, free-agent bidding, etc. Obviously, just spending a lot of time for the sake of spending time doesn't do any good. You need to work smart. One of the reasons I have better in-draft strategy, better sense of value, etc., is because I *take the time* to figure it all out.

I hadn't considered *putting in the time* as a variable worth including in my study. But after I reprinted Larry's note in a follow-up, I received a flood of positive response.

I think Larry sees things more holistically than many of us. While we tend to get glued to the minutia, he finds a way to integrate those news bites into a higher-level decision-making process.

His success—and this book—is proof of that.

At one point, Larry presents a list of more than 30 popular winning tactics and strategies. As I read through them, I kept thinking, "I agree with that, don't agree with that, tried it, use it, never done it," etc. Still, it was a fairly comprehensive list of draft approaches that most other experts espouse.

At the bottom of the list, Larry writes, "I think most of the above is nonsense."

I did a double take when I read that. Many of those were proven strategies!

But I had to keep reminding myself that we don't play this game to find the best strategies. We play this game to win.

To be honest, as I read this book there were some items that I had to quibble with. Some of the assertions conflict with concepts I've been using for the past three decades. Some of them have brought me titles.

But then you have to look at Larry's track record of fantasy baseball championships. It's better than mine, and in fact, better than any expert who currently plays or has *ever played* in Tout Wars. So you simply can't dismiss anything he says, even if it sounds counterintuitive.

Because it's all about winning, and all Larry Schechter does is win.

Ron Shandler is a columnist for USA Today, *author of* Baseball Fore-caster, *and founder of BaseballHQ.com.*

CHAPTER 1

The Longest "Strategies of Champions" Article Ever

Peter Kreutzer is the editor-in-chief of *Fantasy Baseball Guide* magazine and a fellow Tout Wars competitor. For several years, his magazine has run articles called "Strategies of Champions." Written by the winners of some of the experts leagues, the articles are 650-word essays on how the person won that year. When I won Tout Wars in 2005, 2006, and 2007, Peter asked me each time to write an article.

It was an honor to be asked to write these articles, but I found it a difficult experience. First, in just 650 words you can't get into any detail; second, I wasn't sure how much detail I wanted to get into anyway. I didn't necessarily want to give away any of my actual strategies and potentially lose a competitive edge. So I simply wrote 650 words of general information and perhaps gave out a tidbit or two of helpful information.

But I knew that to actually write about my strategy and how I won Tout Wars in a complete and thorough fashion would have taken dozens of pages. And if I included everything from start to finish—projecting player stats for the season, converting those stats into a dollar value, the auction strategy, and the in-season management, it would take even more. It would probably take an entire book.

This was when I first got the idea of writing a book. And for some reason I can't explain, the idea appealed to me. "What the heck?" I thought, "Let me just put it all out there. All of my thoughts and strategies, from beginning to end." I had always wanted to write a book, and this was something I felt qualified to write about.

As I told Peter Kreutzer, the title of this book could have been *The Longest "Strategies of Champions" Article Ever*. And no, 650 words were not sufficient. It took about 95,000.

As I began to write, I realized that I would need to examine everything I do and why I do it, and not only be able to explain it to others, but in some cases also prove the validity. It occurred to me that having to do this would also be very beneficial. So I added as one of my goals for this book to make myself a better player.

And boy, did I ever uncover some areas where there were flaws in my theories. And there were some myths I believed that aren't actually true. And there were things I didn't know and am very glad now that I've learned. Despite my success, I did, in fact, have a lot of room for improvement. Having completed this book, I feel more prepared and knowledgeable than ever.

Fantasy Baseball History

There were some early versions of fantasy baseball, such as the Strat-O-Matic board game, that used major league players' actual performance from prior seasons. But modern fantasy baseball, also known as Rotisserie baseball, was invented in 1980 by magazine writer/editor Daniel Okrent, who came up with the idea on a flight to Texas. It is named after the New York City restaurant La Rotisserie Française, where Okrent and the game's other first participants often met for lunch.

In the early days, before the advent of computers and the Internet, participants would often have to track and calculate the leagues' standings by hand. Participants would need to wait until the box scores appeared in the newspaper to find out how their players had fared the night before. I remember having to wait to get the standings in the mail several days after a stat week had ended. But now almost all leagues have their stats and standings calculated automatically by computer. Most even have *live standings* that can be updated within a few minutes of an event occurring on the baseball field.

In those early days, not many people knew what fantasy baseball was. But it has grown into a huge industry with millions of players. The first time it really hit me how big this game had become was in 2007. I was visiting relatives in Albuquerque. My nephew, who was 13 years old at the time, said he'd heard I play fantasy baseball. He told me that he did, as well. "I've got four teams in Yahoo leagues," he said.

"Wow," I said, "You're in four leagues? That's a lot."

"Well," he said, "there are also my eight ESPN teams."

A 13-year-old boy had 12 teams. My God, I thought, this hobby has really become huge. It used to be people would look at you with a blank stare if you mentioned fantasy baseball. Now it's more likely they'll tell you they have a team.

Later in 2007, my daughter had to pick an elective for the second semester of fifth grade. The choices were dancing, improvisation, or fantasy baseball. She chose fantasy baseball. Her teacher, Mr. Schoemer, was impressed to learn that I had won Tout Wars. And so was one of her classmates. "Wow," he said, "you must be a millionaire!" I had to explain to him that no, winning Tout Wars didn't make me a millionaire.

According to the most recent data, fantasy sports generated $1.9 billion in 2008. In 2011 the Fantasy Sports Trade Association (FSTA) hired its own federal lobbyist and started a political action committee. A study commissioned by the FSTA estimated that in 2011 almost 20% of males in the U.S. and Canada age 12 or older had played fantasy sports in the past year. Also 8% of females in the U.S. and 5% in Canada played. That's an estimated total of 32 million people.

In 2008 CDM Sports sued Major League Baseball Advanced Media, a limited partnership of the club owners of major league baseball, for the rights to use publically available statistics without having to pay a licensing fee. The case went all the way to the Supreme Court and was won by CDM. Three justices recused themselves because they played in a fantasy baseball league comprised of current and past court personnel. Two other justices were also in the league but didn't recuse themselves.

And by the way, my nephew from Albuquerque is Alex Bregman. He was the 2010 USA Baseball Player of the Year. Past winners include Stephen Strasburg, Justin Smoak, Ryan Zimmerman, and Ben Sheets. Alex was the youngest winner ever, at just 16. He's currently playing for LSU, where he was named the 2013

National Freshman Player of the Year. So, keeper league players, go out and grab him if it's not already too late!

How to Use This Book

This book is for total beginners, experts, and everyone in between. If you've never played before, you will learn everything you need to do from beginning to end. And I'm confident that even the experienced and successful will also benefit. I have covered all major formats of play—auctions, snake drafts, salary-cap, and keeper leagues.

Every year, many websites and magazines publish player values for the upcoming season, as well as lists of sleepers and players to avoid. Having a good set of player values is definitely a requirement in order to do well. And this book does cover how to project a player's raw stats and then convert those into a specific value.

But this is only the tip of the iceberg. The real keys to my success have always been my auction and draft strategy as well as in-season management. I doubt I've ever won a league primarily because I had a better set of player dollar values than everyone else.

You don't necessarily need to read this entire book. Chapter 2, "Fantasy Basics for Beginners," is meant only for those who are brand new to fantasy baseball. And, for example, if you have no interest in an auction league, there's no need to read the chapters that deal with auctions.

One exception is that even if you aren't planning to make your own player stat projections, I suggest you read chapter 5 anyway. It gives tips on how to best use the stats and values you see published. That chapter also explains why it's important to use your own value formula. If you don't already use your own formula, I highly recommend that you start doing so. It's a little complicated to understand and set up, but once you have it, it's easy to use and update each year.

While it's not necessary to read the chapters in exactly the order presented, I suggest you read through chapter 4 before you start skipping around. Chapters 3 and 4 (as well as chapter 2 for beginners) lay a foundation for some of the principles discussed in later chapters.

Most of the information in all the chapters also applies to keeper leagues. I've added a separate chapter at the end that includes some additional information that applies only to keeper leagues.

Many of the principles I discuss also apply to fantasy football, basketball, and other sports. So, for example, if you don't participate in fantasy baseball snake drafts but you are in fantasy football snake drafts, I suggest you read the snake draft chapter, because a lot will apply to football. Same for auctions and salary-cap style.

Some of my methods are time-consuming. You aren't necessarily going to have the time or the desire to do everything I do. But many of my suggestions and strategies are fairly simple and not time-consuming. And for some of the time-consuming ones, I give advice on how you can take shortcuts. Some things I'll say may seem a bit complex at first, until you digest them. The good news, though, is that I'm not a math major or rocket scientist, so I don't get too complex. (One day my high school math teacher showed us a formula simply because it plotted a fluegelhorn around the x-axis. I quit calculus the next day.)

Make no mistake, though, putting in time and effort will reap dividends, as long as you work smart—and don't just spend time for the sake of spending time. There are times I've been at an auction or draft and heard people say, "I'm not really prepared, I'm just going to wing it." This has happened even at experts leagues and leagues where you had to pay money to enter. I don't get this. If you aren't going to prepare, why bother? I would never dream of not being fully prepared. As you'll see in this book, that is one of the big keys to my success.

CHAPTER 2

Fantasy Basics
for Beginners

If you already know the difference between a 4×4 and a 5×5
league . . . an auction and a draft . . . Rotisserie scoring and Points
style . . . and a keeper league and a redraft league, then you probably want to skip this chapter. This chapter covers the basics and
is designed for people who are very new to fantasy baseball.

The basic idea behind fantasy baseball is that you get to
own your own team of actual major league players. When they
accumulate stats—such as home runs, stolen bases, wins, saves,
etc.—in real life, you also get those stats for your team. Most fantasy leagues choose their teams before opening day of the real
major league season and then last for the entire 162-game major
league schedule.

Scoring Systems

There are three ways to determine the winner of a fantasy league:

1. *Rotisserie scoring.* Each team is ranked from top to bottom in each scoring category. For example, if there are 12 teams in a league, the team with the most home runs at the end of the year gets 12 points for that category; the next highest total gets 11 points, then 10 points, etc. The point totals for each category are then added up to give a grand total and determine the winner.

2. *Points style.* This scoring gives you a certain amount of points for each achievement, such as one point for hitting a single, two for a double, three for a triple, four for a home run, ten for a pitcher getting a win or a save, etc.

3. *Head-to-Head (H2H).* This competition generally pits one team against another for a weekly game. Opponents rotate each week in a round-robin system. The scoring can be Points style or Rotisserie scoring where the team that wins the most individual categories is declared the winner. At the end of the week, one team gets a win and one gets a loss.

Many head-to-head leagues will have a *regular season* that lasts 22–24 weeks, at which time a certain number of teams with the best won-loss record advance to the playoffs. The playoffs are single-elimination matchups that occur during the last two to four weeks of the actual major league regular season.

Roster Size

Almost all fantasy games include both hitters and pitchers. A typical roster requirement would include 14 hitters and nine pitchers, with the following positions:

> › 2 catchers

> › 1 first baseman

> › 1 second baseman

> › 1 shortstop

> › 1 third baseman

> › 1 corner infielder (either a first or third baseman)

> › 1 middle infielder (either a second baseman or a shortstop)

> › 5 outfielders

> › 1 designated hitter (can be any position except pitcher)

> › 9 pitchers

While the roster shown above is typical, there are many variations. This is an example of a team's starting lineup. In addition, most leagues have a reserve squad of at least four players. These reserves can be moved into the starting lineup as desired.

Commonly a player is eligible at any position in which he appeared a minimum number of games the prior season. Depending on a league's rules, that minimum can be anywhere from five to twenty games.

Most leagues allow lineup changes once per week, at which point you can move players between your starting lineup and reserve squad. Some leagues allow changes midweek or even daily. Also some don't allow any changes. You draft a team and that's your lineup for the entire year.

Selecting Teams

The three most popular formats for selecting players for your team are snake drafts, auctions, and salary cap.

1. *Snake drafts* (also called *straight* or *serpentine* drafts). Draft spots are chosen at random. The team owner with the first pick can select any player he wants, and then the team owner with the second pick chooses someone, etc. The team owner who picked last gets the first pick of the second round, and all teams follow in reverse order of the first round. Then the draft snakes back as the order for round three is the same as the first round, round four is the same as round two, etc.

2. *Auction leagues.* Players are put up for bid, one at a time. Each player is sold to the highest bidder. Teams have a total budget, usually $260, to acquire their roster (usually 23 players). Star players will typically sell for as much as $30–45, while scrubs will go for $1. Once teams have filled their starting rosters, there is usually a reserve draft in which the reserves are selected by a snake draft, rather than an auction. It is rare that reserves are chosen by bidding.

3. *Salary cap* (also called *pick-a-player*). Each major league player is assigned a salary by the game operator. Teams may choose any players they want, provided they fill their

required starting lineup with players whose total salaries fit under a salary cap. The goal is to select the players who will produce the most valuable stats relative to their assigned salary. Reserve players can usually be selected with no regard to a salary cap. However, when players are moved in and out of the starting lineup (usually on a weekly basis), the total salary must always remain under the cap.

Fantasy leagues that use all major league players are called *mixed leagues* and typically have 12 to 15 teams per league. *Mono-leagues*, which use only American League (AL) or National League (NL) players, typically have between 10 and 13 teams.

Logistics

People often get together in person for their snake draft or auction. Snake drafts are less time-consuming than auctions, because no bidding is involved.

Snake drafts can easily be done online, through various websites or Skype. Auctions can be done with Skype or online, but it is more difficult.

For a salary-cap game, participants do not get together to select teams. A player selects his team whenever he wants, prior to the entry deadline (usually opening day of the season), and submits his entry online or by mail or email.

Various companies offer online management services for fantasy leagues. They will calculate the statistics and league standings each day, as well as provide an online place for teams to make their roster moves. Some game operators provide their own websites for this purpose.

Comparing the Formats

Some people prefer the snake draft, because when it's their turn they can simply take whoever they think is the best player available. Some don't like this format because they don't have an equal chance to get every player. For example, if Miguel Cabrera is clearly one of the top few players entering the season and you randomly draw the ninth draft spot, you will not be able to get Cabrera. This is why some people prefer an auction. Everyone has an equal chance to buy every player. If you're willing to spend the money, you can get Cabrera.

With a salary-cap game you don't have to worry about someone drafting players before you do, or outbidding you. You can take whichever players you want, as long as they fit under the cap. This is a nice thing. The downside is that unlike draft and auction leagues, if you own Bryce Harper, you're not the only one. Harper may be owned by 10%, 30%, 50%, or even more of all the teams you're competing against. This makes it less advantageous when he hits a grand slam, but also less damaging when he slumps.

Stat Categories

While Points-style games give credit for singles, doubles, triples, etc., the founders of Rotisserie scoring started with four hitting and four pitching categories:

HITTERS

› Batting average
› Home runs

› Runs batted in

› Stolen bases

PITCHERS

› Wins

› Saves

› ERA (earned run average)

› WHIP (walks and hits / innings pitched)

This original format is called 4×4. Most leagues have now added a fifth category, runs for hitters and strikeouts for pitchers. This is called 5×5.

Some leagues have replaced batting average with *on-base average*, which includes walks.

Some leagues have gone to a 6×6 or even 7×7 format. The 6×6 format typically adds *OPS* (a hitter's on-base percentage plus slugging percentage) and *holds* for pitchers. The seventh categories for 7×7 can be anything.

Free Agents

All players not drafted or bought at auction are considered free agents. There are three common methods used for a team to acquire a free agent, at which time they need to either release a player or place a player on their disabled list.

1. *First come, first served.* Some leagues allow free agents to be picked up at any time. Whoever does it first gets the player.

2. *Reverse order of standings.* Each week teams submit claims on who they want. Players claimed by multiple teams are awarded to the team lowest in the standings.

3. *Blind bidding.* The most competitive leagues use this system. Even many leagues that use a snake draft to create their teams, where there is no bidding, still use the bidding process for free agents.

These leagues will give each team a budget, such as $100 or $1,000 for the season. Each week teams submit a secret bid on any player(s) they want. The player is awarded to the highest bidder. (Ties are usually awarded to the team that is currently lowest in the standings.)

For a salary-cap game, there is no competition for free agents. You are usually allowed a limited number of times during the year when you can add any player not currently on your roster and must release another player.

Redraft, Keeper & Dynasty Leagues

Some fantasy leagues are called *redraft leagues* because you play for one major league season and then it's all over. The next spring you acquire a brand-new team. Some leagues—called *keeper leagues*—allow you to keep all or part of your roster from one year to the next. Players who are not kept by their team are put up for auction or draft. You must plan not only for this year, but also for the future.

Keeper leagues can make minor league players more relevant. You may have a reserve roster with as many as 17 or so spots, which means you can track and roster minor leaguers and college players with good future potential. In a redraft league, a minor leaguer is useless unless he has a chance to be called up and produce in the major leagues during the current season.

The difference between a keeper league and a *dynasty league* is that the keeper league usually involves keeping a smaller portion of your players. Most keeper leagues have some type of salary value or *contract* associated with each player, so you can choose to keep a core group of who you think the best deals are. Dynasty leagues usually have you keep most or all of your players.

Trades

Just as in real baseball, most draft and auction leagues allow trades between teams. There is usually a trade deadline, typically around the end of August. In a keeper league, some teams will decide later in the year that they can't compete for the title and will seek to trade an aging or expensive player for cheaper young talent that may help them in future years.

In redraft and auction leagues where no trading is allowed, it is important to acquire a balanced team because you will be unable to trade excess for your needs. If you have way too much power and need speed, it's difficult to correct that solely via free agents.

Salary-cap leagues do not allow trading between teams, but it is easier to fix roster imbalances. For example, you can use a free-agent move to release a star slugger and replace him with a top stolen-base threat.

National Contests and Prize Money

Many fantasy leagues, especially keeper leagues, are comprised of a group of friends and recruit new players as needed by word of mouth. Some groups play solely for bragging rights, while others might chip in money to buy the winner a trophy and/or to create a prize pool.

Some leagues are run by major companies such as ESPN, CBS Sports, and Yahoo. These leagues are usually free or very low cost. They are easy to join, and you don't need to find friends to play; you will be paired up with others to form a league. The downside of these leagues is that because they are free and easy to join, there is not a great deal of commitment made by the competitors. Many people will stop actively managing their teams during the year.

Some leagues are run by companies who charge an entry fee to join and offer prize money. Aside from competing in a league of 12–15 or so teams, many of these companies hold an overall competition, in which everyone in all of their leagues compete against one another for a national grand prize. Some are high-stakes leagues, in which the cost to enter can range from $500 to $1,000 or more. In addition to the league prizes, the overall grand prize can range from $25,000 to $100,000 or more.

Keeper leagues can't be pitted against other keeper leagues to form an overall competition. They are limited to just their own league.

In-Season Leagues

Most leagues form their teams prior to opening day and last the entire regular season. There are some exceptions whereby the league will form teams after opening day and begin the competition from that day forward. There are also some that have a *second-half* league; teams will be formed around the All-Star break and compete against one another from then forward.

Finally, there are some that hold a playoff competition. Once the MLB regular season has ended, owners will select which players they think will do the best during the playoffs. Most of these leagues tend to be salary-cap style—or even pick-a-player with no regard to salary—because it's impractical to hold a draft or auction during the short amount of time between the end of the season and the start of the playoffs.

A new trend in fantasy sports is companies that offer a daily or weekly game. You pick a team and compete, usually for cash prizes, in a contest that lasts for just one day or one week.

CHAPTER 3

General Auction & Snake Draft Strategy

How to get the most value possible at your auction or draft depends on the format you play. The strategy for a mono-league auction is different than the strategy for a mixed-league auction. And a snake draft is completely different than an auction. Therefore I cover each format with its own chapter.

However, there are some elements of strategy that are similar for all formats. Rather than duplicate them in all three chapters, I'm including them here. The following information applies to both types of auctions as well as snake drafts. (The next chapter has some additional strategy that applies only to auctions.)

It's all about value. I will say this repeatedly.

Every player has a value. Whether he's a superstar or a backup catcher, everyone has a *specific* value.

Obviously, I'm talking here about *projected* stats and a *projected* value. Whenever I say, "Matt Kemp has a value of $40," what I'm really saying is, "I project Matt Kemp will produce stats that according to my formula will correlate to a value of $40." I won't actually know what his true value is until the season is over and he's produced whatever he produced. But before my draft or auction, I need to make my best guess about what his stats will be. In a sense, what I'm saying is that the *over/under* on what his value will be is $40. If the upcoming season were played ten times or one hundred times, I think his value would average $40 for all of those years.

The goals for all formats of fantasy baseball are the same:

1. Make your best prediction of all player stats for the upcoming season.

2. Translate those stats into a specific value (based on an intelligent formula, not just random guessing).

3. Get the most total value possible at your auction or draft.

4. Manage in-season trades, free-agent acquisition, start/ bench decisions, etc.

Goals 1, 2, and 4 are covered in chapters 5, 6, and 11, respectively. This chapter deals with goal 3.

Let's examine what I mean by "Get the most total value possible at your auction or draft." For a moment, I'm going to use an AL-only auction as an example. However, the principles of everything I say can be applied to the other formats.

In an AL-only auction, with 12 teams and a roster requirement of 23 players, you have a pool of players that includes 168 hitters (14 per team × 12 teams) and 108 pitchers (9 per team × 12 teams). If a value formula is done correctly, these 276 players will have a total dollar value of $3,120 ($260 per team × 12 teams). This means that each team can buy $260 of value for their $260 budget.

If you buy a $20 player for $20, and a $14 player for $14, etc., then you're going to end up with $260 of value. This will give you an average team, and you'll finish in the middle of the pack. (Thinking in terms of a snake draft, if you select a $40 player in the first round, a $30 player in the second round, etc., and so does everyone else, then again you'll have an average team and finish in the middle of the pack.)

So when I say, "Get the most total value possible at your auction or draft," what I really mean is, "Get more value than the average team, so that you can kick everyone's butt and finish first."

Everyone has a different opinion as to each player's value. So if I think I have $260 of value, one of my league competitors may think I only have $245. Another league mate might think I have $252 . . . or $270 . . . or whatever.

Because of the differences of opinion in value, and since you are buying players based on your own opinion, theoretically you should be almost guaranteed to think you've bought more than $260 of value. If you think Robinson Cano is worth $33, and nobody else in your league thinks he's worth more than $30, you should be able to buy him for $31 (or $30). If you do this with five players, and the rest of your acquisitions are at fair value, then you'll have approximately a $10 gain, for a total value of $270. (Everyone else in your league may think you have less than $270, but that's okay.)

Due to the differences of opinion, you're virtually guaranteed to come out ahead. Therefore, at the end of an auction (or snake draft) if you think you only got $260 of value, then you've really screwed up!

If we assume that you should probably get $270–280 just based on the differences of opinion—that means if you leave an auction thinking you have $270–280 of value—even then you're probably only average. Again, you're destined for the middle of the pack. If you happen to have superior player stat projections and/or value formulas, then perhaps you really do have an edge, but I wouldn't count on that.

So the question is what strategy can you use to get $290 of value, or $300, or maybe even more?

I typically finish an auction thinking I've gotten more than $300 in value. And this isn't because I'm making "pie in the sky" projections for players and then buying them. I'm typically conservative in my player projections. In the 2011 Tout Wars, for example, I got $333 of value. That gap is so big that it means if you ask my competitors their opinion, probably none of them would agree I had $333, but most of them would probably agree I had more than $260. In fact, after the auction, one of my league mates told me that I was #1 in his computer's projected standings.

Since everyone is buying players based on their own opinion of value, it's very difficult to have someone else think you have a better team than they do. I *always* leave an auction (or draft) thinking I have the best team. And it seems to me that everyone else should also always feel that way about their team.

Before I discuss my strategy, let's consider some other strategies. Here are some ideas I've heard or read from fantasy players, including many fantasy baseball writers and experts:

> I want to get players with a full-time job, because they'll accumulate stats.

> I target age 24 players, because that's when they can improve.

> I want to get a catcher with a decent batting average so he won't kill my team's average.

> I look at K/BB rate (strikeout-to-walk ratio) for pitchers.

> I like age 27 players because that's the peak year.

> I like getting players in a contract year because they're extra motivated.

> You have to get power from your corner infielders.

> I don't want a guy with a .235 batting average.

> Spend big on middle infielders due to the position scarcity.

> I want to avoid injury risks.

> I avoid Colorado pitchers.

> I won't take Miami pitchers because their offense is so bad they don't get wins.

> I employed a stars-and-scrubs approach.

> Go for value. That means not worrying about hitting/pitching splits or specific categories and instead looking for ways to get the most out of my dollars.

> Don't spend big on players without a track record.

> Don't spend big on players unless they are in their prime.

> Make sure my top starters have strikeout potential.

> Corner the market on stolen bases because they are scarce and I can trade later.

> I look for players coming off a down year because they're usually undervalued.

> Avoid players who had breakouts the year before because they will be overpriced.

> I will go an extra buck or two for high-skilled players in volatile situations.

> I was willing to pay a premium at third base because this year the talent really drops off after the big names.

> For my head-to-head league, I like players who are consistent.

> I won't pay more than $25 for any player.

> Don't pay more than $30 for any player.

> Don't spend more than $19 for any pitcher.

> I planned to spend $55 on Dustin Pedroia and Desmond Jennings.

> If I really like a player, I'm willing to go an extra few bucks to get him.

> Avoid one-category players.

> I look for undervalued players who have a very good chance of outperforming their acquisition price.

I think most of the above is nonsense.

First, every player has a value. A *specific* value. The value takes into account all of the variables listed above, such as does the player have a full-time job? Will he hit .235? Does he have breakout potential? Does he pitch for Colorado or Miami?

If a player is projected to hit .235 it will be reflected in his value. If he's a backup and will only get 150 at bats, this will be reflected in his value. If he pitches for Miami or some other low-scoring team and won't get as many wins as pitching for the Yankees, that is reflected in his value.

If done properly, player projections take into account all relevant factors and predict the most likely stats for all possible outcomes. This includes possible improvement for an age 24 player . . . K/BB rates . . . injury risks . . . and every other relevant piece of information. A well-conceived value formula will then convert those raw statistical projections into a specific value.

Then the only thing left to do is get the best deals possible. As the last strategy above states, "I look for undervalued players who have a very good chance of outperforming their acquisition price." In other words, he's saying "pay less than the projected value."

The quote above is from Nick Minnix of KFFL.com, when writing about his 2010 LABR (League of Alternative Baseball Reality) team.

Well, duh . . . exactly! This idea I completely agree with! If a player is worth $10 and you can get him for $8, that's a good deal. If a player is worth $30 and you can get him for $27, that's a good deal. If a player is worth $3 and you can get him for $1, that's a good deal.

If a player has breakout potential, is worth $15, and you buy him for $16, that's not a good deal.

If a player is worth $25 and you pay $27 because you think the talent at that position drops off the table, that's not a good deal.

If a .235 hitter is worth $5 and you pass on a chance to buy him for $4, and instead you buy a .270 hitter who's worth $11 and you pay $12 to get him, that's not a good deal.

The other strategy mentioned above that has got this concept is "Go for value. That means not worrying about hitting/pitching splits or specific categories and instead looking for ways to get the most out of my dollars." This was Jonah Keri, commenting on his 2008 LABR team.

When he says "Go for value . . . get the most out of my dollars," he's saying exactly what I'm saying.

When Jonah says don't worry "about hitting/pitching splits or specific categories," he's saying something that I disagree with. I do worry about the splits, and the categories, because I want to buy a somewhat balanced team. If you have an imbalanced team, you're going to need to make trades later. And making trades can be easier said than done.

Suppose Jonah is in an NL-only auction, and he goes overboard on starting pitchers because there are too many great deals (in his opinion) to pass up. Later he needs to try to trade a pitcher for a hitter. He has several starting pitchers he can trade, for example:

Pitcher	Auction Price	Jonah's Value
Kershaw	$31	$36
Hamels	$24	$29
Bumgarner	$20	$24
Samardzija	$13	$17
Detwiler	$ 8	$12

When he offers these pitchers for a trade, he will be offered hitters more in line with the auction price, not his value. In other words, nobody else thought Kershaw was worth more than $31, so he's not going to receive more than a $31 hitter for Kershaw. He will be forced to trade Kershaw for a $31 hitter, thus negating the gain he thought he had by buying Kershaw. He might as well have passed up the bargain on Kershaw and instead bought a $31 hitter in the first place.

One of the above strategies says, "Corner the market on stolen bases because they are scarce and I can trade later." What's the point of this? Does this person think that by May or June there'll be so many teams clamoring for speed that someone will offer him $35 of value for his $30 speedster? This happens only rarely, if ever.

If this person "corners the market" by overpaying for the high stolen-base guys, then he's really hurting himself. Besides being imbalanced, he's losing overall value.

Let's look at some of the other strategies:

› "I want to get players with a full-time job, because they'll accumulate stats."

For the 2011 Tout Wars AL league, there were 32 players I projected to have 150–300 at bats, yet their value was $1 or more. Fifteen of them had a value from $3–9.

So part-time players are an important part of the player pool. Since you only have $260 to spend on 23 players, you're almost certainly going to need to buy some players for $1–2. If you can get someone worth $2–3 for your $1, or $3–4 for your $2, that's a good deal.

› "I want to get a catcher with a decent batting average so he won't kill my team's average" and "I don't want a guy with a .235 batting average."

If a catcher has a low average but is worth $1 or more, and you can get him for that price, or less, there's nothing wrong with that. I like to go for a balanced roster, so I would avoid getting a lot of low-average hitters, regardless of position. I would also avoid getting a lot of high-average hitters, because I don't want overkill in any category.

An average of .235 is reflected in the player's value. For the 2011 Tout Wars AL-only auction, I projected Mark Reynolds to hit .229, but because of his power, his total value was $20. I bought him for $19.

› "You have to get power from your corner infielders."

Why? No, you don't!

It's true that corner infielders tend to have more power than middle infielders, but there are some middle infielders, some catchers, and lots of outfielders who have power. Some people think they must get a big power bat, someone who will hit 35–40 home runs. But that's not essential. If you get two guys who hit 20 home runs, as opposed to a 35 and a 5, or a 40 and a zero, you still end up with 40 home runs. Again, it's all about the value. If you can buy a 40-home-run hitter for less than his total value, do it. If not, pass.

The same is true for steals. You don't need to have one of the top few stolen-base threats. A few guys who steal 15–20 are as good as a 45 and a couple of single digits.

› "Spend big on middle infielders due to the position scarcity."

I think the concept of "position scarcity" is mostly nonsense. It usually does apply for catchers, but generally not for any other position. For drafts, you do need to calculate the proper time to select various positions, but you don't need to *overpay* for anyone. I'll discuss this in detail in other chapters of this book.

People who target positions based on the flawed concept of scarcity typically are willing to overspend by $1, $2, or even more to land a top player at the *scarce* positions. They are just wasting those extra dollars and are buying players for more than they're worth, rather than getting a bargain.

› "I employed a stars-and-scrubs approach."

Stars and scrubs means you're buying several top, expensive players and several $1–2 players to compensate for how much you spent on the top guys. There is no inherent advantage or disadvantage to this strategy. If you buy a $40 hitter for $40 and two $1 hitters for $1 each, that's a total of $42 spent for $42 value. If you buy a $20, $12, and $10 hitter for $20, $12, and $10, you still end up with $42 spent for $42 value.

If you are so determined to do stars and scrubs that you overpay for a star, then you'll be losing overall value. I almost never will pay more than $40 for a hitter I think is worth $40. I almost never pay more for any player than I think he's worth. I'll discuss the exceptions in other chapters.

› "I was willing to pay a premium at third base because this year the talent really drops off after the big names."

This is along the lines of "position scarcity." Every time you pay a premium you're losing value. Paying a premium is the *opposite* of what you want, which is a discount.

There are undoubtedly lower-value third basemen, let's say in the $1–9 value range, that you'll be able to buy for $1–9. You won't pay a premium, and you might even get a discount. There's no reason to pay a premium to get a top third baseman. You can use that money to get a fair deal—or perhaps discount—for a top player at another position. What's the difference between getting a $25 third baseman and a $3 outfielder as opposed to a $25 outfielder and a $3 third baseman? Or a $15 outfielder and a $13 third baseman? There is no difference! Except if you overpaid to get the $25 third baseman, then you've wasted money and will lose value elsewhere.

› "For my head-to-head league, I like players who are consistent."

If a player is going to end up with 20 homers and 80 RBIs, it doesn't matter if he spreads it out evenly or is streaky. Even for head-to-head leagues. And really, all hitters are streaky, anyway.

› "I won't pay more than $25 for any player," "Don't pay more than $30 for any player," and "Don't spend more than $19 for any pitcher."

This is primarily a question of risk. Some people don't want to buy very high-priced players, because there's always a risk of injury. If you have the misfortune of having a player suffer a long-term injury, it's obviously more devastating if it's a $40 player than a $20 player.

This makes sense, but if you avoid the high-priced player, it means getting more mid-value players. For example, instead of a $33 and a $1 player, you might buy two $17 players. This lowers your exposure to injury risk in terms of not losing a $33 player, but it *doubles* the risk you could lose a valuable $17 player.

It's much worse to lose a $33 player than a $17 player. But it's also much worse to lose a $17 player than a $1 player. So really the risk is the same either way.

> "Avoid one-category players."

Suppose a hitter's main asset is that he'll steal 40 bases. Even if he's not very good in the other categories, he will still score some runs and drive in some runs, and he will have a specific value based on those stats. Even if he won't hit a single home run and has a fairly low batting average, he will undoubtedly still have a positive value.

In fact, many of the hitters that are termed *one-category* are guys that will hit .275, score 85 runs, drive in 35, steal 40 bases, and thus have a value in the $20 range.

If the concern is that this player won't provide any power, that's okay. You can get power from some of your other 13 hitters.

> "Make sure my top starters have strikeout potential."

Why? You can get strikeouts from every pitcher on your roster. What's the difference if your top starters are high-strikeout pitchers or a couple of your lower-value starters get a lot of strikeouts?

> "I planned to spend $55 on Dustin Pedroia and Desmond Jennings."

This could have been a reasonable plan, but after the auction, this person wrote, "I was extended an extra $2 per player and thus spent $59 to get them. But that was okay, I just had $4 less to spend on another hitter later."

Well, no, that's *not* okay! If you overspend by $4 and get $55 of value for your $59, you are on track to get less than $260 total value and finish in the lower half of your league.

I've seen people write similar things after their auction, such as: "I planned to go to $40 for Matt Kemp, and landed him for just $37. With this $3 savings, I was able to get Yadier Molina, although I had to spend $17 rather than the $14 I had planned."

He was very happy that with his $3 savings on Kemp he could now afford to overspend and get Yadier Molina. But he shouldn't be happy! He simply gave back the profit he had made! He should have been looking for more bargains.

There are never one or two players you must get, regardless of cost. It's fine to be targeting Dustin Pedroia or Matt Kemp or anyone else—and I sometimes target specific players—but always with a clear price limit. I am rarely ever going to pay even $1 more than I think the player is worth.

› "I target age 24 players, because that's when they can improve," "I look at K/BB rate for pitchers," "I like age 27 players because that's the peak year," "I like getting players in a contract year because they're extra motivated," "I want to avoid injury risks," "I avoid Colorado pitchers," "I won't take Miami pitchers because their offense is so bad they don't get wins," "Don't spend big on players without a track record," "Don't spend big on players unless they are in their prime," "I look for players coming off a down year because they're usually undervalued," "I will go an extra buck or two for high-skilled players in volatile situations," and "Avoid players who had breakouts the year before because they will be overpriced."

All of these factors are fine to take into account when making a player's statistical projection for the year, and thus they will be reflected in each player's value. But the goal is to buy every player you can at the best price possible. Using any of the above factors as a draft strategy makes no sense.

It is true that a player who just had a breakout year will probably be overpriced, but you still need to make your best projection (most likely allowing for some regression) and place a specific value on that player. If by chance he's available for that price, or ideally less, you may end up buying him.

> "If I really like a player, I'm willing to go an extra few bucks to get him."

Once you make the best possible estimate for a player's projected stats and run that through an intelligently done formula, you have determined his precise dollar value. How much you like him is irrelevant. If you pay an extra few bucks, you've wasted a few bucks.

What some people mean here is that they feel their projections for a player are too conservative, and they think the player really should exceed expectations. In that case, I can't argue with them going an extra dollar or so. But theoretically they should have projected the player to do better in the first place.

Some people who use the above strategies refer to them as "proven" strategies. But how were they proven? If I say that I'm going to avoid players who hit .235 and I'm going to get power from my corner infielders, and then I win my league, that hasn't proven anything. I may have won my league for other reasons. So you can't really prove that any of the above works. Neither can I prove that it doesn't. But I think my opinions here are logical and I'd do well in a debate about all of this.

Throughout this book I'm mostly offering my opinions and the logic behind them. There is very little that can actually be proven. And there is much that can be debated. And there is more than one way to skin a cat. There are some very successful fantasy players I know who appear to use methods quite different than my own.

So what's my strategy? My strategy is to get as many discounts as possible. Buy as many players as possible for less than my projected dollar value. That is the only way you can end up with $300 or more value for your $260 spent.

It's all about the value and ideally paying as little as possible to get as much value as possible! This sounds very simple. Any 10-year-old should be able to figure this out, right? But surprisingly many fantasy players talk themselves into all kinds of reasons to pay more than a player is actually worth.

At the 2008 LABR auction, one participant told me, "LABR always has premium players bid up 15–20% early." This is the ridiculous mentality some people have. They will overpay to land a $30+ hitter, rather than waiting and getting a couple of $20 players for a fair price. And they will overpay due to the myth of position scarcity and various other reasons.

The only other piece to my strategy is that I try to get a somewhat balanced roster. I don't want to start in a position where I know I've got overkill in certain categories and am going to have to trade later.

That's my entire strategy. I don't care if I get power at first base. I don't care what team a guy plays for. I don't care if I get stars and scrubs or not. I don't care about anything else, because every other factor is either irrelevant or it's already built into my dollar value.

To execute my strategy, I could simply show up at an auction with my player values and wait for bargains to appear. But I do much more preparation than to simply just show up. I'll get to the specifics of that for each format in its own chapter.

In all of the above, I've been writing about paying a price at an auction. But all of this logic also applies to snake drafts. Everyone has a specific value, and when it's your turn at a draft, you choose the player based on his value. It doesn't matter if he's a .235 hitter or plays for Miami. It doesn't matter if you get power from your first basemen. And you don't need to draft a third baseman early because the talent drops off later.

Why Don't People Do This One Simple Thing?

Who would you rather have, shortstop A, worth $7, or shortstop B, worth $7?

You have to decide without knowing any other information. In that case, it obviously doesn't matter, right?

Personally, I would take shortstop A. For my dollar values, I include a decimal point. And I know that shortstop A is actually worth $7.4 and shortstop B is worth $6.8.

Simply using a decimal point can get you an extra $5 or so value for your team.

The Speed of an Auction

When I was in college, some friends and I decided to make a trip to Atlantic City. In preparation, I bought a book about blackjack strategy. I learned when to take a hit, when to double down, and how to count cards.

When I sat down at a blackjack table in Atlantic City, I was totally unprepared for the lightning speed at which the dealer dealt the cards and then scooped them up. I barely had time to think about whether or not to hit. Counting cards was out of the question.

Being at a fantasy baseball auction is like this. A player is nominated and a price given . . . and then the bids are very fast.

Someone will say "Evan Longoria, $15." Quickly someone else says "$18." Then the voices shout out "$21 . . . $24 . . . $26 . . . $27 . . . $29 . . . $30 . . . $31 . . ." and then a short pause, when a different voice says "Longoria, $31 . . . going once . . . going twice . . ." Someone shouts "$32." Another pause. "Longoria, $32 . . . going once . . . going twice . . . sold!"

As soon as a player is brought up, you need to locate this player on your spreadsheet quickly, decide if you potentially want him, and at what price. You must make snap decisions. If you take too long to decide, you'll miss your chance to buy the player. If you shout out a bid too quickly, without really thinking it through properly, you might get stuck buying a player you didn't really want . . . or at a price you didn't want to pay.

That's why I prepare as much as possible in advance. When I go to an auction, I use a printout of all the players, listed by position, including my projected stats and dollar values for them. I also have a column where I list my maximum bid for each player. I have decided in advance how high I'm willing to go for each player. (As you'll see in other chapters, this isn't quite as time-consuming as it might sound.)

The point is, I decide all of this in advance, so that I don't have to try to figure it out every time a player is nominated.

As the auction unfolds, I do have to make adjustments. For example, once I buy a top starting pitcher or closer, my maximum bid for the other top starters or closers becomes irrelevant because I can't afford to buy another one. If the prices are unexpectedly high or low for certain positions or pitchers, I may have to adjust on the fly. I might need to go the extra dollar in some situations, or be able to hold out for an even bigger discount than originally expected. Arriving at the auction with my maximum-bid column filled out for every player gives me a very good starting point.

Obviously, the maximum bid doesn't apply to a draft. And the speed of a draft isn't nearly as fast as an auction. Typically everyone has about 60 seconds when it's their turn to draft, so you do have time to think when it's your turn. But you also have plenty of time to think when it's not your turn, so you should be getting ready and know before it gets to you who your couple of top choices will be. Nonetheless, I still do a lot of predraft prep, as you'll see in chapter 9.

Are Pitchers Riskier?

Each team has $260 to spend on 23 players, for an average of $11.30 per player. If you've never been in an auction before, you might think that you should spend this money proportionally between hitting and pitching. Since you need 14 hitters and nine pitchers, this would be $158 for hitting and $102 for pitching.

You could also make a case that since the five hitting categories and the five pitching categories all count equally toward gaining points in the standings, you should spend half your money ($130) on each.

In practice, a small percentage of owners seem to go for roughly the $158/$102 split. But most owners devote more of their money toward hitting. A few will go as high as $200 for hitting and only $60 for pitching. Overall, though, the average split for most leagues is approximately $180/$80. This is a split of 69/31% for hitting.

Equating that to a snake draft, the typical team will draft seven hitters in the first ten rounds and another seven in the next ten rounds, and the pitching selections will be spread out fairly evenly. For example, taking a pitcher in round two or three, then round five or six, round eight or nine, etc.

The only apparent reason people don't use a $158/$102 or a $130/$130 split appears to be a perception that pitchers are more of a risk.

As I discuss in chapter 5, player stat projections should account for the likelihood of all possible outcomes. Therefore, whatever risk a hitter or pitcher has should be accounted for in his projection. Thus by definition a pitcher would have no more risk than a hitter. In practice, though, projections are made by human beings, and it is impossible to accurately predict the exact likelihood of all outcomes for everyone. We just do the best we can. So the question really is, Do most projections do a pretty good job of taking into account the risk for hitters and pitchers in a balanced way?

Fred Zinkie, writing for MLB.com on January 28, 2012, compared his preseason 2009 and 2011 player projections with the actual results. He found that while many pitchers did get hurt and many underperformed, so did the hitters. If anything, pitchers actually did slightly better than hitters overall. This is far from conclusive evidence, and in fact, Fred only looked at players worth $15 or more. However, there don't appear to be any conflicting studies proving that pitchers are indeed riskier.

If Fred was being overly optimistic projecting hitters' values and/or overly conservative projecting pitchers, this could have skewed his results. But Fred states that his predictions "tend to be pretty standard . . . and don't vary widely from the consensus on most players."

I compared my 2011 and 2012 player pool projections against the actual results and found that overall the hitters produced 88.6% of their projected value and the pitchers only 85%. My results indicate that perhaps pitchers are a little riskier than hitters. Although again, if I tend to be slightly more conservative projecting hitters than pitchers, that would skew the results. And only two years of data is not a thorough study. The conclusion I draw from all of this is that perhaps pitchers are indeed slightly riskier, perhaps not.

As for how much to spend, even if you write a manifesto to brilliantly prove that spending $158/$102 (or $130/$130) is really the correct thing to do, since the reality is that most leagues will average a split of $180/$80, you don't want to trend too far from that or you'll be buying a very imbalanced team and will need to trade later. Similarly, in a draft you don't want to do something like take pitchers with your first three picks, or seven of your first ten, or you'll be extremely imbalanced.

One Decision Changes Everything

For a 12-team league, any intelligent value formula is going to have the total value of the 276 players add up to $3,120. However, you have a choice of how you split that money between hitting and pitching when making your dollar values. In the previous section, I was just talking about what people actually spend at an auction. But now I'm talking about how they split the money in their value formula.

It is clear that currently the average money *spent* at auctions is approximately a 69/31% split. What is not clear, however, is the average split used by most value formulas. Very few magazines or websites ever mention how they split the money. I have looked at several and done my best to figure out their split. My best guess is the average is around 67/33%.

My conclusion is that because some people believe things like pitchers are riskier and that premiums must be paid for position scarcity, etc., they spend a little more money on hitters even though the salaries were split 67/33%. I also think most people don't even pay attention to what split was used in a value formula.

You can argue about which money split is the correct one to use. If people who argue that 69% is the correct figure—or people who argue that 50% is the correct figure—or anything in between, are somehow proven to be right about this, it doesn't really matter. The only thing that matters is to know that you have this option and that *what you choose will alter your perception of values*.

If you use a 65/35% split, the hitters will tend to seem expensive and pitchers will be available at discounts. If you use 69/31%, you will have the opposite impression.

For a snake draft, as explained in chapter 6, your values don't necessarily need to add up to $3,120. They can add up to any amount you want. But the ratio between total hitting value and total pitching value will still alter your perception. If you have a 65/35% ratio, you'll find yourself wondering why everyone else seems to think Clayton Kershaw is worth a late-second-round pick, whereas you think he should go early in the first round. If you use a 67/33% split, your values will be close to the norm.

Different Hitting/Pitching Splits

Here's an example of what happens when you use various splits.

HITTERS

69%	67%	65%	Difference Per 2% Change
$40.0	$38.8	$37.6	$1.20
$35.0	$34.0	$33.0	$1.00
$30.0	$29.2	$28.4	$0.80
$25.0	$24.3	$23.6	$0.70
$20.0	$19.4	$18.8	$0.60
$15.0	$14.6	$14.1	$0.45
$10.0	$ 9.7	$ 9.4	$0.30
$ 5.0	$ 4.9	$ 4.7	$0.15
$ 1.0	$ 1.0	$ 1.0	$0.00

PITCHERS

31%	33%	35%	Difference Per 2% Change
$35.0	$37.2	$39.4	$2.20
$30.0	$32.0	$34.0	$2.00
$25.0	$26.6	$28.2	$1.60
$20.0	$21.4	$22.7	$1.35
$15.0	$16.0	$17.0	$1.00
$10.0	$10.7	$11.3	$0.65
$ 5.0	$ 5.3	$ 5.6	$0.30
$ 1.0	$ 1.0	$ 1.0	$0.00

For a 12-team league, when you shift 2% of the total $3,120 from pitching to hitting, or vice versa, you're moving $62.40. The way most value formulas work means that most of that $62.40 is being shifted among the higher-value players. Also it makes more of a difference for pitchers than hitters because the $62.40 is being split among 168 hitters, but only 108 pitchers.

As you can see, this can make a drastic difference, especially for the higher-value players. A top pitcher would be worth $39.40 rather than $35 if you use a 65/35% split rather than 69/31%. A 71/29% split would alter his value by another $2.20.

Why Get a Closer?

Some owners don't want to pay a lot for a closer, because they believe you shouldn't waste a lot of your money (or a high draft pick) on just one category (saves). This is nonsense. Suppose I have Craig Kimbrel projected as a $25 value. It's not just because he gets saves. He contributes to the other four categories as well. His $25 value accounts for everything he contributes. Sure, he doesn't pitch as many innings as a starter, nor does he get as many wins or strikeouts, but that's all accounted for in the value formula. So, just as with hitters and starting pitchers, if you can get a closer for less than his value, that's a good deal.

Some people will avoid buying a reliable closer and buy speculative pitchers who may have a chance at emerging as a closer, or part of a committee. This isn't any better or worse than buying a reliable closer; it just depends, as always, on the price that you pay.

For example, if John Smith is battling John Doe for the closer gig, and your best guess is that Smith has a 40% chance of winning the job, while Doe has a 60% chance, and that the eventual winner will get 35 saves for the season . . . then you're going to project Smith to have 14 saves and Doe for 21. Smith will have a value based on the 14 saves and Doe a value based on 21 saves. If you can buy either for less than that value, it's a good speculative pick. If you pay more than that value, it's a bad pick.

Personally, I usually like to get one of the reliable closers. I don't mind paying a lot for a closer, as long as it's less than his value. I don't like speculating on closers as a strategy, because there's not always a good deal on the speculative ones. Also, I'm confident in my ability to buy a good team and compete for the league title. I don't need to rely on the hope of speculating and getting lucky. Nor do I want to speculate and get unlucky. If I think I can buy a superior team, why take a chance speculating when I might snatch defeat from the jaws of victory?

Most mono-leagues have 12 teams, and there are 15 major league clubs in the AL and NL. This means that getting one reliable closer is sufficient to be competitive in the saves category. There's no point in paying for two closers. If I do that, I'm going to end up with around 70 saves, while most other teams will have 40 or less. I'd just be wasting saves. Undoubtedly, I'd end up trying to trade a closer during the year. As I've said, I don't like putting myself in a position from the start where I know I'm going to have to trade later. There's just no reason or advantage to doing that. There's only downside, where I might have trouble finding a fair trade to make.

However, as the season unfolds, if it turns out I have excess starting pitching or hitting, I will definitely consider trading my excess to get a second closer. There's usually someone willing to trade a closer, and getting a second one once the season is well under way will allow me to move up in the saves standings without having overkill.

For a mixed league, two closers are sufficient to be competitive. If you're in a 15-team mixed league, two closers will be the average. If you're in a 12-team league, the average would be 2.5 closers. This means if you have three closers, you have an edge for saves . . . but a disadvantage for wins and strikeouts. If you have two closers, you have the opposite. Personally, I like to get two good closers to go along with seven starting pitchers. By having two above-average closers, I can be middle of the pack in saves despite the disadvantage of having only two closers. The key here is to get two closers who will get a lot of saves. For example, if Kimbrel and Jonathan Papelbon are both $25 values but one will get more saves than the other, I'll choose the guy with more saves.

Only Punt Saves or Footballs

I'm not opposed to the idea of *punting saves*, which means you ignore getting saves and therefore you can (theoretically) do better in the other nine categories. I don't particularly like the idea, though, because I'd rather try to dominate my league. I don't want to give up having a chance to get points in a category. Also, I don't want to have overkill anywhere. Since I expect to buy an outstanding team to begin with, there's no need to sacrifice one category to try to be even stronger in other categories.

You should never punt any category other than saves at an auction or draft. The reason is that it is very easy to avoid buying pitchers who get saves. You can put together a staff that will get no saves. Perhaps one of your non-closer relief pitchers will vulture a save or two during the year, but that's okay . . . it's not a big waste of value.

However, if you punt any other category, you're going to waste lots of value. You can't put together a team with zero stolen bases or zero home runs or zero of anything other than saves. For example, if you try to punt stolen bases, since most players get at least a few of them, you will undoubtedly end up with at least 30 or 40. These 30–40 stolen bases and the value they represent (approximately $13) are a complete waste!

And, to make it worse, you have to avoid anyone with a fair number of stolen bases. This greatly limits the players you can choose from and your ability to get good deals.

Note that I said never punt anything but saves *at an auction or draft.* During the year is a different story. It's not a good thing if you need to consider punting a category during the season, but sometimes it becomes necessary. I have done it myself. For example, suppose it's the All-Star break, and your team is last in stolen bases with 25. The team ahead of you has 32, and the next team has 41. You evaluate your chances of catching the teams ahead of you and determine that maybe you can catch the team with 32, but that's it. However, if you trade your one or two stolen-base threats and acquire a power hitter (or starting pitcher or closer), you can almost certainly gain a few points (or more) in other categories. Now keep in mind that this is not a good situation, and you have totally wasted your 25 stolen bases—plus whatever other stolen bases your team scrapes together the rest of the season—but yes, in this situation, you should go ahead and trade your stolen-base guy(s).

It might be theoretically possible to make an argument that you can punt batting average. You can say that any average below the mean is a negative contribution and therefore you're not wasting anything. I would argue, however, that you would still be wasting every hit you get. Or, at the least, you'd be wasting every hit each of your players gets above what would be considered the worst possible player in the pool, something like .190 for catchers and .220 for others. If you could fill your team with two .190-hitting catchers and 12 .220-hitting non-catchers, perhaps that would be the equivalent of getting a team with zero saves or zero stolen bases. But, obviously, this would be virtually impossible to do.

I think I'm correct about this, but even if I'm not (let's say getting a team full of .260-and-below hitters could be considered successfully punting and not wasting value), this is still not practical. It's too limiting to try to buy 14 hitters, and spend $180 or so, and avoid everyone who hits above .260 . . . or even .270–.280. You're going to have to buy at least a few players who hit .270 or above. And you won't be able to be very selective and get good deals. Also, if someone else at the auction is avoiding batting average, that can really hurt you.

I could have the same discussion about ERA (earned run average) and WHIP (walks and hits / innings pitched) as I just did with batting average. What's worse with ERA and WHIP is that if you punt one of these, you have to punt both. And punting two categories puts you at such a disadvantage that even if you finish first in the other eight categories, you aren't guaranteed to win your league.

Multi-Position Players

I've heard people say they are willing to pay an extra dollar or two for players who are eligible at more than one position. It is very helpful to have these players on your roster. It can make it easier to alter your lineup when you need to replace someone due to injury, a trade, or when you get the chance to acquire a good free agent. However, since playing more than one position doesn't mean the player will produce any extra stats, he doesn't have any greater an actual dollar value than someone who plays only one position. Therefore, I will not pay a premium for him. If I have a close call between him and someone who plays only one position, then yes, I would take the multi-position player.

Similarly, some people avoid filling their DH spot with someone who is eligible only as a DH. Since the player can never be moved to another position, this makes your roster less flexible. In a close call, I would avoid taking the DH-only hitter. But if it's not a close call, I'm fine sacrificing a little roster flexibility for more value. In some leagues, DH-only hitters tend to go for a nice discount.

Auction and Draft Logistics

I don't think it matters if you use a laptop or not. It's a matter of personal preference. Personally, instead of my laptop, I set myself up with printouts of my player pages, by each position. And I have a worksheet on which I track my team as I assemble it. Every time I buy a player, I enter him on the worksheet. I'll keep a running total of my team's projected statistics, as well as how much money I've spent.

I always have a phone with Internet access. I check the latest news right before the auction or draft, and usually a couple of times during it as well. You never know when a player might get hurt, a new closer might be named, or a pitcher will win the fifth rotation spot. I sure as heck don't want to acquire a player and then find out he broke his leg two hours before the auction. My favorite sources are Rotoworld.com, Rotowire.com, and Rototimes.com, but there are others as well.

Most people like to socialize during the breaks. I like to

socialize as well, but I'm there for a purpose, and I've got work to do. So I mostly save my socializing for before and after the draft and use the breaks to go over my lists and update my strategy.

I Probably Don't Need to Mention This, But Just in Case . . .

If your primary goal is to have fun and root for your favorite players, then by all means, get your favorite players. But if your goal is to win, then whether or not you like a player—or the team he's on—is irrelevant. Try to remain objective. And you can still have fun. Winning your fantasy league will be fun!

I'm a die-hard Red Sox fan, but if the price isn't right, I don't take a Red Sox player. And if the price is right, I won't hesitate to grab a Yankee.

Trust Yourself

When I was in elementary school, one day the teacher asked a question to which the correct answer was either "latitude" or "longitude." The first two kids she asked said "latitude." She asked me and I said "longitude." She then asked a fourth kid, a fifth kid, and everyone else in the class, one at a time. They all said "latitude." She came back to me. "Mr. Schechter?" she asked. "Ummm," I hesitated, embarrassed, "latitude?"

"The correct answer," she said, "is longitude."

This experience taught me to trust myself. I will consider the opinions of other people for player-stat projections, value formulas, strategies, etc., but the buck stops with me. I'll stand by what I think, regardless of what others say.

CHAPTER 4

Additional Strategy for Auctions

This chapter covers some ideas that apply to both mono-league and mixed-league auctions.

As I've said, my goal for an auction is to buy as many players as possible for a discount. That's the only way to buy $290, $300, or more value for my $260 budget. To execute this strategy, I could simply show up at an auction and wait for bargains to appear. But I do much more preparation before I show up.

And there are two important caveats. If I simply wait for bargains to appear and take what I can get, there's a danger that I might pass on too many of the better players and end up not spending my entire $260. Leaving money on the table is the biggest sin for an auction. It is a blunder of huge proportions. If you leave a dollar or two on the table, that is not a huge blunder. But $5, $10, or more? That's a whole lot of value you just gave away.

The other caveat is that if I just take every bargain that shows up, I could end up with an imbalanced roster. What if I'm valuing stolen bases more than my competitors? I could end up with massive overkill for speed and no power. So I do try to get a somewhat balanced team. I don't want to start in a position where I know I've got overkill in certain categories and am going to have to trade later. (Some people think that's a good idea. As I explained in chapter 3, I think it's a terrible idea!)

Identifying Potential Bargains

Rather than waiting for the auction, I attempt to identify potential bargains in advance. On my player-projections pages, I have a column called *Others' Value*. My 2011 AL-only league shortstop projections are shown to the right. The *Value* column is my personal dollar value for that player. Then I have listed the dollar value according to five other sources. For the 2011 season, the sources I used were *Fantasy Baseball Guide* magazine, Rotoworld. com's online draft guide, *Sporting News* magazine, *Fantasy Baseball Index* magazine, and Baseball HQ's website.

I pretty much always use *Fantasy Baseball Guide* magazine, Rotoworld.com, and Baseball HQ. I find their dollar values to be generally pretty well thought out, and—more important—I know that these are popular sources used by many players, including some of my competitors. I often have also used *RotoWire* magazine, for the same reasons. (I didn't use it in 2011 simply because it didn't arrive in my local newsstands until very late in the spring.)

Player	Value	Others' Value				
		FBG	RW	SN	FBI	BBHQ
Derek Jeter	$20.8	19	21	24	21	20
Alexei Ramirez	$20.1	20	20	21	18	21
Elvis Andrus	$18.7	18	25	24	23	17
Cliff Pennington	$13.7	11	8	3	10	10
Asdrubal Cabrera	$13.5	13	15	14	15	14
Tsuyoshi Nishioka	$13.3	1	10	2	16	18
Erick Aybar	$12.9	13	14	3	13	14
Yunel Escobar	$11.8	14	12	12	11	12
Jhonny Peralta	$11.5	11	9	7	11	10
Reid Brignac	$11.0	7	9	2	3	8
Alcides Escobar	$10.3	7	6	2	15	15
Alexi Casilla	$ 8.8	1	8	0	9	15
JJ Hardy	$ 7.6	7	7	2	5	16
Jed Lowrie	$ 7.3	9	4	0	3	8
Orlando Cabrera	$ 7.0	6	3	5	3	7
Marco Scutaro	$ 6.8	12	4	12	10	10
Brendan Ryan	$ 4.4	1	2	1	3	5
Jason Donald	$ 2.6	5	1	1	3	3
Felipe Lopez	$ 1.3	5	2	1	5	2

When I first decided (in 2005) to add this others' value information, my hope was that it would help me identify players whom I thought had more value than what my competitors thought. As it turned out, it *was* a very valuable tool and has continued to be so.

I peruse this information looking for potential bargains. Starting with the shortstops, Derek Jeter is at the top of the list. My value is $20.8. Two of the five others list him at $21, and one at $24. This means it's very likely someone else will be willing to pay at least $21 for him, possibly more. So it's unlikely I'll be able to buy him for less than my value of $20.8. Alexei Ramirez and Elvis Andrus also have many others' values at, or exceeding, my value.

The next shortstop is Cliff Pennington, whom I've valued at $13.7. The others' values are $11–$8–$3–$10–$10. This means it's very possible none of my competitors will be willing to pay more than $11, if even that much. Obviously, my list doesn't include every possible source of values, and all it takes to ruin my chance of getting a bargain is for just one of the other eleven guys at my auction to think he's worth $13 or $14. Nonetheless, I've got a chance here. It's much more likely I'll get a discount on Pennington than on Jeter, Ramirez, or Andrus. As I said, my experience using this system has shown that it works. When I identify a player like Pennington as a potential bargain, there's a good chance he will be available at a price I like.

Going through the rest of the shortstops, I have identified three targets:

Position	Player	Projected $ Value	Discount
Shortstop	Pennington	$13.7	$2.7
	Peralta	$11.5	$0.5
	Brignac	$11	$2.0

My *projected discount* is calculated by simply taking the highest others' value and subtracting that from my own value.

I look at every position, as well as pitchers, and compile a comprehensive target list. There are always many players on the list. For 2011, there were a lot of hitters with projected discounts in the $1–3 range and a lot of pitchers at $3–5. (My complete list of targets for the 2011 Tout Wars auction is shown in chapter 7.)

For a mixed-league auction, as you'll see in chapter 8, I'm

looking to get discounts much greater than just $1–3 for most levels of hitters and more than $3–5 for many pitchers. So the projected discounts here don't exactly apply for a mixed league. However, it still allows me to identify targets. There is a greater chance that Pennington, Peralta, and Brignac will be available for the types of mixed-league discounts I'm looking for than will players such as Jeter, Ramirez, and Andrus where others value them as highly—or more—than I do.

Discount Double Check

In addition to being my list of potential bargains, I must also ask myself, "Could this simply be a list of players where I've got it totally wrong?" For example, if nobody else thinks Pennington is worth more than $11 and I've got him at $13.7, maybe I'm being way too optimistic.

When I project players' stats I try to take a second look at many of them. After generating the above list, I will take a second look at anyone I haven't already considered and perhaps even a third look at some players. For these targets, I want to make sure that I am very comfortable with my projections.

If I change my projected value for anyone, I will adjust the above list accordingly. But for all those who remain, I've now taken two or three looks at them, and I'm going to stand by my projections, even if they're a bit higher than what others think. After doing so, I am confident this is my list of potential bargains.

As I said, my target lists have proven to be extremely helpful. Typically more than half of the players I end up buying were on my target list. And some of the ones I didn't buy still went for a good price, but I didn't have room for them on my roster. Also, that doesn't mean that the other players I bought were all for full price. There are always discounts available for some players I wasn't expecting.

I'm confident that you can compare your own values to others' values to also get a good idea of potential bargains. (If you know that some people in your league like to use certain sources for their information, be sure to include those sources in your *Others' Value* column.)

One Decision Changes Everything

I mentioned in the last chapter that the typical money split used for value formulas is about 67/33%. For 2011, I used a 65/35% split.

I said that my 2011 target list projected a lot of $1–3 discounts for hitters and $3–5 discounts for pitchers. Had I used a 67/33% split, my values for the mid- to upper-level hitters would have all been about 50 cents to $1 higher, and the pitchers $1–2 lower. Therefore, when making my target lists, I would have projected a lot of $2–4 discounts for hitters and $1–4 discounts for pitchers.

So it actually makes no difference in the end. I would have still bought the same players at the same prices. It's just that my opinion of what type of bargain I was getting—or that I had to pay "full price" for someone—would have been altered.

Bidding Tactics

I was invited to join the *USA Today*–sponsored League of Alternative Baseball Reality (LABR) experts league for the 2003 season. It was the first time I had ever been in an auction league. As part of my preparation, I looked for any books or articles that had been written about auction strategy. Some of the ideas I read made sense, some didn't make sense, and some were conflicting. Having now gathered several years of my own experience in auctions, I want to discuss a few things.

One common recommendation is to sit back early in an auction and let other people spend their money. The idea is that your competition will exhaust much of their funds and then you can come in later and scoop up bargains. You will also have "control" later in the auction because you'll have more money than everyone else.

A person following this theory will begin the auction by nominating high-priced players he has no intention of buying. He will make a small opening bid and then let someone else spend the big bucks to land the player.

Some people follow the opposite line of thinking. They know that some are waiting, so they think it's a good buying opportunity to get players early. If, let's say, half the room is waiting, then you're only competing with half the competition for those high-price players.

Which theory do I think is correct? I think they're both wrong.

As always, it's all about value. If a $38 player is available for $36, don't wait . . . grab him! If the bidding gets to $35 for a $34 player, don't bid! It's that simple.

If you wait too long, aside from the possibility that you may have passed up good buys, you also run the risk of having too much money left with too few valuable players remaining. The idea of being able to *control* the auction is nonsense. What are you controlling? You have the ability to overspend on players and pay $18 for a $15 hitter and spend $10 for a $6 pitcher . . . that's about it. Thanks, but no thanks, I don't want that control.

One other reason some people will wait early in an auction is that no two auctions are alike, and they want to gauge the market for players. In some auctions the best hitters might go for more money than in some other auctions, and vice versa. In some auctions there are good discounts on top closers, and in some auctions there aren't, etc.

So it is a legitimate idea to try to gauge the price structure that is going to occur for each particular auction. However, you can only wait so long to attempt to do this. And if you miss a buying opportunity, you can't go back and get a mulligan. So again, if a $38 player is available for $36, I'm going to pounce. The fact that this $38 hitter is available for $36 is most likely not because lots of high-price hitters are going to be going for $2 discounts, but rather because I'm the only guy in the room who thinks he's worth $38. Everyone else thinks he's worth $36 or less.

If the first good starting pitcher nominated is worth $30 and he's available for $29, then I *am* going to wait, because I know that in most auctions I can get a better discount for a top starter. However, if several of them get sold for just a $1 discount, or even full price, then I may have to adjust my thinking and realize that for this particular auction, the price of starters is higher than normal.

Nominating Is an Advantage

Another topic of debate is the question of how often you should nominate a player that you want to buy, as opposed to how often you should throw out a name you have no interest in acquiring. Some strategists will advise that you don't constantly nominate players you want to buy, because others will catch on to this and bid up the price on you.

I think this is ridiculous. If you are going to buy every player you ever nominate, no matter what the price is, then it might be valid. But even then, I doubt that most of your competition is paying that close attention to who you are nominating and buying. If you're in the same league every year with the same people, and they've learned that you always have to own Justin Upton—no matter what the price—then yes, maybe they'll bid up the price.

But for the most part, this idea is silly and I ignore it. The vast majority of players I nominate are players I am willing to acquire—or would *like* to acquire—but always for the right price and not a penny more. So if anyone thinks they're going to bid up the price on me, they're mistaken. When I get to my limit, I drop out.

I doubt anyone is paying close enough attention to me to think, "Gee, Schechter buys a lot of the guys he nominates . . . I think I'll try to bid up the price on him." If I bid $25 on Pablo Sandoval, and you bid $26 . . . you sure as heck better be willing to roster Sandoval for $26 . . . because I may have reached my limit.

This brings me to the notion of *price enforcing*. Price enforcing basically means that if the current bid on Gio Gonzalez is $16, and you think Gonzalez is worth at least $20, and the auctioneer is beginning to say "going once . . . going twice . . . ," you don't want to let somebody else steal Gonzalez for just $16, so you bid $17. You don't want to actually buy Gonzalez for $17; you're hoping (and assuming) someone else will go to at least $18 or more. This means you will have *enforced* that Gonzalez go for a reasonable price.

This is a terrible idea! Unless you are actually okay with buying Gonzalez for $17, don't bid! It's a million times better to let one competitor get a few dollars of discount than to screw up your own team. And you certainly might get stuck with him. Sometimes when you are sure a guy is worth at least $20, you're the only one in the room who is sure of that.

Winning Fantasy Baseball

At the beginning of an auction, some people will nominate players they don't want because they're going to sit back and wait. Some people will nominate players they don't want because they're paranoid that if they are seen to be bringing up players they want, others will try to bid them up.

In either case, I think these people are wasting a valuable tool. When it's your turn to bring up a player, this is an advantage you have. And you're going to have to wait through several more players before it's your turn again.

Even some people who *do* nominate players they want to buy make a different mistake. They make the mistake of not planning anything in advance. When it's their turn, they decide on the spur of the moment whom to bring up.

I usually nominate someone I want to buy—or am willing to buy—and I plan in advance the guys I'm going to bring up. I don't plan it precisely, but I do have ideas, not just spur-of-the-moment, split-second decisions for no particular reason. And when I bring up a player I don't want to buy, I'm doing that for a reason as well. I'm nominating a particular player for a specific reason.

Tout Wars gives the defending champion the honor of the first nomination. If I'm not the defending champion, I try to figure out where the defending champion is sitting and take the seat to his left. This gives me the second turn.

The order in which players get nominated can make a big difference. As much as possible, I want my best targets to be put up for bid before I have to make decisions on other potential buys.

For example, suppose my top two targets to land a #1 starting pitcher are David Price and Clayton Kershaw. I have them both valued at $34. Based on others' values I think there's a good chance I can get a $2 discount on Price and a $4 discount on Kershaw.

60

Suppose Price is brought up before Kershaw, and the bid is $30. I can bid $31 and try to get a $3 discount, or I can pass, hoping to get Kershaw for a $4 discount. It's a tough decision, and there's a good chance I'll regret it either way. I might buy Price for $31 and then watch Kershaw get sold for $30 (or even less), or I might pass on Price and then watch Kershaw's price go higher than $31.

But if Kershaw is brought up first, it's not a tough decision. If I can get him for $30, or even $31 if necessary, I will, because I'm expecting Price will most likely go for at least $31, if not more. It's possible I could buy Kershaw for $30–31 and then watch Price get sold for less, but it's not likely.

In preparing for the auction, I would be aware of this situation, and Kershaw would be among the players I would want to nominate early. I'd really like to get his name out there before Price.

I hate this aspect of auctions—that when you buy a player, you don't know what's going to happen later. At a snake draft, when it's your turn, you know all the players available and you can pick the one you like the best. At an auction, you can buy a player and later regret it because others went for a better price. This has happened to me countless times. So I try to use my nominations to my advantage and think through various scenarios in advance.

More Bidding Tactics

Sometimes people will bring up a cheap player, maybe even a $1 player, very early. The idea is that while everyone is thinking about the studs and spending lots of money, you can catch them off guard and some people will be unprepared to bid on lesser players.

This can work, but it can also easily backfire. Let's say you nominate a $3 player in round one, hoping to catch everyone off guard and snag him for just a buck. But everyone isn't caught off guard; they know that he's worth $3 and bid accordingly. Had you waited, this player might have lasted till the endgame, when most people are running out of money, and you might have landed him for a buck then.

Another tactic is called a *jump bid*. When the bidding on a player approaches his perceived value, people typically start bidding in increments of $1. For example, the bidding might go: "Andrew McCutchen for $10 . . . $20 . . . $24 . . . $26 . . . $27 . . . $28 . . . $29 . . . $30 . . . Sold!"

A jump bid means that when you're getting near the point of the final sales price, you make a bid in an increment of more than $1. You're hoping to end the bidding by doing that. In the example of McCutchen, the person who bid $29 ultimately lost out. If that person was only willing to go to $29, then they were going to miss out on McCutchen. But if they were willing to go to $30, then a jump bid might have done the trick. After the $28 bid, if they had jumped the bid to $30—skipping over $29—they might have gotten McCutchen (depending whether the person who bid $30 would have been willing to go to $31).

A jump bid can be very effective. But it can also waste your money. If the person who bid $29 on McCutchen had gotten him for that price, then a jump bid to $30 would have simply wasted $1.

If you really want McCutchen and suspect $29 isn't going to get it done, and you're willing to spend $30—but not $31—then it's not a bad idea to skip over $29 and go right to a $30 bid.

I have occasionally seen people make idiotic jump bids and waste a lot of money. One way you know you're approaching the sales point for a player is that the bidding slows down. The auctioneer starts saying "going once . . . going twice . . ." a lot. I've seen people at that point make a jump bid of $3 or even $5, which is just crazy. A $2 jump bid would almost certainly have been sufficient. And there's a good chance they would have even gotten the player for just a $1 increase.

Personally, I'm reluctant to make jump bids, because I'm always looking to get the best bargain possible. I'd rather take a shot at getting the player for $29 rather than jump to $30 and possibly waste $1.

My Gabe Kapler Story

That's right, I want to talk about Gabe Kapler. Right now, you're either thinking, "Why in the world would he want to talk about Gabe Kapler?" or "Who the hell is Gabe Kapler?"

The 2003 LABR NL-only league was my first ever auction. I had Kapler, an outfielder for Colorado at the time, valued at $14. Fairly late in the auction, he was still available. I nominated him for $10, figuring that would be a good bargain price, and I'd probably go to $12 after someone bid $11. After I said "Gabe Kapler, $10" you could have heard a pin drop. Complete silence. And then I owned him.

What I learned from this experience was that I'd made a rookie mistake. The first lesson is that just because I valued him at $14 doesn't necessarily mean anyone else agreed with me. So it was possible that nobody else in the room even thought he was worth $10, let alone $14.

The second lesson is that when you get to the later stages of an auction, there can be great bargains because not many people have much money left and/or open spots on their roster. If I'd opened at $9, maybe someone would have bid $10. But who knows, maybe I could have gotten him for $8 . . . or $6 . . . or even less.

So the important lessons here are never make an opening bid that is higher than the price you are absolutely sure some others in the room will value the player at; when it's getting to the later stages of an auction, open with very low bids, because you never know when you might run into a huge bargain.

If you are entering every pick into a draft software program— or the league is doing it for everyone to see—then it's easy to know what teams have open slots for various positions during the later stages, and how much money everyone has left.

Control the Endgame?

Some people think it's good to save money to control the end game. There's a chance that a pretty good player, let's say a $9–10 value, might slip through to the end. And since most people are almost out of money, whoever can afford to spend $5–6 can snag him. And the person who snags him will think how wonderful it was that he saved a few extra dollars for this endgame coup. However, it was just as likely he'd have gotten stuck and left a few dollars on the table, completely wasting them, or would have gotten a $5–6 player for a buck or two, which would have been just as good a bargain.

Bidding on Closers

I've developed, and then discarded, some theories about bidding on top closers. At one point, I came to the conclusion that since there are only a limited number of owners willing to pay for a top closer, it's better to wait until two or three of them have been sold. This eliminates some of your competition, and then you have a chance to get a better discount on the third or fourth or fifth good closer. As soon as I created this theory and tried it, it blew up in my face. I missed a couple of acceptable discounts and then got stuck. It turned out there were more owners willing to pay for a good closer than there were good closers. So once a few were gone, there was now more desperation among those owners who didn't have a closer yet.

There are many theories in auctions, some of which I've mentioned, that sound reasonable, but then it turns out there's also a perfectly reasonable counterargument. It's like you're damned if you do, and damned if you don't.

CHAPTER 5

Projecting Player Stats

Determining a player's value before your draft or auction is a two-part process. First, you must project what statistics you think the player will produce for the upcoming season. Second, you must enter those statistics into a formula that determines the precise worth of those statistics for the fantasy format you are going to play.

This chapter covers projecting the raw stats. The following chapter discusses how to convert those stats into a specific value.

Once the season is under way, projections can and should be revised based on events and the players' actual performance. This is useful for evaluating trades, free-agent pickups, start vs. bench decisions, etc. I discuss in-season management in chapter 11.

I prefer to make projections myself. I like to be completely in charge and confident with all of my values. I begin in early February, look at all potentially relevant players, and make my best prediction for the raw stats I think they will produce. As the season approaches, I will take a second look at many players, and I also make adjustments as injuries, position battles, trades, etc. warrant. I then use my own formula to convert those stats into a specific value.

I realize that not everyone wants to take the time to do all this work. So first, I want to offer advice for everyone who would rather just use the projections and values from their favorite magazine or website. After that, I'll get into the specifics of what I do, for those who would like to do it all themselves or are at least curious to learn how I do it. I actually recommend that you read the entire chapter even if you don't want to make all your own projections, because you'll learn things that will be useful when looking through other people's projections and comments that you read about players. For example, there are several myths floating around the fantasy baseball world that aren't necessarily true.

Real Clear Projections

Fantasy magazines and websites always look very authoritative and tell a good story about their supposed expertise. Even my son will quote them. "Dad," he said when he was 12 years old, "you think Jason Bay will hit 15 homers, but this magazine says 20!" Because it's in print, he assumes the magazine must know more than I do.

Most magazines and websites publish projections that are based on the opinion of just one person, or perhaps just a few people. These people are not God. Just because they are in print or on the web, you can't take their values as the gospel truth. If you rely on only one source, you're taking a big gamble.

So if you don't want to do it all yourself, I suggest you find at least three good sources, preferably more, and calculate the average of their projections and values. This is similar to what RealClearPolitics does with polling for elections. Each individual poll has its own assumptions and methodology, and a margin of error. So to rely on one is very risky. RealClearPolitics publishes the average of all the polls, which is more reliable data.

Some of your sources will have outdated information. For example, if you use a magazine published in February, and a player subsequently got injured or was named the closer, etc., you'll need to adjust for that.

It can be difficult to know what a good source is. Everyone will have statistical projections for the standard categories, but when using someone's dollar values, you need to be sure they are calculated for the same format you're playing. If you're playing 5×5 and someone has published values for 4×4, they're not going to be exactly what you need. If you're in a mono-league, values created for a mixed league aren't what you need.

A properly done value formula should have all the salaries add up to a total of $3,120 for a 12-team league (12 × $260) or $3,900 for a 15-team league (15 × $260). But how that money is split between hitting and pitching is at the discretion of whoever is making the values. I have examined several sources to see how they split the money when creating their values, and that average appears to be approximately 67% for hitting and 33% for pitching. Some use a 69/31% split, or a 65/35% split, or other splits. Thus, even if two sources predict identical raw stats for a player, their dollar values may be very different.

To be clear, I'm talking here about the split people use in their value formula. As for how much money people actually spend at an auction, that average is currently 69% for hitting and 31% for pitching. So while value formulas are typically only giving hitters 67% of the money, people are actually spending 69% at auctions. This means that, overall, people are slightly overpaying for hitters and getting small discounts on pitchers.

Some value formulas being used just don't add up. One source I looked at was showing values for a 12-team mono-league, and the 108th-best pitcher was valued at $5. This is just flat-out wrong. The 108th-best pitcher should be worth $1. (I would obviously never use this as one of my sources for values.)

Another warning sign is when a source's projections mostly make sense, but there's a smattering of absurd values. I've seen situations, for example, where you have a player who has been a $10 value three years in a row—nothing substantial has changed regarding his situation—and he's projected for $18. Or a player who is age 34 and has hit between seven and ten home runs the past six years, is now projected to hit 15 home runs. Again nothing substantial has changed. This is either a typo, or just plain dumb.

I also suggest you pay attention to injury-prone players. There are some sources that will at times project a player for 575 or more at bats, despite the fact that his injury history dictates that it is foolish to expect that many.

I'm Also Not God

While I like to do my own projections, I will also look at some sources I like in order to see what they think. The key here, though, is that I'm looking at their projections of *raw stats*, not dollar values. I don't care what their dollar values are.

In a 2013 interview, Patrick Davitt of Baseball HQ asked me

"Why is it better for people to make their own value formula rather than just taking the average of values from several magazines and websites?"

This was a really good question. Even if someone is willing to put in the time and effort, is it any better to do it yourself?

My answer is yes. As I say throughout this book, it's all about value, the *precise* value. If I spend $20 on a player, I want to be confident he's really worth $20. I don't want to hope he's worth $20. And a magazine won't tell you that one player is actually worth $20.4 while another is worth $19.6.

Value formulas are based on the exact format you play, and the exact number of projected stats in your total player pool. And the values should add up to $3,120 for a 12-team league. And the 168th hitter and 108th pitcher should be worth $1.

If you simply take the average of dollar values you see published, you probably won't fulfill all of these criteria. If you play 4×4 or 6×6, use on-base average instead of batting average, have an 11-team league, etc., the dollar values you see published won't fit your format.

So I strongly recommend you use your own formula. If you don't want to take the time to project stats for players, that's okay. But you should still use your own formula. You can take the average stat projections from your favorite sources and plug them into your formula.

In addition to having the precise value for your exact player pool and format, this will allow you to do many useful things. For example, during spring training 2013, Curtis Granderson, Mark Teixeira, Chase Headley, and others got hurt and were going to miss time during the year. If you have your own formula, you can adjust the stats and see what Granderson will be worth now that you know he's going to miss eight weeks. You can add the stats that you're likely to get from a replacement player for the first eight weeks and see what the total value will be. This gives you a precise value. Someone who simply took the average of dollar values for Granderson from magazines has to make a guess. Or they just write off Granderson entirely. This is a mistake, because with a precise value for Granderson, he may actually be a good buying opportunity.

Many other developments occur during spring training, and throughout the year. People are named the closer, part-time players get a full-time role, etc. You can't look at magazines to find out their new exact value. With your own formula, you can.

During the year, when you're considering trades, you can use your formula to know the exact value of what you're getting and giving up.

So there are many reasons to use your own formula. The good news is that projecting raw stats is the time-consuming chore. Making your own formula is not so bad. Value formulas are a bit confusing and take a little time to understand and set up in Excel or a database, but once you've got it set up, it's easy to use and not particularly time-consuming.

The other good news is that I'm not a rocket scientist or even a math major. My chapter on value formulas is relatively easy to understand. If I can do it, so can you.

Sabermetrics

Sabermetrics is the statistical analysis of baseball data. The most prominent sabermetrician is Bill James, who was one of the pioneers of the field.

Some people reading this are probably thinking, "Since Larry's been successful I'll bet he uses a lot of sabermetrics. I wonder how much emphasis he puts on OPS (on-base percentage plus slugging percentage), BABIP (batting average on balls in play), K/BB rate (strikeout-to-walk ratio), and the rest of it?"

The answer is that prior to writing this chapter of my book in the fall of 2012, I paid very little attention to it. However, as stated in my introduction, one of my purposes in writing this book was to make myself a better player. So to that end, and for the sake of having this chapter be a more complete discussion of how to project players' stats, I delved into the world of sabermetrics during the winter of 2012. I will get into that shortly.

Maybe it was to my detriment that I didn't study sabermetrics sooner, but I mostly kept it very simple. If a pitcher had a 2.70 ERA (earned run average) and 1.30 WHIP (walks and hits / innings pitched) last year, I didn't need any more data to realize that a 2.70 ERA wasn't going to be sustainable with that poor of a WHIP.

And if a hitter had averages of .300, .295, and .330 the last three years—all for the same team with nothing much being different—I didn't need sabermetrics to tell me that the .330 was probably a fluke and he'd likely regress back toward .300 next year.

So all in all, I kept it pretty simple and didn't go looking for sabermetric data. Sometimes, though, sabermetrics would find me. For example, in 2011, Jeremy Hellickson pitched 189 innings with an ERA of 2.95 and a 1.15 WHIP. In the 2012 *Fantasy Baseball Guide*, Alex Patton (from Alexpatton.com) wrote this about Hellickson: "By sabermetric consensus, the luckiest pitcher last year. Averaging five different 'should have been' ERAs (Bill James's ERC, *Baseball Forecaster*'s xERA, Baseball Prospectus's FRA and FIP, and Fangraphs' xFIP), his ERA should have been 4.14."

So when I saw that, it did get my attention. I did know that there was some value in sabermetrics.

I wait until early February to start making my projections so that I can get magazines and web-based draft guides. When I evaluate each player, I will look at their last three years of production, and I read the capsules in two or three sources to see if they say anything I need to know. There are enough people into sabermetrics that if a player was very lucky or unlucky, it will probably be mentioned in the comments, such as what Alex Patton wrote about Hellickson.

I choose the magazines and other sources based on the usefulness of the comments. Some will say, "Johnny Smith started out 2011 strong but faded down the stretch, ending with a 13–7 record, with a 3.75 ERA and 1.30 WHIP. He throws a fastball and slider." Well, thanks! That's really helpful! Can you also tell me his zodiac sign, mom's maiden name, and favorite TV show?

I don't use magazines full of player capsules like that. I use the ones that will, at least for some of the players, offer some insight into why a player did what he did, and what that might mean for next year. Maybe the player struggled due to an injury but is expected to be 100% again. Maybe the pitcher was more successful because he added a new pitch. Maybe the player faded during the second half because he never played a full season before, but spent the off-season working on his conditioning.

All Possible Outcomes

Obviously, you can't predict in advance exactly what a player will do in the upcoming season. But your job is to make the best prediction possible of what that player is *likely* to do.

A projection takes into account *the likelihood of all possible outcomes*. This includes factors such as job security, injury risk, breakout potential, potential decline for old age, changing teams, etc.

There should be no such thing as "I project Troy Tulowitzki for 600 at bats, with 32 homers, and 100 RBIs, but he's a big injury risk." If he's a big injury risk, you need to project how many at bats you can reasonably expect. If the upcoming season were played ten times, or 100 times, what do you guess would be his average number of at bats? If the answer is 450, then you should project him for 450 at bats (24 homers and 75 RBIs).

There should be no such thing as "I project Eric Hosmer will hit .290, but his walk rate is rather low." You need to project what you think his average will be, including the fact that his walk rate is rather low.

If you think a player has a 50% chance of being a setup man and vulturing two saves, and a 50% chance of being the closer and getting 38 saves, then you need to take the average of all possible outcomes and project him for 20 saves.

There are always players with job-security issues. Let's say you think it's very likely that Ryan Ludwick will play full-time until June 1, when the Cincinnati Reds will call up Billy Hamilton from AAA, relegating Ludwick to a fourth-outfielder role for the rest of the year. This means Ludwick will get about 190 at bats the first two months, and then something like 160 over the final four months. You project him for a total of 350. And you project Hamilton for four months of every-day at bats.

Sometimes it's more difficult. Entering the 2011 season, the Yankees signed free agent Russell Martin to be their starting catcher. He had the potential to get 450 or more at bats. However, he was a big injury risk, having issues with both his hip and a knee. In addition, the Yankees had a hotshot prospect, Jesus Montero, who had a chance to not only be called up during the season, but possibly even make the opening-day roster. He would play catcher as well as DH.

So this leads to a lot of questions. If Martin stays healthy and Montero stays at AAA, would he be likely to get 450 at bats? 475? 500? How much do I downgrade him for the injury risks? What are the chances Montero makes the team on day one? If he doesn't, what are the chances Montero gets called up June 1? If Montero is on the Yankees, how much will he be the DH and how much will he catch?

I'd need a computer programmer to help me figure this out. I took my best guess and projected Martin for 350 at bats. But I still felt like there was a lot of risk, so in my comments section I wrote "very risky, best to avoid." When his name came up at my Tout Wars auction, he was available for a price that would have been acceptable based on 350 at bats, but I couldn't pull the trigger. I didn't trust that I was being conservative enough with my projection.

Examples

Here are a few examples of how I arrived at my 2012 projections. I'll start with Dustin Pedroia:

	AB	AVG	RUN	HR	RBI	SB
2009	626	.300	115	15	72	20
2010	302	.288	53	12	41	9
2011	635	.307	102	21	91	26

Pedroia broke his foot in 2010 and only played 75 games. This was a fluke injury; he's had no other history of injuries, so it can be chalked up as a one-time event. It's safe to assume he'll be healthy all year. (Yes, there's always a chance anybody could get hurt, but unless someone has a real history of being injury-prone—or is beginning the year with a known risk—we can assume everyone will be healthy.)

Had Pedroia played his usual 155 games or so in 2010, he would have had 625 at bats again. Adjusting his 2010 figures to full-time gives us this:

	AB	AVG	RUN	HR	RBI	SB
2009	626	.300	115	15	72	20
2010	625	.288	110	25	85	19
2011	635	.307	102	21	91	26

At age 29, he's probably not going to improve much, but is in his prime and should continue at his current levels. He is still expected to hit second in a potent Red Sox lineup, so nothing has really changed. Therefore, I'm going to project him for:

	AB	AVG	RUN	HR	RBI	SB
2012	625	.300	108	21	85	22

As a rule, for a player with a solid three-year track record—and no unusual BABIP or other anomalies—I (almost) simply take a three-year average of stats. But I do place extra emphasis on the last year or two, and try to decipher any trends.

In this case, his three-year average is a .298 batting average. But that's giving too much weight to 2010, since he really only had 302 at bats. Taking his actual number of at bats to calculate the three-year average, it is .299. I suspect that if he hadn't gotten hurt in 2010, his final average would have been better than .288, because he missed most of the warm summer weather when hitting usually improves. So I feel confident that projecting a .300 average is safe.

He was mostly age 25 during the 2009 season, so it's not surprising that his power increased some in 2010 and 2011. So I'll keep him at the 21 homer and 85 RBI level. I'm going to assume his stolen bases will regress toward the 2010–2011 levels.

You can see my approach is subjective and not very scientific. If I were to take another look at Pedroia a few days later and not look at the projections I'd already made for him, I might come up with something slightly different. In fact, when I've gone through projecting all relevant players, if time permits, I will look at many a second time to see how that look matches my first opinion. I will then either take an average of my two opinions, or go with the more conservative one. I always like to be conservative.

Next let's look at Brett Lawrie:

	AB	AVG	RUN	HR	RBI	SB
2010 AA	554	.285	90	8	63	30
2011 AAA	292	.353	64	18	61	13
2011 TOR	150	.293	26	9	25	7

Lawrie is a very highly touted rookie, who is supposed to be the Blue Jays everyday third baseman in 2012. As you can see, he was very successful in his first big league action in 2011. But with only 292 AAA and 150 major league at bats, we don't have much of a track record to go by.

There's always a chance a rookie will falter and be sent back to the minors, but Lawrie is a blue-chip prospect who's already had great success at every level, so he appears to be a pretty safe bet. Chances are he'll get 575–590 at bats, but since there is a small chance of failure, and it's unknown where he'll hit in the order—but most likely sixth or lower—I think projecting 550 at bats is safe.

Projecting the batting average for someone with such little experience is very difficult. As a player moves from AA to AAA to the majors, obviously the pitching gets a lot better, but the player is also young and improving. Considering Lawrie hit .285 in a full year at AA, and then .353 in half a year at AAA, my guess is he would be likely to hit somewhere in the .270–.280 range in his first full season. This is clearly an unscientific guess.

His major league average of .293 is better than .270–.280, but was only for 150 at bats. So I'm going to go with a .275 projection. Again, I like to be safe. If I buy him, and he hits .290–.300, that will be a bonus. If someone else outbids me because they think he will hit .295, that's not a problem. I don't need to buy this guy.

He only hit eight home runs in a full season at AA, but if you extrapolate his 2011 AAA numbers he was on pace for about 34, and extrapolating his major league numbers you again get about 34. Could he keep this up and hit 34 in 2012? Yes, he could. When young players age they often develop power. And Toronto is a good hitters' park.

However, in general if a AAA hitter had 34 homers, I'd only expect him to hit roughly 20 in his first big league season, and 150 major league at bats is a very small sample size. Thus I'm going to project 20 homers. It certainly wouldn't shock me if he hit 25, but it also wouldn't shock me if he hit 15.

Extrapolating his stolen bases for a full season would be about 25–26 for both AAA and the majors. Again, I wouldn't expect a 25-stolen-base AAA player to come to the majors and immediately keep that pace. I'd typically project about 15. But ever since John Farrell took over as the Blue Jays manager, they love to run, so I'm going to go with 20.

When projecting a player based on his minor league stats, I basically ignore his run and RBI totals. He was hitting in a different spot in the order for a different team. Instead, I have to ask myself this question: "If a guy gets 550 at bats, and hits .275 with 20 homers, probably hitting sixth, seventh, or eighth for Toronto—which is a pretty decent hitting lineup and ballpark—how many runs and RBIs would I guess he'll have?"

My guess is 70–75 runs and 70–75 RBIs. So my projection is:

	AB	AVG	RUN	HR	RBI	SB
2012	550	.275	73	20	72	20

Clearly there is a *lot* of guessing involved here. I have much less confidence in this projection than the ones for established players like Pedroia. So for Lawrie, I also want to incorporate a bit of the RealClearPolitics logic. I'm curious to see what others say about him. Looking at some sources I like, I see the following projections:

	AB	AVG	RUN	HR	RBI	SB
	533	.273	77	32	85	21
	576	.286	98	23	86	25
	570	.283	82	19	71	22
	560	.276	77	24	84	22
	550	.281	82	18	71	12
Average	558	.280	83	23	79	20

Overall, I'm pretty close to these averages, but a little less optimistic across the board (except stolen bases). This is okay, because I like being conservative. But I am willing to be swayed a bit by these other projections. I was leaning toward putting him down for another home run or two, anyway, and I can admit that maybe I was a little conservative on the runs and RBIs. So I'll adjust my projection to:

	AB	AVG	RUN	HR	RBI	SB
2012	550	.276	76	21	75	20

Next we'll look at Matt Garza:

	GS	IP	ERA	WHIP	W	K	K/IP
2009 TB	32	203	3.95	1.26	8	189	.93
2010 TB	32	205	3.91	1.25	15	150	.73
2011 Cubs	31	198	3.32	1.26	10	197	.99

When evaluating starters, I always want to include the number of games they started (GS) in my analysis. This helps project the number of innings they'll pitch and the number of wins they'll get. A starter who stays healthy all year will typically get 32 starts, maybe 33–34 if he's one of the team's top aces or only 30–31 if he's the team's fifth-best starter.

Garza has been healthy three years in a row, so I'm going to pencil him in for another 200 innings. At age 28, and projected to be the #1 or #2 starter for the Cubs, it's possible he could increase his innings, but when in doubt, I always like to err on the side of being conservative.

His ERA dropped from the 3.91–3.95 level with Tampa Bay to 3.32 with the Cubs. This wasn't too surprising, since he had moved out of the DH league—and the tough AL East in particular. It was perhaps a little more of a drop than I would have expected, and it was a bit too good for a WHIP of 1.26, so my guess was that his ERA would probably regress back toward 3.50.

It was surprising to me that in 2012 he didn't have a corresponding drop in WHIP. My best guess was to surmise that his WHIP should still drop a little now that he was in the NL, to the 1.24 range.

Ten wins seemed low for as good a pitcher as Garza, but the Cubs still weren't going to be a very good team, so my guess was that he'll get 11 or 12 wins.

It's common for people to talk about a pitcher's K/9 rate—how many strikeouts he gets per nine innings pitched. Most of the sources that I use don't show a K/9 rate, so I simply divide Ks by IP to get a percentage. Garza dipped from .93 in 2009 to .73 in 2010, and then jumped to .99 with the Cubs. It's not surprising that he had a nice increase once he started facing pitchers instead of designated hitters. If his 2010 had also been .93, or even .90, I'd be confident predicting him to stay at .99, but the .73 concerns me, so I'm going to project him for .92. Thus, I have the following:

	IP	ERA	WHIP	W	K
2012	200	3.50	1.24	11.5	184

Again, there's nothing scientific or profound about my method. As with Lawrie, it's now helpful to see what others think:

	IP	ERA	WHIP	W	K
2012	218	3.43	1.20	12	205
	203	3.42	1.18	14	190
	200	3.58	1.25	12	183
	197	3.89	1.30	10	176
	209	3.23	1.20	15	203
Average	205	3.51	1.23	12.6	191

My wins and strikeouts are slightly conservative compared to these, but nothing jumps out at me that I've erred and should alter anything. What does jump out is that someone has projected a 1.30 WHIP. Garza has had three full years at 1.25–1.26 and is now entering his prime at age 28. There's no reason in the world to think his WHIP is likely to increase to 1.30. Even looking back further, in 2008 he pitched a full year with Tampa Bay at 1.24.

This is an example of why I like to do my own projections, because others will often not make sense.

The bottom projection with a 3.23 ERA, 15 wins, and 203 strikeouts is optimistic and assuming improvement. I think it's certainly possible Garza can improve, and these numbers are doable. But I'm not going to say this is the average of all possible outcomes. I think this is on the optimistic side, and I wouldn't want to pay for Garza as though he was likely to achieve this. There's very little upside and a lot of downside.

Broken Footnote

When writing this chapter, it occurred to me that I've always done something that doesn't make sense. And, I imagine, pretty much everyone else does as well. In the examples above, I am quick to write off Pedroia's broken foot as a fluke, one-time occurrence and project him for full-time at bats. For Tulowitzki, there is a clear history of injuries, so I'm not willing to pay for more than 450 at bats.

What's missing in this equation is that there is always a chance every player will get hurt. Each year, many players with no apparent extra risk will spend time on the disabled list. So really, all players who aren't already being downgraded for risk such as

Tulowitzki should not be projected for full-time. There is always a chance a guy like Pedroia will miss time.

To account for this, my guess is that I should downgrade everyone by about 10% (except the guys like Tulowitzki whom I have already downgraded). If I do this, what will happen is the total stats for my player pool will decrease by almost 10%. And when I convert those stats to a dollar value, I'll end up almost where I was going to be in the first place. A guy like Pedroia would most likely lose only 10–20 cents of value. But for Tulowitzki and the other injury risks, their value would increase. I would have kept him at 450 at bats and the other risks at their current level, and downgraded everyone else. I'm guessing a guy like Tulowitzki would gain a dollar or so.

Rather than downgrade everyone by 10%, which I think would be a pain in the butt, I think the thing to do is either be a little more generous when projecting the injury risks and give them an extra 10% at bats to make them level with the non-risks, or don't change the projections but be aware of this at my drafts, which would make me just a bit more likely to take a guy like Tulowitzki.

Commonsense Factors

Rather than show more examples, I'm going to list some items to consider. I call these *common sense*, as opposed to scientific or sabermetric.

- *Changing teams*. Moving from a hitters' park to a pitchers' park, or vice versa, will obviously have a big effect. Not to mention that the strength of the lineup will change. This is another situation, such as Lawrie, where I'll take my best guess but then look to see what other people's opinions are as well.

- *Regression.* When a player has an unexpected terrific year, the question is always has this player had a permanent breakout or was it a fluke career-year? If the player moved to a hitters' park, is at an age such as 26 or 27 when players are still improving, or had Lasik eye surgery or a new conditioning program prior to the season, there may be reason to think the improvement—or at least some of it—is here to stay. Unless I see a pretty concrete explanation, I will assume he will regress toward his prior numbers. Again, it's best to be conservative. If I pay for the breakout to continue, and he regresses, I've blown it.

- *Platoon to full-time (or vice versa).* Suppose a left-handed hitter has been getting 400 at bats per year playing mostly against right-handed pitchers, and has averaged .290 with 20 homers. But now he's going to play every day and you project him for 575 at bats. You can multiply his production (575/400 × 20) to arrive at a projection of 29 homers. However, you must remember that against left-handed pitching, he isn't likely to hit home runs at the same pace, nor is he likely to keep up the .290 average.

- *Fill-in value for injury risks.* There are some players who rarely can make it through a full season without spending time on the DL. Look at Troy Tulowitzki:

Year	AB
2007	609
2008	377
2009	543
2010	470
2011	537
2012	181
Average	453

Since his first full year in the big leagues in 2007, he's spent time on the DL every year. To project him for 550 or more at bats is foolish. For 2013, assuming he's healthy entering the season, I wouldn't feel comfortable paying for an expectation of more than 450 at bats.

However, for a player like this, you can add a fill-in value. For some of the games he misses, you will be able to replace him in your lineup. At some points he'll have a minor injury and be day-to-day, and unless your league allows daily moves, you'll need to stick with him. And if he goes on the DL on a Tuesday and your weekly lineup deadline is Monday, you'll be stuck with him for six days. But if he really ends up with only 450 at bats, he'll likely spend a good chunk of time on the DL and you'll have someone else in your lineup.

Let's say—and this is just a random guess—you get 100 at bats from a replacement. This replacement's production for 100 at bats can be added to your projections for Tulowitzki. If you're in an NL-only league, the quality of the replacement will add little or no value. In a mixed league, there will be value added. Thus, you could actually estimate how valuable a replacement you'll be able to get and project Tulowitzki's value with the added production. If you don't want to bother doing that, you can at least know that if you buy him based on 450 at bats, you'll actually be getting an extra buck or two of value (in a mixed league).

- *Second-half stats.* If a player showed a marked improvement (or decline) in 2013, and you're trying to figure out if it was a trend or a fluke, it's helpful to look up what he did during the second half of 2012. If the improvement (or decline) actually started during the second half of 2012, it's more likely to be here to stay.

Some people suggest it can also be helpful to look at second-half stats of the most recent year, especially for older players who may start to decline or younger players who may be improving. However, I don't place a lot of emphasis on this, because it can often be a mistake. I've sometimes gotten sucked into thinking a young player's great second-half stats mean that something has clicked and he's reached a new level, only to be disappointed.

For the vast majority of players who were significantly better (or worse) in the second half of a season, it is not the start of something new. It's just that some players tend to start well and then fade; some tend to start poorly and get better; and most players aren't going to have two halves of a season that are very close in production—one will be better and one worse—with no rhyme or reason.

- *Recovery time from some injuries.* Pitchers coming off Tommy John Surgery (TJS) and most shoulder surgeries typically take up to a year after resuming pitching to regain their past form. It can be easy to get sucked into glowing reports of how good a pitcher looks when he first comes back from surgery, but they almost always struggle.

Adam Wainwright was one of the game's best starting pitchers, averaging a 2.53 ERA and 1.13 WHIP for 2009 and 2010. He missed all of 2011 after TJS. He looked so good in spring training 2012 that I started to believe maybe he'd barely skip a beat, but, sure enough, his first-half ERA was 4.73 with a 1.34 WHIP. He improved markedly during the second half, posting an ERA of 3.18 and a 1.16 WHIP, but even those numbers were worse than 2009 and 2010. His total for 2011 was 3.94 and 1.25.

Similarly, hitters coming off shoulder or wrist surgery can take half a year or more to regain their full power.

- *Japanese player stats.* Trying to ascertain how a Japanese player's stats will translate to the U.S. should be treated similarly to those of a AAA player. One key difference is that the fences in Japan are mostly shorter.

- *Spring training stats.* These are mostly irrelevant. Don't alter your projections because a player is hot or cold or has hit a couple of home runs. Players get hot and cold all the time, not to mention that during the spring they may be working on things other than just trying to get great stats. And they are probably facing a lot of AA and AAA players. Many hitters' hot springs quickly turn into a slump when they head north and into the cold April weather.

  There can be some useful spring stats; for example, if a player is coming off a leg injury, it's a good sign if he steals a couple of bases.

- *Batting-order changes.* Changing spots in the batting order can make a big difference. Being moved from the bottom of the order to the top can increase a hitter's at bats by 50–100 over the course of a full season. The hitter's runs scored and RBIs will also be affected if they change spots in the order. For example, #1 and #2 hitters tend to have lots of runs scored and fewer RBIs.

- *New starting pitcher.* When a pitcher moves from the bullpen to a starting role, they have to throw more pitches and can't keep up the velocity they display when only pitching an inning or two at a time. Therefore, their ERA and WHIP should increase and their strikeout rate will decline. When a pitcher goes from the rotation to the bullpen, the opposite will occur.

- *Playing time estimates.* This can be difficult to project for many players. As your draft or auction approaches, check the latest player notes and depth charts to help your estimate.

Wins and Saves

Some people say that wins are a crapshoot and therefore very difficult to predict. I disagree. They can be a bit fluky, but if you consider the ability of the pitcher—what's his ERA likely to be, and will he last deep into games? plus the run support he's likely to get—you can make a reasonable guess at how many wins he will have. Sure, he could end up +/– 2 wins or even +/– 4 wins, but the job of projecting is to predict the average of all likely outcomes. So that's what you have to go by. (This is really no different than projecting home runs, stolen bases, or any other stat.)

People also say that saves can be a crapshoot. One year a closer might get 35 saves and then the next year 42. Many closers will lose their jobs. However, it is very possible to make good, reasonable projections. You know before the season starts how much of a track record the closer has, how much job security he appears to have, and if his team is likely to win a lot of games.

If a guy has clear job-security issues, then don't project him for 35 or 40 saves. Project the average of all possible outcomes. If a guy has been successful at closing—having saved 112 games over the last three years—and appears to be healthy and without competition, then there's no reason not to feel comfortable projecting him for 37 or so saves.

It appears obvious that the better the team, the more wins they'll get, and thus the more saves. However, some people wonder if the really good teams win a lot of blowouts, therefore missing out on many saves. Similarly, some have hypothesized that if a team doesn't score a lot of runs, they will generate a lot of saves because when they do win, it's usually a close game.

Let's examine these. The numbers below combine the 2011 and 2012 MLB seasons:

# Wins	Avg. Wins	Avg. Saves	% Saves/Wins
90+	94.4	47.6	.504
80–89	84.3	41.7	.495
70–79	74.2	40.5	.546
<70	64.3	34	.529

We can see that it is true that the worse teams (those who won 79 or less games) did generate a higher percentage of saves per win. However, the really good teams (90+ wins) still generated a much higher volume of saves (47.6). So if everything else is equal, it is clearly best to get a closer from a team you expect will win a lot of games.

To analyze saves by runs scored, I'm again using the 2011 and 2012 seasons combined, but have separated the stats by league, since more runs are scored in the AL:

AL

Runs/Gm	Avg. Wins	Avg. Saves	% Saves/Wins
4.6+	92.5	42.8	.463
4.3–4.59	79.5	37.5	.472
<4.3	74.9	41.2	.550

NL

Runs/Gm	Avg. Wins	Avg. Saves	% Saves/Wins
4.5+	83.3	44.1	.530
4.0–4.49	85.5	47.1	.551
<4.0	73.3	40.2	.548

You can deduce from this that the lower-scoring teams do, in fact, have a higher percentage of saves. It's interesting to note that the NL, which scores fewer runs, has an overall higher percentage of saves than the AL. That also proves the point that lower-scoring teams do get a higher percentage of saves.

However, the sheer quantity of saves still favors the teams that score more, but by a smaller margin than the "# Wins" chart above. (Obviously, teams that score more tend to win more games.)

Age 27 Breakout?

There's a lot of hype among fantasy players that the age 27 year is when many hitters have their breakout season. However, the facts show that this isn't really true. It is a myth.

First, there are variables such as does a player turn 27 in February before the season starts? Or what if he turns 27 in December after the season is over? Those two players are really almost one year apart in age. There are some 27-year-olds who have already been in the big leagues playing full-time for a few years, and there are others who didn't get called up until recently. So experience is a big variable.

Tristan Cockroft, writing for ESPN, did a study of this that was published in 2008. He concluded that, overall, players tend to show improvement from age 24 to 28. A player is just as likely to make a leap in productivity at any of those ages. The prime years are roughly age 26 to 32, after which many players will start to decline.

I have not conducted any analysis myself, but based on my experience, I totally accept Tristan's conclusions. There is nothing magic about age 27. I have seen many players improve anywhere from age 24 to 28. There are some analysts who now think players don't actually peak until 29 or 30.

Derek Carty published a similar study in 2011 for *Hardball Times*. He also concluded this is a myth.

High-Innings-Pitched Risk?

Tom Verducci, a writer for *Sports Illustrated*, came up with a theory called the Year-After Effect. The idea is that a pitcher age 25 or younger who throws 30 innings more than the previous season will be less effective as well as more susceptible to injury the following year. So if a pitcher accumulates 100 innings pitched in 2011, then throws 130 (or more) innings in 2012, he is likely to suffer ill effects in 2013.

Verducci keeps publishing his list of such pitchers every year, and many fantasy baseball players recite it as a truth. Other writers have forwarded similar ideas, such as changing the age limit or increasing the threshold to a 50-innings-pitched jump.

However, research by many has shown that these theories don't hold a lot of validity. Sure, there are many pitchers in this category who get hurt or decline the next season, but not necessarily more than the norm. Various studies have been done that show the results of these pitchers are not significantly better or worse than a control group.

Some of the problems with Verducci's rule include that he's looking at innings pitched rather than total pitches thrown; he does include minor-league and playoff games, but not winter ball or spring training, and he uses a rather arbitrary cutoff; it doesn't include someone who is age 25½ or has a 29-inning increase.

Contract-Year Effect?

There's a theory that players in the last year of their contract will perform well because they want to get a new contract. Since a player's motivation can affect how hard he trains in the off-season, how much he hustles, etc., this certainly makes sense. However, research doesn't back this up. For every study that shows a possible grain of truth to the theory, there's another one that shows it's false.

Eric Mack, writing for CBSsports.com in 2010, explains one of the reasons:

> Free agents tend to be past their prime. Most players have gone through at least six years before they can become a free agent: three years on one-year tenders and then three years in salary arbitration. And there's a modern trend of locking up players through their arbitration years and first couple years of free-agent eligibility. If you arrive in the majors at age 25, six years puts you at 31 and therefore on the way down, not up.

And for the relatively small number that are only 26 or 27, any improvement can just as easily be attributed to the fact that they are still in their improving years, not necessarily because of the impeding free-agency.

The other side of this theory is that having just signed a new long-term contract, a player may tend to slouch off. Again, this sounds good, but research doesn't prove it. Any studies showing that there tends to be a slight decline after signing a contract can just as easily be attributed to the fact that, as Eric Mack says, most of these players are on the way down, anyway.

My Sabermetric Research

As I mentioned, I started to look into sabermetrics during the winter of 2012. There were a few things I learned.

1. Sabermetrics can definitely be helpful in projecting performance.

2. A little knowledge can be a dangerous thing. If you don't fully understand what you're looking at, you can draw the wrong conclusions.

3. Sabermetrics can be very confusing. Having an economics degree is helpful. Unfortunately, I don't have an economics degree. I could only read about *regression analysis* and *correlation to the mean* for so long before my eyes would glaze over and I'd begin to feel light-headed.

Let's start with ERA. ERA is clearly a flawed measure of a pitcher's performance. It doesn't take into account luck factors, such

as how many bloop fly balls fell in for a hit, how many grounders found a hole, how many inherited base runners the bullpen
allowed to score, etc. Sabermetrics can adjust for much of this and
tell you what a pitcher's ERA *should* have really been had the luck
been more neutral.

But one of the problems is that sabermetrics mostly eliminates all factors, including where you play. So when, as mentioned before, they say that Jeremy Hellickson's 2.95 ERA should
have been 4.14, this means if he pitched in a neutral park with
a neutral defense and bullpen. If Tampa Bay had a neutral park,
defense, and bullpen in 2011, then that's a pretty good statistic.
But if Tampa Bay was above (or below) average in those areas,
then Hellickson's ERA should have been better (or worse)
than 4.14.

One of the key statistics is batting average on balls in play
(BABIP). That measures how many hits were made when the ball
was put in play. Therefore, it doesn't count walks, strikeouts, hit
by pitch, and home runs. The league average is usually around
.295–.300, so if a pitcher had a BABIP of .325, the assumption is
that he was either unlucky, had a bad defense, or a combination
of both.

The sabermetric measures, such as the ones Alex Patton cited
(ERC, xERA, FRA, FIP, and xFIP) will typically adjust that .325
BABIP to the league average for that season in order to *normalize* it.
They are looking to see what the pitcher's ERA would have been
with normal luck. This can be helpful, but the problem is that it
assumes everyone should have the same BABIP and discounts the
defense and park factors. Even the pitcher himself—if a good (or
bad) fielder—can save himself (or cost) a few hits a year.

In the case of Hellickson, his 2011 BABIP was an incredibly

low .223. The American League average was .291. The Tampa Bay pitching staff had a team BABIP of .265. It could be that Tampa Bay, as a team, was quite lucky. But more likely it means that park factors, such as the height of the infield grass, height of the outfield walls, etc. played a part. And it's quite likely the defense was exceptional and made an out on a lot of balls that other teams wouldn't have. Joe Maddon, manager of the Rays, was one of the first to use a lot of defensive shifts, which also may have played a part.

So when sabermetric measures say that Hellickson should have had a BABIP of .291 (and hence an ERA of 4.14), they are overstating it. Perhaps he should have had a BABIP of .265 (like the rest of his team).

In 2012, Tampa Bay had a team BABIP of .277, while the league average was again .291. So once again, they beat the average. And once again, Hellickson was even better, with a .261 BABIP. (His ERA was 3.10.)

And here is the *strand rate* data, which measures the percentage of men left on base:

	2011	2012
MLB average	72.5%	72.5%
AL average	71.8%	72.5%
Tampa Bay	75.5%	75.5%
Hellickson	82.0%	82.7%

Tampa Bay left 3% more runners stranded on base both years than the MLB average. And Hellickson did even better than that.

And it makes a big difference. If Hellickson's 2011 strand rate had been the Tampa Bay average of 75.5% rather than his actual 82%, his ERA would have been 3.55 rather than 2.95. If we normalize his strand rate to the league average of 71.8%, his ERA would have been 3.89.

This statistic only partially represents the job done by the bullpen when inheriting base runners left by the starting pitchers. It is mostly comprised of base runners stranded by the starter—or reliever—who put them on base in the first place. But it does indicate the bullpen was probably better than average, and Hellickson himself was excellent both years. Some of it may be luck, but some pitchers have a better ability than others to bear down with men on base and get out of a jam. Some are less effective when they have to pitch out of the stretch rather than a full windup. Therefore, any sabermetric measure that normalizes a pitcher's strand rate to the league average, as some do, is probably not being fair to a guy like Hellickson.

Some measures also normalize the home-run to fly-ball rate (HR/FB). The assumption again is that if the average pitcher has 10% of his fly balls leave the park for a homer, any pitcher who strayed far from that percentage was either lucky or unlucky. Here's that data:

	2011	2012
MLB average	9.7%	11.3%
AL average	9.8%	11.6%
Tampa Bay	9.8%	10.7%
Hellickson	8.1%	12.4%

For this, Hellickson beat the average in 2011 but was worse than average in 2012. So for this stat, perhaps he really was a little lucky in 2011 and a little unlucky in 2012.

I would infer from all of this that for 2013, assuming the Tampa Bay defense and bullpen stays relatively the same, Hellickson will continue to do better than average with BABIP and strand rate, while his HR/FB rate should normalize close to the league average.

This is why I say a little knowledge can be a dangerous thing. If you simply read that Hellickson's ERA should have been 4.14, this is misleading. In fact, prior to my looking into this topic, that is exactly what I thought it meant. I thought they were saying his ERA should have been 4.14 and that's all there was to it. But to get a clearer picture, you need to take a look at the league and team averages, not to mention Hellickson's own averages.

And consider these HR/FB rates:

	2011	2012
NL average	9.6%	11.0%
Colorado	11.6%	13.7%
San Francisco	6.9%	9.9%

It's clear that balls fly out of the thin air at Coors Field more than the average park, and it's also well known that San Francisco is a tough place to hit one out. Therefore, if you use a system that normalizes the HR/FB rate to the league average, Rockies pitchers are going to look a lot more attractive than they should, and Giants pitchers will be undervalued.

The sabermetric systems that normalize everything to the league average may be useful for a real MLB general manager evaluating talent. He can estimate how good a pitcher would be pitching in a neutral park with a neutral defense. And if you need to forecast a player who's moved from one team to another, this can be useful. But when a player will stay with his team and ballpark, normalizing everything to the league average is not necessarily helpful for forecasting future performance.

How Much Does a Pitcher Really Control?

There are more sabermetric measures for ERA than just the five referenced by Alex Patton. The genesis for all of these was a study done in 2000 by Voros McCracken. His research discovered that pitchers basically have no control over their BABIP. For example, Greg Maddux (one of the best pitchers at the time) was no better at inducing weak contact and thus preventing hits than any other pitcher. Once a ball was put in play, the BABIP was similar for all levels of pitchers.

McCracken created a formula, called DIPS, meaning Defense Independent Pitching Stats. This looked only at elements fully under the control of the pitcher . . . strikeouts, walks, hit batters, and home runs. Everyone's BABIP was regressed to the league average.

Since then there has been much subsequent research and debate. Some researchers came to the conclusion that pitchers also don't really have much control over their home-run rate. They take McCracken's original formula and add an element to normalize the pitcher's HR/FB rate to the league average.

There are several examples of pitchers, such as Matt Cain, who consistently beat the league averages. Some will argue that this is simply by random chance. And yet you see a guy like Cain consistently beating his expected ERA and have a hard time believing it's random. You watch Justin Verlander pitch and have a hard time believing the balls put in play have as good a chance of getting a hit as the balls in play against a weaker-throwing pitcher with an ERA of 5.00.

Indeed, many researchers now believe that pitchers do have an effect on their BABIP. When analyzing the types of balls in play—grounders, fly balls (not including homers), line drives, and infield pop-ups—it is clear that more grounders turn into hits (about 25%) than do fly balls (about 15%). Line drives (about 70%) have the highest percentage of being a hit, and infield pops almost never become a hit. Thus, some expected ERA formulas will adjust the BABIP based on the percentage of fly balls/ground balls a pitcher allowed.

Some research also suggests that higher strikeout pitchers do tend to induce weaker contact and can sustain a BABIP that is lower than league average. There may actually be an overlap here, because pitchers with a high strikeout rate tend to also get more fly balls than grounders. So a pitcher with a high strikeout rate who doesn't get a lot of fly balls may be less likely to beat the league BABIP.

Matt Swartz, who helped develop a system called SIERA for Baseball Prospectus, and then later refined it, wrote this in a July 2011 column on FanGraphs.com:

Looking at all 3,328 pitcher-seasons (with at least 40 innings pitched) between 2002 and 2010, I sorted players into four groups by strikeout rate. The higher the strikeout rate, the lower the BABIP and HR/FB at each level:

Strikeout Group	BABIP	HR/FB
High	.286	9.1%
Medium-High	.295	10.2%
Medium-Low	.298	10.7%
Low	.301	10.7%

Assuming Matt did this correctly, it's hard to accept McCracken's hypothesis that pitchers have little control over their BABIP and the subsequent hypothesis by others that pitchers don't control their home-run rate. The only outstanding question here is how much is really because of a high strikeout rate and how much is due to a higher percentage of fly balls.

Going back again to Jeremy Hellickson, I was curious to see how he compared in the strikeout and ground-ball rate. I looked at all American League pitchers who threw at least 150 innings in 2011 and 2012:

Pitcher	Year	Best K/9 Rate	Lowest GB%
Hellickson	2011	37th of 47	4th of 47
Hellickson	2012	31st of 42	13th of 42

His strikeout rate was actually very low both years, and yet he allowed very few ground balls. The lack of ground balls (GB) is another explanation for why Hellickson's BABIP was so low.

My Conclusions

I think there is definitely value in considering data such as BABIP when projecting a pitcher's future performance. However, it isn't easily applied. The various systems that try to estimate what an ERA should have been mostly regress everything to the league average, but there are clearly some teams with above (or below) average defense, some parks that allow more (or fewer) home runs, and some pitchers who are consistently better (or worse) than the averages.

Hellickson is a great example of this. To say that his 2.95 ERA should have been 4.14 misses that Tampa Bay has a good defense and lower home-run rate, and that Hellickson himself appears to be very good with runners on and gives up fewer grounders than most. Could this all be a fluke and random occurrence? Yes, but I wouldn't want to bet on it.

To be fair, the people who produce these sabermetric measures aren't necessarily saying that you should use their exact numbers as a future prediction. Ron Shandler, founder of the Baseball HQ website, told me, "You can't just use xERA in a vacuum. It's just one data point." And in his annual *Baseball Forecaster*, they explain that you should ignore a variance of only .50 between an actual ERA and the xERA. *Baseball Forecaster* instructs, "Any variance more than one run per game is regarded as an indicator of future change." So they aren't saying they necessarily expect the ERA to increase by a full run. In this context, xERA and the other measures do have a use.

Besides the likes of Hellickson and Cain, there certainly are a lot of pitchers who did indeed get lucky, or unlucky. If a pitcher had a high BABIP, high HR/FB rate, and low strand rate—playing for a team that has fairly neutral team averages—he is a good bet to improve his ERA. Knowing this gives you an edge on your competitors who are simply looking at his ERA.

Most of the systems to determine what should have been or predict what will be use a one-size-fits-all formula or algorithm. Some of them claim that FIP, xFIP, SIERA, etc. are better at predicting future ERAs than simply looking at the ERA itself. I don't doubt that this is true. But the problem is that you don't need to draft 150 pitchers. Usually you only need nine or ten. So you don't want to think certain pitchers are a good deal and draft them when in fact the system didn't properly account for their numbers. Not drafting Hellickson or Cain because they are mistakenly undervalued won't be a problem, but you will draft pitchers who are mistakenly overvalued, and that *will* be a problem.

I think that you've got to evaluate each pitcher individually, and take a look at his BABIP, HR/FB, and strand rates, as well as GB% and strikeout rate. And comparing them to his team average is much more useful than looking at the league average. Better yet is to look at the pitcher's own history and compare him to himself. Finally, you also have to consider if there have been any meaningful changes to the team's defense or bullpen during the off-season.

When I made my player projections for 2013, in addition to my usual magazines and web sources, I also used FanGraphs.com. They show each pitcher's yearly history for all of these stats.

I learned that using sabermetrics is absolutely helpful in trying to predict future performance, but it's more an art than a science. There's no easy way to know how much a pitcher controlled and how much was luck, and exactly what his ERA really should have been or will be next year.

Other Pitching Stats

I've been discussing ERA because it is the most flawed and dissected pitching stat. There are not a lot of systems and theories to project WHIP. But if you take what we've learned about BABIP, you can make a simple estimate. Suppose you have a pitcher with a .264 BABIP who allowed 190 hits and 50 walks in 185 innings pitched for a WHIP of 1.297. However, based on his previous few years' BABIP, as well as his ground-ball rate and his team's BABIP, you suspect his low BABIP was mostly due to luck and should regress to around .282. Therefore, he should have given up $.282/.264 \times 190 = 203$ hits, which would have resulted in a WHIP of $203 + 50/185 = 1.368$.

For WHIP, the strand rate is not relevant. The HR/FB rate is essentially irrelevant. Perhaps a couple of more balls should have left the park rather than being caught on the warning track or dropping in for a double, but it won't make much difference.

If you search the Internet for "xWHIP" you can find a few formulas that break down the pitcher's BABIP and team BABIP and analyze them by types of batted ball. These formulas try to estimate what the WHIP should have been, similar to the estimated ERA formulas.

For projecting wins and saves there aren't any particularly useful sabermetric methods. For strikeouts, there is some analysis that correlates a pitcher's swinging strike percentage with his strikeout rate. A pitcher with a high swinging strike percentage and low strikeout rate should improve his strikeouts, and vice versa.

Hitting

BABIP applies to hitters as well. When they aren't walking, striking out, or hitting a home run, they put the ball in play. Some of those are hits and some aren't. While McCracken and some others think that pitchers have very little control over their BABIP, virtually nobody disagrees that hitters do have more influence over their BABIP.

Some hitters make hard contact more often than others, which results in more hits. Some have more speed, which results in more infield hits. Some hit more line drives or ground balls, which leads to more hits than those with a higher percentage of fly balls. And some are hurt more than others by defensive shifts.

You can use an xBABIP formula to determine what a hitter's BABIP maybe should have been. These formulas typically regress the hitter's percentage of ground balls, fly balls, etc. to the league average of hits. This is far from perfect, because it usually doesn't account for where they play and their speed. It can give you an idea if a player was lucky, or unlucky, but you need to use some common sense to adjust for their park and speed.

It can be more useful to compare a hitter against his past history. Most hitters tend to establish their own hit rate that stabilizes over time. If a player has a three or more year track record in the majors, his BABIP from those years should give you a good estimate of future performance. If he's changed teams, or is getting older and has maybe lost a bit of speed, you can adjust for those.

You can search the Internet for "xBABIP" or "baseball xAVG" to find formulas and a list of expected batting-average estimates for the current or prior year. You can also find them in some publications and websites such as the *Baseball Forecaster* and BaseballHQ.com. For a player's historical BABIP and breakdown by type of ball in play, check out FanGraphs.com or Baseball-Reference.com.

Home Runs

The ratio of home runs to fly balls (HR/FB) is a leading indicator of whether a hitter was perhaps lucky to hit as many home runs as he did—or should have hit more. But it's not something that can be easily compared to the league average. Aside from some parks being easier to hit home runs in, the sluggers will have a much higher rate of HR/FB than an average or weak hitter.

Again, if a player has been around for three years or more, you can compare his own rates. If his HR/FB rates the last three years were 18%, 17%, and 23%—and there's no apparent logical reason for the increase—then it's likely the 23% was an outlier and he should regress back toward 18–19%. (A logical reason might be that he's at an age where his power was still developing or that he had been playing hurt or in a park that's worse for hitters the prior two years.)

The number of fly balls hit is, obviously, an important part of this equation. If a player has a meaningful change in his percentage of fly balls, that should correlate to a change in home runs hit. If a hitter's fly-ball percentages the past three years have been 40%, 40%, and 34%, it's likely to revert back toward the 40%. However, you need to be careful when making that assumption, because it could also be a sign of a player who is past his prime starting to decline, or perhaps even a conscious change in approach to sacrifice power to get more hits.

ESPN has a home-run tracker (Hittrackeronline.com) where they chart each home-run by the distance it traveled. They categorize the homers by *No Doubt*, *Plenty*, *Just Enough* and *Lucky*. *Just Enough* means it barely cleared the fence and *Lucky* means it was aided by wind and/or excessive humidity. If a player had an unusually high percentage of Just Enough and Lucky home runs, then he's probably due for a decrease—and vice versa. You may not have time to go through every hitter and look at his historical FB%, HR/FB%, and the home-run tracker, but for at least some tough cases you might want to.

For example, Curtis Granderson had this three-year record:

Year	Team	ABs	HRs	FB%	HR/FB
2009	DET	631	30	49%	12.6%
2010	NYY	466	24	47%	14.5%
2011	NYY	583	41	48%	20.5%

When he left the Tigers and went to Yankee Stadium, with its friendly short right-field porch, it was not a surprise that this left-handed hitter saw an increase in his HR/FB rate, from 12.6% to

14.5%. Had he gotten as many at bats as he did in 2009, he would have hit 32 or 33 homers instead of just 24.

But when his HR/FB rate jumped to 20.5% in 2011 and he hit 41 homers, it *was* a surprise. His overall FB% stayed essentially the same all three years, and was actually slightly lower at Yankee Stadium. When the 2011 season began, he had just turned 30, so a power increase due to age was not likely much of a factor.

When projecting him for 2012, the obvious question was "Can he keep this up?" Looking at a home-run trend like this, my instincts would tell me that the 41 homers were an unusual leap, and he should regress back toward the low 30s. But the home-run tracker tells us that in 2010 only 13% of his homers were of the Just Enough or Lucky type—far below the normal rate (about 27%). In 2011 this normalized, as exactly 27% of his homers were Just Enough or Lucky. With this knowledge, it's not as surprising that his rate jumped in 2011.

And look what he did in 2012:

Year	Team	ABs	HRs	FB%	HR/FB
2012	NYY	596	43	44%	24.2%

His FB% actually decreased, but the percentage that left the yard increased yet again. His 2012 Just Enough and Lucky percentage was a little low at 21%.

So what do we make of all of this? There's no concrete conclusion to be drawn, but considering the home-run tracker, along with the FB% and HR/FB rates, we can get clues as to what is likely to occur in the future. This is better than guessing based solely on how many homers a guy hit in the past, where he's played, and how old he is. Some people also like to consider how many doubles a player hit the prior year. The logic is that if a lot of doubles were hit, some of them may turn into home runs, especially if the player is young and at an age where he's likely to get stronger.

Runs and RBIs

Some sabermetricians will try to normalize a hitter's run and RBI production based on criteria such as his spot in the batting order and the strength of his team's lineup.

Some will try to predict future performance using an algorithm based on factors such as how often he gets on base, how he gets on base, stolen bases, and the strength of the team.

Stolen Bases

Sabermetric analysis can't trump the biggest factor in determining future stolen bases, which is the manager's decision to run. If a manager has always liked to steal a lot, that trend will probably continue. But a managerial change or a player switching teams can have a big impact—positive or negative—on his attempts. If a team has added, or lost, a couple of power hitters, that can change a manager's philosophy.

Besides the obvious factors such as how often will a player get on base, and how much has he run in the past, there is another factor—which, frankly, is also pretty obvious: How often has he been caught stealing in the past? If he has been caught a lot, his manager may stop giving him the green light.

Minor League Equivalents

Some projection systems try to estimate what a minor leaguer would have done in the majors. They examine data from players who make the jump from AAA (or AA) to the majors as well as players who get demoted from the majors to AAA (or AA). They also adjust for park factors.

The goal isn't to predict future performance, but rather to convert minor league stats into a major league equivalent. For example, if a player hit .300 with 30 homers at AAA, perhaps that would convert to .260 with 23 homers at the major league level. Knowing this can help you predict the future performance of a player who is getting called up.

However, minor league equivalents are not very reliable, partly because it's a very inexact science and partly because the sample sizes are often small. Some players don't even spend a full year at AAA.

Draft Skills, Not Role?

A lot of fantasy experts preach that you should draft players who have good fundamental skills, such as K/BB rate, contact rate, etc. and not worry so much about their role on the team. The idea is that roles change and talent will win out.

All things being equal, sure, I'll take talent and skills over someone with less talent and skills. But you can't just ignore roles. At draft time, we usually have a good idea who's going to be in the starting lineup for major league teams, who their starting pitchers will be, and their closer. If there are two guys battling for a closer job, and you can get them for the same price, and one is clearly more skilled, then sure, take the skilled guy.

But if there is no competition, the less-skilled guy has been the closer for two years and has been fairly successful, and the manager has given no indication his job is in danger then guess what? His role trumps the setup guy who may have better skills but is still going to be the setup guy! He is almost certainly going to be the more valuable fantasy asset for the upcoming year.

A player's talent and skills, as well as his expected role, should all be factored in when you are making your stat projections. And then, as with everyone, it's a question of can you buy the player at a good price? If you can get the talented setup man for $2 it might be a better deal than spending $17 to get the closer.

CHAPTER 6

Value Formulas

Once you have projected statistics for all relevant players, as described in chapter 5, those raw statistics must now be converted to a value.

For an auction league, every team should be able to buy $260 worth of value for their $260 budget. So for a 12-team league, the total value of the 276 players in the player pool should equal $3,120. And the value of the 168th-best hitter and 108th-best pitcher should equal $1. That's because at the end of the auction, you won't have to spend more than just $1 to buy the last hitter and pitcher. Also, since $1 is the minimum bid, you can't have anyone in the player pool valued at less than $1. (For a 15-team auction you must have a total of $3,900 value, and the 210th hitter and 135th pitcher would be worth $1.)

For a snake draft or salary-cap game, it is not necessary to have the values conform like this. Nor is it necessary to even think of values as a *dollar* value. You could create a formula where Clayton Kershaw's projected value is 350 or 35,000 or 3,500,000.

If you are playing a Points-style game, it is very simple to know what the correct value formula is. If the scoring system is one point for a run, four points for a homer, ten points for a win, etc., any fifth-grader can easily calculate the projected value of each player. You simply take the number of runs, plus four times the number of homers, plus ten times the number of wins, etc. If you only play a Points-style game, then you can stop reading this chapter right now.

But when you're dealing with Rotisserie baseball, it's not nearly so simple. You accumulate runs, homers, wins, etc., but how do you know if a homer is worth four more than a run? Is a win worth ten more than a run? That may be the scoring system some Points-style games use, but that's quite different than Rotisserie scoring. And when it comes to batting average, ERA (earned run average), and WHIP (walks and hits / innings pitched), it gets even more complicated. Now you have to place a value on a ratio statistic. And you must ask yourself questions such as "If one player has a .300 batting average with 600 at bats, that is clearly more valuable than someone with a .300 batting average with just 200 at bats, but how much more valuable? How do I quantify that into a specific value?"

If you could use a perfect valuation system—while most of your competition is using something not quite so perfect or even flawed—that would obviously be a big advantage for you. That would be fantastic! Correct?

Well, not necessarily. It would be a good thing in some respects, but it also might lead you to draft a team with too many stolen bases, too many home runs, too few saves, or various other problems. This is because when it comes to drafting a team, everyone has their own set of values.

Let's say that everyone else in the world values a save at somewhere between 20 and 35 cents each, and you value a save at 45 cents. Even if you're right, and everyone else is wrong, that only helps you so much. You would buy a closer or two, and you'd have gotten a good deal, because everyone else was undervaluing saves. You might have bought a closer you know is worth $25 and only had to pay $20 to get him. But you can't keep buying more closers—even though you know they are bargains—because you'll just end up with too many saves. And if you try to trade your excess closers, you'll never get what you consider a fair trade, because nobody else thinks the closer is worth as much as you do.

Meanwhile, if everyone else is undervaluing saves, then they must be overvaluing something else. Let's say it is stolen bases. This means you might have to overpay to get stolen bases and be competitive in that category. Your overpaying for steals offsets the bargains you got for saves. So you haven't really gained anything.

Does this mean the value formula is irrelevant? No, it's still a very important aspect of being a good fantasy baseball player. If you are using a good, sound formula, you will be better off than someone else who is using a very flawed formula. However, when it comes to drafting your team, you'll need to be aware that your formula may value certain things a little differently than most of your competitors, and you'll need to adjust for that.

I know some fantasy players who spend a lot of time making projections and preparing for their drafts, and yet they are using flawed or ill-conceived formulas. They are spending lots of time and effort, but then hurting themselves by not having a decent formula. That's like preparing a car for the Indy 500 and then just picking up some tires off the rack from a discount tire store.

There are two popular and widely used value formulas. One is called SGP, which is short for Standings Gain Points, and the other is PVM, short for Percentage Value Method. People who use either SGP or PVM are typically not using the same exact formula, because they make different assumptions and tweaks along the way. So if you have a player who hits .270 in 600 at bats, with 85 runs, 10 homers, 55 RBIs, and 15 steals, and you ask ten different fantasy players what his value is, you're likely to get ten different answers.

I would rather be going to the dentist to get a root canal than have to write this chapter. This is a very complicated and confusing subject. I could write an entire book about it. There is much debate about which formula is best and what can or cannot be proven mathematically. And what may be mathematically and logically accurate must be adjusted to account for everyone else's flaws to become practical and useful.

So I'm going to discuss these formulas as simply as I can, so that your eyes don't glaze over too quickly. I'm going to just write a chapter, not an entire book. I'm going to explain the basic way that they work—the strengths and flaws—and the tweaks that need to be made. The good news is that I'm not a mathematician, so I couldn't make it too complex even if I wanted to.

SGP Formulas

Alex Patton, writing in the late 1980s, was the first person to publish some of the concepts of the SGP formula. Art McGee wrote the book *How to Value Players for Rotisserie Baseball* in 2007. McGee discusses in detail his version of the SGP formula.

SGP formulas are based on the idea that the best way to determine value is to see the effect of raw stats on the actual standings in your Rotisserie league. For example, if you've been in a 12-team league for six years, you can calculate the averages of the final standings per category each year. Suppose the six-year history shows that the team who finished with the most home runs averaged 224 per year, and the team with the fewest averaged 150. This means it took an average of (224 − 150)/11 = 6.73 home runs to gain one point in the standings.

This logic makes sense since, after all, the primary objective is to gain points in the standings. If it took an average of 6.5 steals to gain one point in the stolen-base category, then we know that steals are a little more valuable than homers. If we get six and a half stolen bases we gain a point, but it takes a little more than 6.7 homers to gain a point. Doing this for all categories gives us the exact value of each statistic.

In the home-runs example above, I simply subtracted the lowest average from the highest and divided by 11. This only measures two values, the best and worst teams. A more exact way is to use the average for all 12 spots. Enter the home-run standings—from the best, next-best, third-best, all the way down to worst—into a spreadsheet and run a regression (called the Slope function in Excel). This value will almost certainly not be 6.73 and will be a more accurate value to use.

For now, though, I'll stick with 6.73. Also, let's say that the average number of runs to gain one point is 21 and for RBIs it's 20.6.

The average number to gain one point becomes the

denominator in the formula for the appropriate category. Our formula would look like this:

$$(RUN/21) + (HR/6.73) + (RBI/20.6) + (SB/6.5) = SGPs$$

I've left off batting average, because that's a little more involved. We can calculate that it takes, for example, a .0018 increase to gain a point in batting average. But you can't simply divide a player's batting average by that. You need to figure out the effect the player will have on your team's total average. To do this, you assume that you have a roster of 13 average hitters, and then see what happens when you add a particular player.

If you examine the six-year history of your league, you can calculate that, for example, the average team had 1,596 hits in 5,880 at bats for a batting average of .2714. So a roster of 13 average hitters would have $(13/14) \times 1,596 = 1,482$ hits in $(13/14) \times 5,880 = 5,460$ at bats, for an average of .2714.

If we now add someone who is projected to get 150 hits in 500 at bats for a .300 average, we can see his effect on the total. We would now be at 1,632/5,960 = .2738. This player has increased the team average by .2738 − .2714 = .0024. Since we determined that it takes .0018 to gain one point in the standings, we divide .0024 by .0018 to calculate this player's SGP value for batting average. In this case it is 1.33.

So the entire formula is:

$$(RUN/21) + (HR/6.73) + (RBI/20.6) + (SB/6.5) +$$
$$((((1482 + HITS)/(5460 + AB)) - .2714/.0018) = SGP$$

Pitchers' SGPs are calculated in a similar fashion. For ERA and WHIP, you use the same logic as with batting average. You examine the league history and find the team averages for innings pitched, earned runs allowed, and hits and walks allowed. Use

8/9 of the team average, and you can see the effect a particular pitcher has on your team ERA and WHIP when he is added as your ninth pitcher. Your formula would look something like this:

$$(WIN/2.79) + (SAVE/4.34) + (K/26.5) +$$
$$((3.98 - ((ER + 469) \times (9/(IP + 1060))))/.08) +$$
$$((1.302 - ((1380 + H + BB)/(IP + 1060)))/.013) = SGP$$

In this example, the average pitcher threw 132.5 innings with a 3.98 ERA and 1.302 WHIP. This example is from a mono-league, but the procedure is the same for a mixed league, it's just that the denominators and averages would change accordingly.

You'll note that for batting average, ERA, and WHIP, approximately half the players will be worse than average and thus have a negative SGP contribution for that category.

Now that we know the formula, we can calculate the SGP value for all hitters and pitchers. We then identify the best 168 hitters (provided we have at least 24 catchers, 60 outfielders, etc.) and the best 108 pitchers.

For my 2011 AL-only league, the 168 hitters' total projected production was 1,410 SGPs and the pitchers' was 850, for a grand total of 2,260 SGPs. Since we have a total budget of $3,120, this means each SGP is worth 3,120/2,260 = $1.38.

Hitting/Pitching Breakdown

I'm going to talk about dollar values for a little while, but these values can also be used for a draft or salary-cap game. And later on I'll specifically discuss drafts and salary-cap values.

Whether you use an SGP-based formula or something else, you have a choice of how to allocate the $3,120 between hitting and pitching. While most people these days tend to spend an average of 69% of their money on hitting at auctions, as best as I can estimate I think the average value formula uses a split of 67/33%. To be clear, what I'm saying is that when people make their values, the average split they use is 67/33% (it can range anywhere from 65/35% up to 71/29%), but at auctions the average amount actually spent is close to a 69/31% split. Therefore, people tend to overspend slightly at auctions for hitters and get slight discounts on pitchers.

The point isn't whether you can justify and prove that you're right for choosing the split that you use. Heck, you can even make a case for a 50/50% split, since pitching categories count for 50% of the standings, just like hitting. But the point is to be aware of what split you use, and how that will alter your perception of auction prices. If you use a 65/35% split, you will be putting more money into pitchers than the average. You will be at your auction thinking pitchers are being sold for discounts and hitters are very expensive. If you use a 69/31% split, you'll have the opposite impression.

My 2011 league had 1,410 hitting SGPs and 850 pitching SGPs. This is a breakdown of 62.4/37.6%. I could make a case that this is the correct split to use, since these are the actual SGPs that will be produced. But doing this would make my pitching prices much too high compared to others, and my hitters much too low. So let's continue this example by using the more typical split of 67/33%.

This means we will allocate $2,090 (67%) to hitters and $1,030 (33%) to pitchers. Therefore, the value we place on hitting SGPs is 2,090/1,410 = $1.48. Pitching SGPs are worth 1,030/850 = $1.21.

Calculating Dollar Values

The best hitter, Carl Crawford, is worth 20 SGPs, so his dollar value is 20 × 1.48 = $29.60. The worst hitter, catcher Hank Conger, is worth 1.98 SGPs, so his value is 1.98 × 1.48 = $2.93.

But there's a problem with this. As I've stated before, the 168th hitter must be worth only $1. Since we can automatically get Conger at the end of the auction for just $1, there's no need to spend $2.93 for him. Therefore, we can subtract $1.93 from everyone's value to bring him down to $1. We now have an extra $324.2 ($1.93 × 168) to spread among the other hitters.

We had our hitting value at $2,090, but have removed $324.2, so it now stands at $1,765.80. This means we can multiply everyone by 2,090/1,765.8 = 1.184. Doing this brings our total value back to $2,090, but unfortunately it has also made Conger worth $1.20.

Doing another round of adjustments, we subtract 20 cents from everyone. This removes .20 × 168 = $33.60 from the pool, so we multiply everyone by 2,090/2,056.40 = 1.016. Now we're back to $2,090 total value, and Conger's value of 1.016 is rounded off to exactly $1.00.

Doing this has put more money into the top players. Crawford is now worth $33.

In his book, Art McGee explains his concept of marginal SGPs. This is another way of describing what I just did to lower Conger's value to $1. The idea is that since we automatically get at least Conger's 1.98 SGPs for a dollar, we won't place any extra value on the first 1.98 SGPs for anyone. We assign everyone a base value of $1 and deduct their first 1.98 SGPs. This leaves us with:

Total Dollars	$2,090	Total SGP	1,410	
Base Dollars	– $ 168	Base SGP	– 332.6	(168 × 1.98)
Marginal Dollars	$1,922	Marginal SGP	1,077.4	

Subtracting $1 and 1.98 SGPs from all 168 hitters leaves us with $1,922 marginal dollars to spend on 1,077.4 marginal SGPs. This means the value of each marginal SGP is worth $1,922/1,077.4 = $1.784. The dollar value formula is therefore:

$$(SGP - 1.98) \times 1.784 + 1$$

You will arrive at the same exact dollar values whether you adjust them as I did or use McGee's marginal SGP method. Either way, what you're doing is lowering the value of the 168th hitter to $1 and then redistributing money elsewhere. I would guess McGee's method is easier to use, but you need to be aware of the first method because if you don't use an SGP-based formula, you still need to tweak the values (up or down) such that the 168th hitter is worth $1.

Pitchers' values are calculated in the same fashion. The 108th-best pitcher contributes 3.58 SGPs. Multiplying that by $1.21 equals $4.33. I must adjust him down to $1 and redistribute the money elsewhere such that the total for all pitchers is $1,030.

Sometimes people would rather leave an injured player in their lineup rather than replacing him with someone they perceive will do more harm than good. And if a player's value is negative, that would appear to be the case. However, even most players with a negative dollar value actually contribute positive SGPs, so you're better off using them.

Position Scarcity?

Conger, worth $1, is the 168th-best hitter. Let's look at the bottom ten:

Rank	Pos	Value
159	OF	$2.6
160	3B	$2.0
161	SS	$1.9
162	2B	$1.9
163	1B	$1.8
164	C	$1.8
165	C	$1.5
166	C	$1.3
167	C	$1.2
168	C	$1.0

My bottom ten will look fairly similar to this each year, whether I'm using an SGP-based formula or something else. Not surprisingly, the worst five hitters are all catchers. There were six non-catchers who didn't make the player pool, yet they had more SGPs than these five catchers.

Because of this, you can make an argument that catchers should be looked at separately. With these values, I'm assured of getting at least a $1 catcher for my last $1. I'm also assured of getting at least a $1.8 corner infielder, a $1.9 middle infielder, or a $2.6 outfielder for my last $1. So it would be better to spend my last dollar on a non-catcher:

Position	Value	Price	Value	Price
Catcher	$5.0	$ 5	$ 1	$ 1
1B	$1.8	$ 1	$ 5	$ 5
Total:	$6.8	$ 6	$ 6	$ 6

If I pay full price for a $5 catcher and use my last dollar for a first baseman, I'm better off than if I pay full price for a $5 first baseman and use my last dollar for a catcher. In essence, catchers are worth 80 cents more than corner infielders, 90 cents more than middle infielders, and $1.60 more than outfielders. Here's another example:

Position	Value	Price	Value	Price
Catcher	$4.0	$ 5	$ 1	$ 1
OF	$2.6	$ 1	$ 5	$ 5
Total:	$6.6	$ 6	$ 6	$ 6

This example demonstrates that even if I overpay by a dollar to get the $4 catcher, I have still gained 60 cents by not saving my last dollar for a catcher. And in reality, to say that I overpaid by a dollar isn't correct, because catchers are really worth 80 cents more than non-catchers.

The way to adjust for this is to add 80 cents to the values of the catchers in my player pool. When I do this, I must then reduce the value of everyone by $19.20 (80 cents × 24 catchers) to get my total values back down to $2,090.

At this point, my 168th-best hitter is now a tie between Conger and a first baseman, both worth $1.80. So I must make the necessary adjustments to lower their values to $1 and then restore the total pool back to $2,090.

These adjustments have also made the values of the various worst players more reasonable. For my last dollar, I am guaranteed of getting a corner worth $1.0, a middle worth $1.1, or an outfielder worth $1.9. And doing all of this has also put more money into the better hitters. Crawford is now worth $34.3.

If the top 168 hitters don't contain at least 36 corner infielders, 36 middle infielders, or 60 outfielders, then you can theoretically treat the values of the other scarce position separately as well. This rarely happens, though.

This adjustment for catchers will be relevant whether using an SGP-based formula or something different.

Art McGee does provide a shortcut for this process. In the marginal SGP example above, I subtracted a base SGP of 1.98 for all hitters. But we could have made a distinction at that point between catchers and non-catchers. The worst non-catcher in my pool has 2.43 SGPs. Since we don't want to pay more than $1 for him, we should deduct a baseline of 2.43 SGPs for all non-catchers. This makes our total base SGPs (24 × 1.98) + (144 × 2.43) = 397.4:

Total Dollars	$2,090	Total SGP	1,410
Base Dollars	– $ 168	Base SGP	– 397.4
Marginal Dollars	$1,922	Marginal SGP	1,012.6

The marginal SGPs are now worth $1,922/1,012.6 = $1.898. And you need to set up your spreadsheet with two separate formulas (or use a "what if" function regarding position):

Catchers: (SGP – 1.98) × 1.898 + 1
Non-Catchers: (SGP – 2.43) × 1.898 + 1

So if we had just done this from the beginning, we would have solved the issues of reducing the 168th hitter to $1 and adjusting for catcher scarcity at the same time.

Hitter vs. Pitcher Scarcity?

Since the 168th hitter and 108th pitcher have a different number of SGPs, one quirk of the formula is that a hitter and pitcher with the same number of SGPs will end up with different dollar values.

In fact, since I've chosen a money split of 67/33% and the actual SGPs are split 62/38%, the dollar values would be different even if both worst players had identical SGPs.

Since the 168th hitter is worth 1.98 SGPs and the 108th pitcher contributes 3.58 SGPs, you could make an argument that we should adjust for hitter vs. pitcher scarcity, just as we did for catchers and non-catchers. If we pay $1 for a hitter, we get at least 1.98 SGPs. If we pay $1 for a pitcher, we get at least 3.58 SGPs. Therefore, we're better off buying the $1 pitcher.

Since we have a choice to buy a $15 non-catcher and a $1 catcher—rather than a $1 non-catcher and $15 catcher—we must make the scarcity adjustment for catchers.

We also have a choice to buy a $15 hitter and $1 pitcher, or a $1 hitter and $15 pitcher. Therefore, you can assert that we must also make the scarcity adjustment between hitters and pitchers. The problem, though, is that we can't just buy nine crappy pitchers. Even the most lopsided auction budgets still spend $50–60 on pitching, and the norm is around $80.

So we really need to treat hitters and pitchers separately. That's why I recommend you choose your dollar split (69/31%, 67/33%, or whatever) first, and then calculate the hitting and pitching dollar values separately, based on the total SGPs available for each category.

Differences of Opinion

I explain in other chapters that due to differences of opinion with my competitors, many players not in my pool will be bought by others. Therefore, for a mono-league, I can pretty much count on at least one catcher, five non-catchers, and eight pitchers to be bought (for a 15-team mixed league, even more).

Therefore, I'll further adjust the worst players a little to account for this. I'll end up showing a handful of hitters (and eight pitchers) with a value less than $1. I'll have the bottom values such that I feel confident I'll still be able to get at least $1 players for my last $1 at various positions. For example, if my pool of corner infielders has 40 players (36 plus 4 allotted at DH), I'll be counting on being able to buy at least the 38th- or 39th-best guy, so I'll have his value at approximately $1. And the 100th-best pitcher will be worth $1.

Again, this is a manipulation I'll make whether I'm using an SGP-based formula or not. The effect of this is it allows me to put a little more money into higher values. This is really just a psychological ploy to help me justify buying some of the top hitters and pitchers.

When using an SGP formula, an easy way to do this is to use the SGPs of the 23rd-best catcher, the 139th-best non-catcher, and the 100th-best pitcher as my baseline SGPs when calculating the marginal SGP value.

The Problem with SGP Formulas

SGP formulas are predicated on historical data. The problem is that getting enough good data can be difficult. And the denominators are very league-specific. If you have more or less than 12 teams in a league, or more or less than 23 players per team, this will make a difference. If you use nonstandard categories, such as *on-base average* or *holds*, it can be even tougher to get good information.

If you've played in the same league with the same people and same rules for 25 years, then that would be pretty reliable. Although even then, changes have occurred such as entering and ending the steroid era, and Houston moving to the American League.

I've examined many leagues that I've been in over the years, separating them by mono or mixed, American or National League, and calculated average denominators for the various categories. Even then, I don't feel as though I have definitive, concrete answers. Should I divide home runs by 6.7 or 6.8? I'm not really sure. And it wouldn't shock me if the correct answer is really 6.6 or 6.9.

Some sources have published data they've collected from a variety of leagues, and while I'm sure they've compiled accurate data, some of the results don't jibe well with the results from my leagues.

In his book, Art McGee mentions several times how you can tweak the denominators if you want to. For example, on page 46 he writes, "Think that these denominators are placing too much value on steals? Just increase the denominator and watch everyone's steals become less valuable." He implies that the ability to tweak the formula is a good thing. But here is where the whole problem lies! This formula is supposed to be based on historical data. If we could actually get reliable data, tweaking would not be an option! With a perfect formula, he would write, "Think that these denominators are placing too much value on steals? Too bad, that's what history tells us! Use this value because it's accurate!"

Having said all of this, overall I actually do like the SGP formula. Some critics of SGP say that it's only good looking back after the fact. I think this is a lazy argument. While it is true that we don't know in advance what the actual denominators will be in any given year, we can make our best guess based on the history we have. If I'm not sure if home runs should be divided by 6.7 or 6.8, I'll divide by 6.75, and that should be close enough.

When I am comparing my dollar values to other people's values, if I notice I tend to be higher (or lower) than most on home-run hitters, I'll know that I need to adjust my planned bids accordingly. Maybe using 6.75 was correct and everyone else was wrong—or maybe they're all right and I'm wrong. Either way, I simply need to alter my expectations for what I'll need to pay for a home-run hitter.

PVM Formulas

Percentage Value Method formulas assign values based on an individual's contribution to each stat category. For example, if the total 168 individuals in the player pool are projected to steal 1,000 bases, and Elvis Andrus is projected for 40, then he is assigned 4% of the value allocated to SB.

This is very simple and logical. And unlike with SGP formulas, no historical data or guessing is required. All you need are your projections for the upcoming season.

To demonstrate, we'll again use a 67/33% money split. This means we have $2,090 to allocate for hitting, which is $418 per category.

Ideally we want to know the projected stats for our best 168 hitters. The problem is, when we begin we don't know who those hitters are. For my 2011 AL-only league, I projected all players who I thought had a chance to be relevant. There were 230 of them. The total projected stats were 10,500 runs, 2,150 homers, 9,800 RBIs, and 1,450 steals. (I've rounded off to make it simpler.)

Therefore, each run is worth 418/10,500 = .0398, or about 4 cents. A hitter who will get 100 runs would be assigned a value of $4. A home run is worth 418/2,150 = .1944. Hitting 40 of them would be worth $7.78. And a steal is worth 418/1,450 = .2883. Stealing 40 bases is worth $11.53.

Again, figuring out what to do with batting average (ERA and WHIP) is more complex. One of the first well-known fantasy analysts, John Benson, wrote a 1993 book called *Rotisserie Baseball: Playing for Blood*. He explains in detail his PVM formula. His idea is to start by estimating the lowest team average in your league, because you start earning points when you're better than the lowest team. His rule of thumb for doing this is to use the median average of all players forecasted. My 228 projected hitters have a total batting average of .266, but the median average—which is the 114th and 115th hitters—is .257. His formula takes a player's batting average minus the mean and then multiplies by at bats. You then calculate the positive value (everyone above .257) and the negative value (everyone below .257), then adjust the total so that you have an absolute value of $418. *Absolute* value means, for example, that if everyone above the median has a total positive value of +300 and everyone below the median has a total negative value of –118, then that adds up to 418 of absolute value. That's what you want.

After creating the values for each category, we can identify the 168 hitters for our player pool. Since I've divided the $418 per category among 230 players rather than 168, and since the batting average has a total net value less than $418 ($300–$118 = $182, in the example above), this means that we will have to manipulate the total values. We manipulate them such that the total is $2,090, and the 168th hitter is equal to $1. We can also make a catcher-scarcity adjustment the same way that we did with the SGP formula.

For pitchers, you follow the same procedure. Benson subtracts pitchers' ERA and WHIP from the median and then multiplies by innings pitched.

I'm Not a Mathematician, But . . .

For the counting stats, PVM couldn't be simpler or more logical. But for batting average we're subtracting from the median and multiplying by the number of at bats? Where did this come from? Is this really the way to calculate the *percentage* of hitting value? Is it just me, or does this all seem very arbitrary?

Benson says he has done much research to indicate that using the median average of the projected players is a very good estimate of what the lowest team's batting average will be.

John Mosey came up with the idea of measuring *extra* hits. This calculates how many hits above (or below) the median a player gets per his at bats. For example, if the median is .250, a hitter with 600 at bats would get 150 hits. So if you project Mike Trout will hit .300 in 600 at bats, he produces 180 hits, which is 30 *extra* hits. Some analysts who questioned the validity of Benson's method have accepted Mosey's as being mathematically sound. And the interesting thing is this method leads to the same exact results as Benson's.

The Problem with PVM Formulas

While I'm not 100% convinced Benson's method for dealing with average, ERA, and WHIP makes perfect sense, there's no doubt that for counting stats it does make perfect sense. It is a completely logical and accurate way to measure scarce commodities.

However, for some categories it just isn't practical. If there will be 2,150 homers and 1,450 steals produced, it is accurate to say that steals are scarcer. And therefore stealing 40 bases is worth $11.53 while hitting 40 homers is only worth $7.78. That's almost 50% more valuable. But in practice this leads to dollar values that place way too much emphasis on steals. Top speedsters are assigned values that are typically $3–5 too high.

SGP data, inexact as it is, does show that when it comes to gaining a point in the standings, the true relationship between home runs and stolen bases is very close to even. When I first examined this, I wondered since steals are, in fact, much scarcer, how can this be? Why wouldn't a stolen base matter more in the standings? Well, they just don't. Everyone has an average of 50% fewer steals, but that doesn't mean the gap between teams in the standings must be 50% closer. In fact, they aren't much closer at all.

One of the reasons I'm not totally convinced about the logic behind the ratio category adjustments is that the batting averages I get with a PVM formula seem to place too much emphasis on average. The hitters with the highest batting average gain too much, and the lower average hitters lose too much. Again, it just doesn't seem practical.

Similar to steals, saves are valued excessively high.

So while PVM may be theoretically correct, its practical use is severely flawed. Many proponents of PVM give in to this reality and adjust their formulas to make their values more realistic. They'll use proper PVM theory to calculate the value of a homer and a steal, and then weight homers by 1.1 or more and steals by .9 or less to bring them into more of a balance. Once they've done this, they no longer really have a PVM formula. It's closer to an SGP formula.

Some who do this still argue that PVM is correct and SGP flawed, and that they are forced to do this because of the prevalence of SGP theory. They may be correct. When it comes to value formulas, being practical is more important than being right.

Adjusting for Replacement Level

Some value formulas think that the proper method is to subtract the stats that you should essentially get for free. For example, if all 168 hitters will score at least 20 runs, you don't need to pay for those. You can subtract the baseline of 20 runs and place a value on runs above that. This is similar to the marginal SGP valuation, where we didn't want to pay for the first 1.98 SGPs.

This sounds very logical, and I think it's a great idea. The problem is, for many formulas it ends up making no difference. You end up with the same exact dollar values.

When learning about SGP formulas, I tried a version subtracting the free stats, and it makes no difference. The marginal SGP, baselines, etc. all change proportionally such that you end up with the same exact dollar values.

More Criticism of SGP Formulas

Now that we've covered PVM, I can explain something else about SGP formulas. Look at the breakdown of hitting SGPs per category for my 2011 AL-only player pool:

Category	SGPs
Runs	9,592/21 = 457
HR	2,060/6.73 = 306
RBI	9,042/20.6 = 439
SB	1,365/6.5 = 210
Average	0
Total SGPs	1,412

It is a quirk of SGP formula that each category doesn't contribute the same amount of SGPs. Critics say this is a flaw. Why should runs contribute 457 SGPs and steals only 210? I don't have a brilliant answer. All I can say is that's just the way it is, and SGP formulas are logical and work.

You can try to correct this flaw by adjusting values to give categories equal contributions. If we multiply HR SGPs by 1.49 they would now be worth 457, the same as runs. If we do a similar multiplication for RBIs and SB they would all be equal at 457.

And you know what's happened? We've just turned this into a PVM formula!

For example, steals are now worth about 50% more than homers, just like with PVM. So I guess maybe that's my brilliant answer. If you correct the flaw, you get PVM. And PVM isn't practical.

You'll note that batting average (as well as ERA and WHIP) has no net contribution of SGPs. Approximately 50% of the players are above the mean and produce positive SGPs, and 50% are below the mean and produce negative SGPs. Therefore the net is zero.

Some analysts have argued that this is a flaw. Batting average, ERA, and WHIP count as much as any other category—they are each 10% of the total value in a 5×5 league—so how can one possibly assign them a value of zero?

John Benson, on page 35 of his book, says that an analyst named Mike Dalecki proved this can't be correct. He says that, for example, if the player-pool total batting average is .263 and you have a team made up of all .263 hitters, then you would finish in the middle of the pack and get six or seven points in the category, not zero. He writes, "Any valuation method that assigns zero to the average batting average (.263 in this example) fails to account for those six or seven points and is therefore wrong."

I disagree with this logic. I think it is fine to start with an assumption that a hitter should be average and then can produce either positive or negative value. When you go through the machinations of converting SGPs into a dollar value, players are properly rewarded (or penalized) for their contribution. Benson's own formula uses absolute value, rather than net value. So if his positive hitters produce +300 and negative hitters produce –118, we can think as if the SGP formula produces +209 and –209. Yes, Benson does have a positive net value, rather than zero. But he has less net value for batting average than for the counting categories. So Dalecki could argue that he should have as much net value for all categories since they all count as much. I don't have a problem with Benson using absolute value, because as with SGP netting at zero, I think in the end everyone gets properly rewarded or penalized.

Another way of looking at this is to consider that we normally award points in Rotisserie standings from 12 (for the best) down to 1 (for the worst). If we awarded points from +6 to –5, the end result would be the same.

Standard Deviation Formulas

Some people use formulas that calculate a player's contribution per category by the number of standard deviations above or below the average player. For example, suppose the average player in your pool is projected to hit 12 home runs and the standard deviation for home runs is 7.17. If you project Josh Hamilton will hit 40, then his value for home runs would be $(40 – 12)/7.17 = 3.9$.

Since everyone is being compared to the player pool average, the net value for all players will end up being zero. To allow for this, when converting raw values into dollar values you can assign everyone a base value to start, such as $2,090/168 = $12.44 for hitters and $1,030/108 = $9.54 for pitchers.

For practical purposes, I don't like these formulas any better than PVM. For example, whereas with PVM stolen bases will be valued much too highly compared to a home run, with a standard deviation the value of a stolen base is usually *less* than a home run. For my 2011 AL-only pool, a steal was only worth .93 of a homer. For a 2011 mixed league it was .76. This is just much too low. SGP data shows that a steal and a home run are actually very close in value.

Some people will measure a player's standard deviation from replacement level, rather than from the average. This leads to a different result, but is still no more practical.

Even if using standard deviations is logical, it isn't practical enough. As with PVM, I've seen some people who swear by using standard deviations, but then they add weights to the results, which makes their formula no longer truly based on standard deviations. They are now closer to SGP-based formulas.

My Conclusion

It's probably obvious by now that I think the SGP formula is the best choice to use because it is much more practical. As for the problem of needing to get accurate historical data, I've said that I do struggle trying to figure out the exact figures I should use. But I can get a pretty good idea. Estimating that the SGP for home runs will be 6.73 is not really much different than estimating that

Albert Pujols will hit 40 home runs or Salvador Perez will get 400 at bats. All you can do preseason is make your best projections for everything.

So while I may struggle deciding if I should use 6.6, 6.7, or maybe even 6.8 for home runs, how much of a difference will that make? It seems as though for my 2011 projections if I were to use, let's say, 6.53 instead of 6.73, that should make a pretty decent difference. Intuitively, I would think a good home-run hitter should probably gain a buck or two in value. Let's see what happens:

Player	HR	6.73	6.53
Miguel Cabrera	37	$33.1	$33.2
Jacoby Ellsbury	8	$30.8	$30.7
Michael Bourn	2	$23.7	$23.5
Adam Dunn	40	$23.5	$23.7

Miguel Cabrera with 37 homers had his value increase only ten cents? How is this possible?

The total home-run SGPs were 2,060/6.73 = 306.1. Now they are 2,060/6.53 = 315.5. That's an increase of 9.4 SGPs, which were valued at $1.48 each. That's an increase of $14 total value. Dividing by 2,060 home runs equals .0068 per homer. That means Miguel Cabrera added 37 × .0068 = 25 cents more value.

However, the $14 added value must be deducted from the 168 hitters to get us back to a total salary of $2,090. As explained before, when money is added or deducted from the pool it will affect the higher-value hitters the most. So Cabrera loses back most of his gain. His actual increase was only six cents, from $33.10 to $33.16. Adam Dunn, who isn't quite so high in value, does gain 20 cents.

This is a quite different result than what my intuition told me would happen. It's going to take a much bigger difference in the SGP denominator to have any real impact on the dollar values.

What if we make steals less valuable by changing the denominator from 6.5 to 6.7?

The total SGPs were 1,365/6.5 = 210. They are now 1,365/6.7 = 203.7. We have lost 6.3 SGPs × $1.48 = $9.30. Dividing by 1,365 steals equals .0068 per stolen base, the same exact figure as home runs. The top stolen-base threat, Jacoby Ellsbury, projected for 58 steals, ends up losing 30 cents value. (Initially he lost 40 cents, and when the $9.30 was added back to the pool, he regained 10 cents.)

What if we change the batting average denominator from .0018 to .0017?

Player	Avg	AB's	.0018	.0017
Miguel Cabrera	.320	585	$33.1	$33.4
BJ Upton	.246	550	$24.9	$24.8
Joe Mauer	.328	510	$20.9	$21.2
Mark Reynolds	.229	525	$20.2	$19.9
Jeff Mathis	.203	300	$ 1.2	$ 1.0

Even the very best and worst hitters only change by about 30 cents. Again, nothing meaningful has happened.

This all gives me more confidence in the SGP formula, because even if I'm a bit off choosing my SGPs it won't make a big difference.

Snake Drafts & Salary-Cap Games

I've been using as an example a 12-team AL-only league. When making a formula for a mixed league, you follow the same procedures, only your player pool will consist of players from both leagues. If it's a 15-team league, you'll have 210 hitters and 135 pitchers. And you'll want to get historical SGP data for the exact type of league you're in.

You can do this to create dollar values for a mixed auction. However, as I explain in chapter 8, these dollar values will be extremely flawed. Chapter 8 explains what you should do about this.

Salary-cap games typically don't have an easily identifiable player pool. You can't say, for example, that since everyone needs two catchers there will be 24 (or 30) catchers used. Theoretically, every team could choose the same two catchers, so there might only be two catchers in the actual pool. While that's very unlikely to happen, it's also unlikely that a 12-team league would actually have 24 different catchers being used.

For determining values for a salary-cap game, my opinion is the best way to do it is to act as if it were a 12-team mixed league. This is going to give a good approximation of the number of players who will appear on at least a handful of teams. It will also give you reasonable values. There may be situations where only, let's say, six shortstops appear on more than just a couple of rosters. But basing a player pool on just six shortstops and perhaps a total of only 70–80 or so total hitters will give you some pretty whacky values. Also, you can't know in advance that only six shortstops will actually be taken, or who those six will be.

In any event, it's not going to really matter much. If you follow my method of comparing salary-cap values, described in chapter 10, you'll almost certainly end up with the same team whether you used a 276-player pool, or 345, or even something a bit less than 276.

When you create values for a snake draft or salary-cap game, you can think of them in terms of dollar value. You can take all of the SGPs and have them conform to the $2,090 total, with the 168th hitter being worth $1, etc., and you can use those values.

However, it's not necessary to do this. You don't need to think in terms of dollar values at all. For drafts and salary cap I find it easier to use values such as 435, 265, and 118 rather than $39.7, $24.1, and $11.6. (When you read chapters 9 and 10 you'll understand why.)

For a 15-team league, I simply multiply the SGPs by a number so that the total hitters' value is 52,500, the pitchers' is 25,858, and the grand total is 78,358. The 52,500 figure is because I randomly decided to make the average hitter worth 250 value points (210 hitters × 250 = 52,500). The 25,858 figure was chosen to make the hitter-to-pitcher ratio 67/33%, similar to my auction dollar values. It's not necessary to do this. However, if you were to make the pitchers also worth an average of 250, then in effect you'd have a 61/39% split. This would make your values for pitchers seem too high relative to others. You'd find yourself wondering why everyone else seems to think Stephen Strasburg is worth a late-second-round pick, whereas you think he should go in the early first round.

You could argue that the *true* value of an average pitcher should also be 250, or even that your total pitching value should be equal to the total hitting value of 52,500. But if you draft based on those ideas, your team will be extremely pitching heavy. It's just more practical to use a 67/33% split.

To be clear, it doesn't matter what multiplier you use. You could make the average hitter worth 250, or 2.50, or 147,000. The only thing that matters is to keep the ratio of 67/33% (or whatever ratio you prefer).

I could convert all of the SGPs into auction-style dollar

values and then multiply them all to make values I find easier to use. However, this isn't necessary, because it would all work out the same in the end.

It's also not necessary to make the 210th hitter and 135th pitcher worth a specific amount. Nor is it necessary to make an adjustment for catchers. I simply multiply whatever the total SGPs happen to be so that the hitters have 52,500 total value and the pitchers have 25,858. That's all there is to it.

For snake drafts, there is a comparison of values that must be done to allow for catcher scarcity. I explain that in chapter 9. As you'll see in chapter 10, no scarcity adjustment is needed for salary-cap games.

Keeper Leagues

When creating values for a keeper-league auction, you need to deduct the salaries of the kept players from the $3,120 available, and deduct the value (or SGPs) of the kept players from the available total. Since the kept players will mostly be great values, there will be less value available than there is money to be spent. This will cause the prices to be inflated. This is also discussed in chapter 12.

You may know before your auction the exact list of kept players for your league. If not, you'll need to estimate. The inflation rate most likely will be different for hitters and pitchers, so once again, you want to look at them separately.

I'll use again my 2011 mono-league as an example. Suppose we know that 54 hitters will be kept, representing a total value of 550 SGPs, which translates into $847 of dollar value. Since most of them are being kept at bargain rates, let's say their total frozen salaries are only $577. This leaves us with:

Total dollars	$2,090	Total value	$2,090	Total SGPs	1,410
– Kept	$ 577	– Kept	$ 847	– Kept	550
Net dollars	$1,513	Net value	$1,243	Net SGPs	860

We now have $1,513 to spend but only $1,243 of available value. This means there will be an inflation rate of 1,513/1,243 = 1.217%.

It's not necessary to redo your entire value formula. You can just increase everyone's value by 21.7%. If you do want to redo your formula, you would start from scratch with the 54 hitters removed from your pool. Your new numbers would be:

Total dollars	$1,513	Total SGP	860
Base dollars	– $ 114	Base SGP	– 269.7
Marginal dollars	$1,399	Marginal SGP	590.3

The value of a marginal SGP is now $1,399/590.3 = $2.37. Using this figure, you create your values the same way that we did previously. Once you have adjusted for catcher scarcity and made the 114th player worth $1, etc., you're done.

You'll find that the inflation rate is very consistent around the 21.7% mark for all levels of values. This is why it's not really necessary to bother redoing your formula. You can just as easily multiply everyone's pre-keeper value by 21.7%. As discussed in chapter 12, the actual bidding will often inflate the star players by more than the 21.7%, which will leave some of the lower values available for a price of less than 21.7% inflated.

SGPs You Can Use

If you don't have your own fairly reliable SGP data or would just like another opinion, I'm going to show you the denominators I'll be using for the 2013 season. As always with SGPs, these are far from exact, but they are my best estimates based on everything I know and have examined. Houston moves to the American League in 2013, and that will change things a bit. Most NL-only leagues that used to have 13 teams will drop down to 12 teams, so I'm going to show 12-team values here. (This book won't be out in time for the 2013 season, but if you can't get your own data, it will give you a good estimate of what to use for 2014 and beyond.)

Category	12-Team AL-Only		12-Team NL-Only		12-Team Mixed		15-Team Mixed	
Avg	.0021		.00195		.00165		.0021	
Runs	20.1	(1.015)	20.1	(1.015)	15.52	(1.05)	18.57	(1.05)
HR	6.48	(3.15)	6.48	(3.15)	5.93	(2.75)	7.1	(2.75)
RBI	20.4	(1.0)	20.4	(1.0)	16.3	(1.0)	19.5	(1.0)
SB	6.48	(3.15)	6.24	(3.27)	5.93	(2.75)	7.1	(2.75)
W	2.82	(9.4)	2.76	(9.6)	2.58	(9.5)	2.89	(9.5)
ERA	.0923		.0815		.0723		.079	
WHIP	.0149		.0142		.0125		.0138	
K	26.5	(1.0)	26.5	(1.0)	24.5	(1.0)	27.5	(1.0)
S	4.65	(5.7)	4.65	(5.7)	4.9	(5.0)	5.5	(5.0)

Player Pool Averages

AB	420	415	500	515
BA	.264	.262	.271	.2733
IP	133	133	157	160
ERA	3.95	3.79	3.68	3.61
WHIP	1.285	1.280	1.245	1.23

The numbers in parentheses show the relative value of each category. For example, in an AL-only league, when you divide RBIs by 20.4 and divide home runs by 6.48, that is essentially the same as if you were to multiply RBIs by 1 and home runs by 3.15 (20.4/6.48 = 3.15). You are making a home run 3.15 times more valuable than an RBI.

The reason I mention this is because when you're trying to adjust SGPs for leagues of various sizes, it's important to realize that the raw value of the SGP isn't very important, but rather the ratio of values. So if you're going to be in an 11-team AL-only league, you don't need to go nuts trying to figure out the exact SGP for a run, homer, etc. Yes, the SGPs would be slightly different for an 11-team league, but the ratios should be pretty much the same. A home run will still be worth about 3.15 times more than an RBI. As you can see above, the relative value for all counting stats is the same for either a 12-team or a 15-team mixed league.

I've mentioned before that steals are a scarce commodity compared to homers, yet for SGPs their value is almost identical. Another counterintuitive item is that runs are worth slightly more than RBIs, despite the fact that runs are a little more plentiful.

Once you have identified the 168 (or 210) hitters and 108 (or 135) pitchers who comprise your player pool, before you calculate the marginal SGPs and dollar values, I suggest you calculate the batting average, ERA, WHIP, and average number of at bats and innings pitched for your pool. Then alter your formula to use those numbers rather than the historical estimates shown above. It probably won't make a big difference, but it will make your formula more precise. After doing this, check to see if there are any changes to the players that made your pool. Then proceed to calculate the dollar values.

Based on the chart above, formulas for a 2013 AL-only league would be these:

$$(RUN/20.1) + (HR/6.48) + (RBI/20.4) + (SB/6.48) +$$
$$((((1441.4 + HITS)/(5460 + AB)) - .264)/.0021) = SGP$$

$$(WIN/2.82) + (SAVE/4.65) + (K/26.5) +$$
$$((3.95 - ((ER+463.5) \times (9/(IP+1056))))/.0923) +$$
$$((1.285 - ((1357 + H + BB)/(IP + 1056)))/.0149) = SGP$$

The 5,460 at bats figure is 13 hitters multiplied by the pool average of 420 at bats. And 5,460 multiplied by the pool batting average of .264 results in 1,441.4 hits. The figures for ERA and WHIP are calculated in a similar fashion.

You can substitute whatever SGP denominators you want to use for the denominators shown in my formula. And substitute your player-pool average number of at bats, innings pitched, batting average, ERA, and WHIP. Remember that the formula is showing what an average 13 hitters and eight pitchers would do, so that you can measure the effect of any particular player on your team. (You can alter this, if needed. For example, if your league requires ten pitchers, then show an average of nine pitchers rather than eight.)

Recapping the Dollar Value Conversion

Once you have identified your player pool, you can total their SGPs. You must decide how to split the $3,120 between hitting and pitching. I'll again use a 67/33% split ($2,090 and $1,030) as the example. You then calculate the marginal hitting SGPs:

Total Dollars	$2,090	Total SGP		1,410	
Base Dollars	– $ 168	Base SGP	–	397.4	(24 × 1.98 + 144 × 2.43)
Marginal Dollars	$1,922	Marginal SGP		1,012.60	

The base SGPs are calculated by finding the SGPs of the 24th-best catcher and multiplying by 24, plus the SGPs of the 144th-best non-catcher multiplied by 144. (In this example, those figures are 1.98 and 2.43.) The value of a marginal SGP is the marginal dollars divided by the marginal SGPs. In this case $1,922/1,012.6 = 1.898. (If you prefer to allow for differences of opinion, as I do, you can multiply the SGPs of the 23rd-best catcher by 24 and the SGPs of the 139th-best non-catcher by 144.)

You then have one formula to calculate the catchers' values and another for the non-catchers.

$$\text{Catchers: (SGP} - 1.98) \times 1.898 + 1$$
$$\text{Non-Catchers: (SGP} - 2.43) \times 1.898 + 1$$

If you are using software that makes it difficult to enter two different formulas or a "what if" equation, you can just use the non-catcher formula and make a manual adjustment for catchers. In this case, the adjustment is $2.43 - 1.98 = .45 \times 1.898 = 85$ cents. Adding the 85 cents to the catchers' values has allowed for position scarcity.

If there weren't at least 36 middle infielders, 36 corner infielders, or 60 outfielders in the top 144 non-catchers, you could create a third formula to allow for their scarcity. This shouldn't happen very often.

For pitchers, you calculate as follows:

Total dollars	$1,030	Total SGP	850	
Base dollars	– $ 108	Base SGP	– 386.6	(108 × 3.58)
Marginal dollars	$ 922	Marginal SGP	463.4	

In this case, the 108th-best pitcher has 3.58 SGPs. The marginal SGP is worth $922/463.4 = 1.99$. (Again, if you prefer to allow for differences of opinion, you can multiply the SGPs of the 100th-best pitcher by 108.) Therefore, the formula to calculate pitchers' dollar values is:

$$\text{(SGP} - 3.58) \times 1.99 + 1$$

Once you're done, double-check to make sure that your total dollar values are equal to $2,090 and $1,030. Between the time you do this and your auction, if you've made many updates to your projections, you should check just before your auction and see if you need to adjust your formulas.

For a non-auction league, you can simply multiply a player's SGPs by any number you like. Just be sure that the total ratio of value is a 67/33% split, or whatever split you prefer.

Conclusion

It is extremely important to use a good value formula. If you make good stat projections and use a good value formula, you can have confidence in your dollar values.

However, you must always remember that everything is relative. If you're finding lots of great bargains for power hitters, it could be that you're placing more value on a home run than everyone else. You'll want to be selective and buy the best bargains, rather than overloading your roster with too much power. It's okay to have a lot of power, but you don't want overkill.

As you'll see in other chapters, before an auction or draft I always compare my values to those published in various sources. This allows me to identify targets for good bargains. It also gives me a clue as to whether my formulas are in line with the mainstream or not. For example, if my target list has a disproportional amount of closers, then I'm probably valuing saves more than most others.

If we could assemble a thousand of the world's best mathematicians for a weekend summit and debate the virtues of various formulas, perhaps we could prove which one is the most logically sound. But for now, all I care about is being practical. Being right is the booby prize.

CHAPTER 7

Mono-League Auctions (AL or NL Only)

The obvious difference between being in a mono-league rather than a mixed league is that the talent pool is a lot worse. Instead of having starters at virtually every spot on your roster, you need to have some bench players and scrubs. This makes your roster look more similar to an actual major-league team. With a mixed-league team, there's more action to follow during the year, because all of your players are constantly playing. With a mono-league team, some of your players are constantly on the bench. However, when your scrub player gets a couple of hits and steals a base, it can be more satisfying than when your superstar goes 3–4 with a home run and three RBIs.

For this chapter, I'm going to use my 2011 Tout Wars AL-only league as the example. This is a 12-team league, standard 5×5 format, with a roster requirement of 23 players. This means you have a pool of players that includes 168 hitters (14 per team × 12 teams) and 108 pitchers (9 per team × 12 teams). If a value formula is done correctly, these 276 players will have a total dollar value of $3,120 ($260 per team). This means that each team can buy $260 of value for their $260 budget.

As mentioned in chapter 3, because of differences of opinion about value, and the fact that you are buying players based on your own opinion, everyone should leave an auction thinking their team has more than $260 of value. If we assume that you should probably get $270–280 just based on the difference of opinion, then the question is what strategy can you use to get $290, or $300, or maybe even more?

My strategy is simply to get as many discounts as possible. Buy as many players as possible for less than my projected dollar value. That is the only way you can end up with $300 or more value for your $260 spent.

To execute my strategy, I could simply show up at an auction and wait for bargains to appear. But I do much more preparation before I show up. The first thing I do is examine the player pool.

Position Scarcity?

The *player pool* is comprised of the players who, based on my values, should be selected to fill out the starting lineups for all the teams in an AL-only league. If I was drafting all 12 teams, this would actually happen. However, since the other owners will have different opinions than I have, undoubtedly some players not included in my player pool will be bought at the auction. This is fine. In fact, the more players outside my pool that are bought, the better, because it leaves me with more valuable players to scoop up at the end for just $1.

There are always players who qualify at more than one position. I slot each player where he will typically be the most valuable. I put Mike Napoli at catcher rather than first base, because the talent at the bottom of the catcher pool is usually very bad. If a player qualifies at shortstop or second base and another position, I put him at shortstop or second base. And I give first and third base priority over the outfield.

Since 12 teams will each need two starting catchers, this means that 24 catchers will be part of my player pool. The 24th-most-valuable catcher on my list is Hank Conger, a $0.5 value.

Next I identify the top-12 first basemen and third basemen, and the next 12 most-valuable first basemen or third basemen, who would occupy the corner spot. I do the same for second basemen, shortstops, and the middle infielder. There will be five outfielders needed per team, so I note the 60th-most-valuable outfielder.

The designated hitter can play any position, so I identify the next 12 highest values not already included in my player pool. In this case, it includes the top-four hitters on my designated hitter list, three second baseman, three outfielders, and two shortstops.

In my opinion, the key to any discussion of position scarcity is the question of what value player can you get at the end of an auction for $1?

With this player pool, it breaks down as follows:

Position	# Players	Last Player Value
Catcher	24	$0.5
First Base	21	$0.0
Second Base	21	$0.1
Shortstop	20	$0.0
Third Base	15	$1.4
Outfield	63	$0.9
DH only	4	$3.4
Total	168	

You may be wondering why I have players included in the pool with a value of less than $1. Theoretically, the value formula should be done such that the 168th-best hitter (and 108th-best pitcher) have a value of exactly $1. In chapter 6, I explain in detail why I do this. The short answer is that if I were drafting against 11 Larry Schechter clones, I would make the 168th player worth $1. But the reality is that I can fully expect that a handful of players who are not in my pool will be taken, and thus I have "bumped up" a player or two at most positions. For example, at the end of the auction, if I have $1 left and need a corner infielder, I'm counting on being able to buy the 34th or 35th player in the corner infield pool, rather than the 36th player. If I need an outfielder, I'm expecting to be able to get approximately the 59th- or 60th-best outfielder, rather than the 63rd. In a typical mono-league auction, there are usually at least six hitters not in my pool who are bought by others.

I wanted to show you the breakdown for each position, but the reality is that I can't necessarily wait at third base and be guaranteed to get at least a $1.4 value for my last $1. The third basemen may all get taken to fill out corner spots, or even a DH spot. By the end, I might have to take one of the last first basemen to be my corner, and his value is going to be less than $1.4.

Therefore, to properly analyze this, the first basemen and third basemen need to be combined to account for the corner pool, and likewise the second basemen and shortstops for the middle pool:

Position	# Players	Last Player Value
Catcher	24	$0.5
1B/3B	36	$0.0
2B/SS	41	$0.0
Outfield	63	$0.9
DH only	4	$3.4
Total	168	

So there's no guarantee of much at the end, except that I can safely wait for my last outfielder(s) and get at least a fair deal (spend $1 for at least 90 cents value).

The least valuable designated hitter is worth $3.4, but there are only four of them, so if I wait until the end, they will probably be gone, and I'll need to get someone else to fill my designated hitter slot.

As you can see, there's no scarcity. First and third basemen are just as scarce as middle infielders. There are some people who will pay a big premium for a catcher or middle infielder. Why? In the above chart, the most you could justify—if anything—is to spend an extra buck for an infielder, so that you don't get stuck with a $0 value. I won't do that, because as I said, I'm counting on a few players not in my pool to be taken. And if I weren't counting on that, I'd adjust my formula to make the worst infielders equal to $1. Again, middle infielders would not be scarcer than corner infielders.

People who target positions based on the flawed concept of scarcity typically are willing to overspend by $1, $2, or even more to land a top player at the *scarce* positions. They are just wasting those extra dollars and are buying players for more than they're worth.

To be clear, though, there is some scarcity with catchers. But as explained in chapter 6, this was already accounted for in my value formula. An adjustment was made to equalize the catchers' values. For 2011, it was 85 cents. Without this adjustment, Conger would have a value of negative 35 cents. So in reality, I am willing to pay a premium of $0.85 for catchers. (In some years, the adjustment has been as much as $2.00 or more.)

Pitchers

I will want to have a certain balance on my roster between starting pitchers and relievers. However, the only league requirement is that each team starts nine pitchers, regardless of their role, so for the purposes of identifying the player pool, all the pitchers can be lumped together. This means I simply have to identify the top 108 values.

For 2011, the 108th value is worth $0.7. It's pretty much certain that every year at least eight pitchers—and probably more—not in my pool will be bought by other teams. This means that I should be able to get a pitcher worth at least $2 at the end of the auction for just $1. In fact, most years I'll end up getting a pitcher I think is worth $3–5 and occasionally even more.

Tout Wars Targets

I explained in chapter 4 that I identify potential bargains in advance by comparing my values to others' values published in popular magazines and websites. If I value a player more than most everyone else, there is a good chance I'll be able to buy him at a discount.

For 2011, I was in three different AL-only leagues. The poker-training website CardRunners.com invited some fantasy "experts" to compete against some of their poker experts; this auction was held on March 2. The *USA Today*–sponsored LABR (League of Alternative Baseball Reality) had their auction on March 5. And the Tout Wars auction was on March 19.

I created a list of potential bargains, which I call my *target list*, and used it for the CR (CardRunners) and LABR auctions. The list was based on dollar values published by five sources. Since the Tout Wars auction was held after CR and LABR, this gave me additional valuable data. Knowing the actual prices paid at two experts leagues was very helpful. I revised my target list for Tout Wars based on the prices paid at CR and LABR, which gave me this:

2011 TOUT WARS HITTERS TARGET LIST

Position	Player	Projected $ Value	Discount	HR/SB
Catcher	Olivo	$ 8.5	.5+	11/5
	Jaso	$ 8	E	5/4
	Avila	$ 5	E	9/2
	Kendall	$ 2	E,1	0/5
	Castro	$ 2	E	7/0
	Mathis	$ 1.5	.5	6/3
	Shoppach	$ 1.5	.5	8/0

Position	Player	Projected $ Value	Discount	HR/SB
First Base	M Cabrera	$33	E,+1	37/3
	Konerko	$22	E	31/0
	Cuddyer	$17.5	.5	17/6
	Barton	$13.5	2	11/5
Second Base	Pedroia	$27	E	18/18
	Izturis	$ 8.5	E+	5/11
	M Ellis	$ 8	2	7/6
	Getz	$ 7	2+	1/20
Shortstop	Pennington	$13.5	2.5	7/25
	A Cabrera	$13.5	1.5	6/11
	Brignac (2B)	$11	2	12/6
	B Ryan	$ 4.5	3.5	2/9
Third Base	Kouzmanoff	$11	1	16/1
	Inge	$ 9.5	3.5	15/3
	Betemit	$ 5.5	2.5	11/0
	Teahen	$ 5.5	1.5	7/4
Outfielder	Ellsbury	$31	1	8/58
	Choo	$28	1	22/21
	Rios	$27	1	19/29
	Pierre	$26	2	1/58
	Gardner	$24	2	4/47
	Abreu	$22	2	16/21
	Adam Jones	$20.5	.5+	21/10
	Swisher	$19.5	.5+	28/1
	Vladdy	$19	.5+	22/3
	Lind	$18	1	26/0
	Gutierrez	$17.5	3.5	14/21
	Kubel	$16	1	21/0
	DeJesus	$14.5	3.5	9/5
	Francoeur	$10.5	3.5+	12/5
DH	Big Papi	$17.5	3.5	26/0
	Thome	$ 8.5	3.5	18/0
	Hafner	$ 7.5	3.5	12/1

2011 TOUT WARS PITCHERS TARGET LIST

Position	Player	Projected $ Value	Discount	
SP	F Hernandez	$36.5	4.5+	
	Verlander	$31	4	
	C Lewis	$21	4	
	Buchholz	$20	4	
	Cahill	$18.5	5.5	
	Romero	$17.5	4.5	
	Braden	$13.5	4.5	
	W Davis	$12	4	
	Niemann	$11	4	
	Guthrie	$10	4	
	Carrasco	$10	4	
	Vargas	$ 8.5	4.5	
	Carmona	$ 8	4	
	Fister	$ 7.5	5.5	
	Bergesen	$ 5	4	must nominate for $1
	Chen	$ 4.5	3.5	must nominate for $1
RP	Soria	$25	3	
	Rivera	$23.5	1.5	
	C Perez	$19.5	1.5	
	Breslow	$ 4.5	3.5	must nominate for $1

As I've said, I'm looking to get discounts. However, it's not always easy to do that for catchers and the very best hitters. That's why I've got a lot of catchers and a few top hitters where I'm showing the discount as "E." This means *even*. In other words, I would be willing to pay full price. It is not essential to get a top hitter, but if I can get one for a fair price, it's usually a good idea. I'll explain that in detail shortly.

Many fantasy players discount the price of designated-hitter-only players, because they don't want to fill up that roster spot with someone who can't be moved. Personally, I don't mind it, because since so many people have this idea, I can usually get someone only eligible at designated hitter for a very good discount.

I'm expecting to be able to get at least a $4 discount for all levels of starting pitchers (except just $3.50 for Bruce Chen). For Brad Bergesen ($5), Craig Breslow ($4.5), and Chen ($4.5), I've made myself a note that I must nominate them. If I wait too long, and someone else brings them up for $1, it means I'd have to bid $2—or pass on them. Either way, I wouldn't get the $3.5 and $4 discounts I want.

As I mentioned in chapter 3, when you create your value formula, you have a choice of how to split the $3,120 total salary. For 2011, I used a 65/35% split. Had I used something else, such as 67/33%, it ultimately wouldn't matter. My target list would have all the same players. It's just that I'd be looking to get about a $2 discount on starting pitchers rather than $4, and I'd be targeting an extra $1–2 discount on the various hitting levels.

Being Fully Prepared

As I mentioned in chapter 3, the bidding happens very fast and you need to make snap decisions, often in a split second. Therefore, I prepare as much as possible in advance and think through various scenarios. On my player pages, which I print out and bring to the auction, I have a column where I list my maximum bid for each player.

Here are the maximum bids for the shortstops:

Player	Value	Max Bid
Derek Jeter	$20.8	$18
Alexei Ramirez	$20.1	$18
Elvis Andrus	$18.7	$16
Cliff Pennington	$13.7	$11
Asdrubal Cabrera	$13.5	$11
Tsuyoshi Nishioka	$13.3	$11
Erick Aybar	$12.9	$10
Yunel Escobar	$11.8	$10
Jhonny Peralta	$11.5	$ 9
Reid Brignac	$11.0	$ 9
Alcides Escobar	$10.3	$ 8
Alexi Casilla	$ 8.8	$ 6
JJ Hardy	$ 7.6	$ 5
Jed Lowrie	$ 7.3	$ 5
Orlando Cabrera	$ 7.0	$ 5
Marco Scutaro	$ 6.8	$ 4
Brendan Ryan	$ 4.4	$ 2
Jason Donald	$ 2.6	$ 1
Felipe Lopez	$ 1.3	$ 1

As you can see, I'm mostly looking to get at least a $2 discount. The target discount will vary a little by position and by value range. For example, at first base I only have one player (Daric Barton) on my target list where I'm hoping to get a discount of as much as $2, so I might need to accept only a $1 discount at first base.

The point is, I decide all of this in advance, so that I don't have to try to figure it out every time a player is nominated. When a player is put up for bid, I can very quickly find him on my player pages and see what my maximum bid is.

As the auction unfolds, I do have to make adjustments, but arriving at the auction with my maximum bid column filled out gives me a good starting point.

Distributing the Dollars

As I explained in chapter 3, in most leagues the average team spends $180 on hitting and $80 on pitching. And you don't want to stray too far from these averages or you'll be imbalanced and need to trade later.

Entering the 2011 season, I had always been of the opinion that there were typically better discounts on pitchers rather than hitters. Therefore, I used a split of $170/$90 in order to acquire more pitching value. You might assume that if I only spend $170 on hitting, my hitting will be weak relative to others. However, this isn't the case, because I'm buying good values. I'm not overspending and wasting my money. My hitting is typically just fine, usually above average. Meanwhile, my pitching typically dominates.

During the winter of 2011, I did more research into value formula theory—as part of writing this book—and came to the realization that the discounts for pitchers weren't any better than for hitters. It was just my perception, because of what I described earlier about splitting the $3,120. Using a 65/35% split while most others used a 67/33% gave me the false impression that others were valuing hitters too much.

So for 2012, I started using a 67/33% split for my value formula. And I also changed my planned spending from a $170/$90 split to a $180/$80 split to be in line with the norm.

But for 2011, my spending plan was a $170/$90 split. I used the following template to execute my plan of spending $170 to acquire my 14 hitters:

Plan	Actual	+/−	
32			
27			
22			
20			
17			
15			
12			
8			
6			
4			
2			
2			
2			
1			

$170

At the auction, when I buy a player, I write the amount in the *Actual* column, and adjust my future buys accordingly.

This template is just a rough guide. I said earlier that it's more difficult to get a discount on a very-high-priced hitter, so you might wonder why I even include a spot for a $32 hitter. Rather than buy a hitter in the $32 range, where I might have to pay full price, why not buy a couple of $17 hitters instead of the $32 and one of the $2 spots? Theoretically, this could work out to my advantage:

	Value	Price	Value	Price
	$32	$32	$19	$17
	$ 4	$ 2	$19	$17
Total:	$36	$34	$38	$34
Gain:		+$2		+$4

If I only had to buy a handful of hitters, I would avoid the $32 hitter. The problem, though, is that I need 14 hitters and I already have spots for a $15, $17, and $20 hitter. If I have to buy several hitters in the same price range (that is, $15–20) then it's harder to be selective and find discounts. So if I add more spots in the $17 range, I may end up being forced to buy someone at full price anyway.

Also, I need to spend $170. The worst thing you can possibly do at an auction is to be left holding money. If you fill your roster and haven't spent your $260, that's a complete waste. Buying some of the higher-price hitters helps enormously toward the goal of spending my $170.

While I said it's more difficult to get a discount on a top hitter, it's certainly not impossible. I will always hold out hope to be able to get a discount. My target list does include a $31 Jacoby Ellsbury, whom I'm hoping to get for $1–2 less. But, in general, I'm okay with the notion of spending full price for a top hitter, if necessary.

If I have to spend full price for a top hitter or two, and maybe for one or both of my catchers, and then I get discounts on everyone else, I'll be in good shape. Also notice, I'm saying pay "full price," not "overpaying."

I've spread out the hitter spots from $32 to $27 . . . to $8–$6–$4, so that I can be selective in various price ranges. It's easier to find a good bargain if I only need one player from each range.

Some people use a template along the same idea as mine, except that they assign certain dollar amounts to specific positions. For example, they might allot a $32 spot for a first baseman and a $27 slot for a shortstop. I don't like this. There's no reason to lock yourself into spending big—or small—on certain positions. With my template, there's complete flexibility. Most likely, the people who go by position are doing so because of some false notion of scarcity.

My pitching template looks like this:

Plan	Actual	+/−	
29(SP)			
21(RP)			
17(SP)			
9(SP)			
6			
3			
2			
2			
1			
$90			

I have the $21 spot reserved for my closer. Of course, I could end up spending anywhere from probably $17 to $23 for a closer and will add or subtract the difference from one of the other spots. I only want to buy one reliable closer, so the other three expensive spots are reserved for starting pitchers.

I have a top spot of $29 because I usually buy one of the best pitchers. The reason is because they often come with the best discounts. Many fantasy players are reluctant to spend big on a pitcher. And even those who are willing to spend big often don't want to go past $29, even if a pitcher is worth more than that.

However, I certainly don't *need* to buy one of the best. If the price isn't right, I can wait and get someone for less. If I end up spending, let's say, $20 for my best starter and take the saved $9 to use elsewhere, that's not going to be a problem.

The Saga of Jacoby Ellsbury

I have my target lists, and I have my templates. Now I need to get more specific about my plans. First, I'm going to consider the question of where will I spend big on a hitter?

Other than possibly Ellsbury, it appears that I have no chance at landing a $30+ hitter for a discount. Even for full price is unlikely, except for perhaps Miguel Cabrera. I value Cabrera at $33.3, and he went for $34 at CR and $35 at LABR. So if he's available at $33, or perhaps even $34, I might be willing to take him.

As for Ellsbury, I have my own personal saga. In 2009, he hit .301 with eight home runs and 70 stolen bases, for a value of $36. I am a die-hard Red Sox fan, and he's one of my favorite players. Watching him play, I drool over how good he is, especially his speed. (My wife, also a Red Sox fan, watches him play and drools over how good-looking he is.)

Heading into the 2010 season, I had him conservatively valued at $34. I bought him for $34 for my 2010 LABR team. (I did not buy him at Tout Wars, because I was in the NL league in 2010.) I also bought him on my mixed auction team, and I drafted him for some of my snake draft leagues. Heading into the 2010 season, considering how many teams I had him on, and his high value, he was the single most important player for my overall fantasy hopes.

And he didn't disappoint . . . for six days. After starting out 10 for 30, with two stolen bases, he collided with Adrian Beltre chasing a foul ball, hurt his ribs, and missed most of the rest of the season. He ended the season with just 78 at bats, a .192 batting average, and seven stolen bases. And he was the biggest single reason most of my fantasy teams didn't do well in 2010.

After this disastrous 2010 season, there was some reason to be skeptical heading into 2011. Some of his teammates labeled him "soft" and thought he should have been able to play through his injury. However, my feeling was that, by all accounts, Ellsbury just needed time for his rib injury to heal, which the off-season provided.

So my opinion was that since I thought he was a bargain in 2010, if anything he should be an even bigger bargain for 2011 since some people would be scared of him. The others' values had a high of just $29.

At the start of spring training, he appeared 100% healthy. My big concern was that there was speculation Ellsbury might bat ninth, at least to start the season. As a result, I lowered his projection to 575 at bats and a $31.1 value. If other people weren't willing to go past $29, this made him a great target.

For the CR auction, I planned a maximum bid of $29. I nominated him for $24. Someone bid $25, and I went to $26. Then there was a $27 and a $28. I quickly bid $29, not wanting anyone to beat me to the punch. For a couple of seconds, I was confident I'd get him. Then Shawn Childs bid $30. And that was that.

My reaction was "oh, damn" because I didn't get him. Then it occurred to me that Shawn Childs was also going to be in the LABR auction with me. "Double damn," I thought. If he's willing to go to $30 now, he's probably willing to do it again.

Prior to the LABR auction, I considered upping my maximum bid, but decided against it. At LABR, I nominated Ellsbury with a bid of $27. I assumed someone would go $28 and I'd immediately say $29 before anyone else could get the words out of their mouth. However, after my opening bid, someone immediately bid $29. I was screwed.

I had started with $27 just on the very slight chance I might actually get him for $27, but in retrospect that was pretty stupid. I should have just opened at $29. As it turned out, Shawn Childs did again go to $30, so it didn't matter. I wouldn't have gotten Ellsbury anyway.

In preparing for Tout Wars, I wasn't going to beat around the bush. I planned to nominate Ellsbury for $29. And if anybody brought him up before I did, I would immediately bid $29. And, since Shawn Childs wasn't going to be in Tout Wars, hopefully I had a chance of actually landing Ellsbury this time.

More Planning

I have one slot for a $27 hitter. There are 13 hitters whom I give a value of $25–30. This means I have a lot of players to choose from in this price range. With 12 teams in Tout Wars, there will be an average of one for each of us. If I miss out on Cabrera and Ellsbury, I'll want to try to get two in this range. I've got four guys on my target list—Pedroia, Choo, Rios, and Pierre.

There are 22 hitters in the $20–25 range, and I have a spot for a $20 and a $22. Again, this is a good distribution. I should be able to find two good buys from these 22 hitters. Five of them— Konerko, Gardner, Abreu, Adam Jones, and Guerrero—are on my target list.

I have plenty of targets available in the lower price ranges as well.

Category Balance

After identifying the 168 hitters I think should be in the player pool, I can easily add up the projected stats for these players and determine the average per team in Tout Wars. For 2011, the averages are a .269 batting average, 805 runs, 173 home runs, 759 RBIs, and 116 stolen bases.

I'm going to try to buy a team that is at least average in a couple of these categories and above average in a few, without getting overkill. So I need to pay attention to this, and I even give it some thought before the auction. If I land Ellsbury, I'll avoid Pierre and Gardner—even if they are available at a good price—because otherwise I'd have overkill on stolen bases. Ellsbury, along with either Pierre or Gardner, would give me 105 or 116 stolen bases. Even if I then try to avoid getting steals, the rest of my roster would undoubtedly get 30–40 more, which would put me into overkill territory.

This is one reason I want to hold out for a price of $29 on Ellsbury. I have many other good stolen-base options. I don't want to spend $30–31 on Ellsbury and then quite likely have to pass up a $2 or more discount on Pierre and/or Gardner.

I said that if Miguel Cabrera is available at $33, or perhaps even $34, I might be willing to take him. The phrase "might be willing" is not sufficient. When his name is brought up at the auction, I need to know in advance *exactly* what I want to do. Am I willing to take him for $33 or not? What about $34? I have to make that decision before the auction, not in the split second I would have to decide when his name is brought up.

After some thought, I came to the conclusion that while stolen bases were plentiful, batting average was potentially a problem. I really liked what his .320 batting average could do for my team. So I decided I'd go to $34.

Who Should I Nominate?

Not only was I willing to go to $34 for Cabrera, but I also hoped I would get him. He would make a very nice high-priced foundation for my offense, especially for average and power. While there was a chance I might get him for $34, it seemed almost certain that I wasn't going to get him for less than that. So when his name was brought up, I wanted to immediately bid $34 before anyone else. It's not guaranteed, though, that I can react quicker than everyone else in just a split second. Somebody could beat me to $34. Therefore, it would be nice if I were to nominate him myself, and open at $34. That's the only way I can guarantee I'll get my $34 bid in. Since Cabrera's one of the top handful of hitters, he'll undoubtedly be brought up early. So if I want to nominate him, I'd better do it in the first round.

Another guy I want to bring up early is Ellsbury. He's my best target for buying a high-priced hitter, and whether or not I get him will affect my plans later when other stolen-base threats are nominated.

If I don't bring up Ellsbury, there's a decent chance someone else will bring him up before too long. But what if Pierre or Gardner come up before him? That gives me a problem. If I can grab one of them for a $2 discount, I probably have to do it. But then I'm going to have to pass on Ellsbury. I'd rather be in a position of getting Ellsbury for a $2 discount, and then having to pass on Pierre and Gardner. Although a $2 discount is still a $2 discount, my preference is to spend the bigger money, and Ellsbury is better than Pierre and Gardner for batting average.

So I definitely want to bring up Ellsbury early, maybe even in round one.

After Cabrera and Ellsbury, who I nominate will depend a lot on whether I got Cabrera and/or Ellsbury. If I don't get them both, I'll be looking for at least one high-value hitter. Choo and Rios are my prime targets. I'd like to see if, in fact, I can get one of them for a dollar off, before I possibly go full price for the likes of

Pedroia, or someone not on my target list who might potentially be available for full price.

After these guys, who I bring up will depend on what's happened, but I'll mostly be using my target lists. I might want to bring up Brandon Inge, because he's my biggest potential bargain at third base. I like getting my biggest potential bargains out of the way, so that I can see what happens before other lesser bargains are on the table. For example, if Kevin Kouzmanoff is brought up before Inge and he has a $9 bid, I would hesitate to bid $10. I don't want to settle for the $1 discount since I think I can do better with Inge (not to mention Betemit and Teahen). On the other hand, if I bring up Inge first, and to my surprise someone else bids $8, then I'll let him go. And in that case, I'd be more likely to take Kouzmanoff for $10 if I can. (And I'd still have the corner slot available for Betemit or Teahen.)

Bringing up my outfield targets isn't as critical, because I have five spots for outfielders. Even if I buy a couple of outfielders, I still have three more spots left. When it gets to the later stages of the auction and I've filled some outfield spots, I will want to make sure I get my best targets nominated before I run out of room for them.

The Dilemma of Brandon Inge

Some people would argue that for some of these players I might do better if I wait. For example, if I bring up Inge fairly early, everyone still has plenty of money to spend and they still need a third baseman (or at least a corner or DH). So someone might be willing to pay $7 or $8 for him. On the other hand, if I wait, and hope that nobody else nominates him, when we get to the later stages some people won't have a lot of money left and/or won't have a spot for him on their roster. This could lead to a very nice price, maybe even less than my targeted $6.

This is certainly possible. But on the other hand, you can make just as strong a counterargument. If I bring him up early, many people will think "I don't need or want Inge, because there are plenty of better options still available." If I wait, there may be someone with too much money and too few decent players to spend it on, and they might pay more for Inge than they would have earlier.

So I can lose if I wait, and I can lose if I don't wait. The bottom line is that Inge is on my target list for a reason. I value him at $9.5. The others' values don't go higher than $6. He went for $6 at CR and $7 at LABR. This means that few people besides me think he's worth more than $6 or maybe $7. When his name comes up, it's very likely that nobody else will be willing to go past $6. If he comes up before the late stages, nobody will have reason to (in their mind) overspend on him. If he comes up late, there's a chance someone might have money to burn and feel justified to overspend.

A player like Inge does present a bit of a bidding dilemma. My hope is that I can get him for $6. There appears to be an excellent chance that I can. There's even a possibility I'll get him for $5. But there's also a chance someone else will go to $7 or that someone will beat me to the $6 bid and I'll need to go to $7.

If I have to pay $7 to land him, that's a $2.5 discount, which is still a good deal. But I'm greedy, and I'd certainly prefer to get him for $6.

The dilemma is, do I bid $6 and hope that nobody is willing to go to $7? Or do I wait and let someone else bid $6, then trump them with a $7 bid, which almost certainly will be the winning bid?

I can try to be the person who bids $5, knowing there's even a small chance I might get him for $5, and, if not, then being pretty certain I'll safely get him for $7. Or I can be the person who bids $6, and hope it's enough. So I'm either going to take a little gamble that I can get him for $6, or I'm going to go for more of a sure thing and get him for $7.

So what do I do?

The answer is . . . there is no answer. This *is* a dilemma.

When the time comes, what I do may be based on what other options I think I'll have. If I think I can get a $2.5 discount on someone else like Betemit, then maybe I'll gamble on getting Inge for $6. If Betemit is already gone and/or I'm at a point where I think I'd better spend more than just a few bucks on this slot, then I'll probably play it safe and go for the $7 bid.

Another factor is going to be what others bid and how fast they bid. For a player like Inge, I would expect the bids to go in increments of just $1 (at least once it got to $3 or $4, anyway). But if someone jumps the bid from $4 directly to $6, then they've taken the decision out of my hands. My only choice is to bid $7.

On the other hand, if there's a $5 bid, and the room is silent, and the auctioneer says "going once . . . going twice . . . ," then I've got to quickly make the $6 bid. Again, the decision is out of my hands. I can't wait for someone else to bid $6 and then trump it, because once the auctioneer has said "going twice . . ." there's a good chance nobody else is going to bid $6.

Similarly, if there's a $4 bid, and the auctioneer says "going once . . . going twice . . . ," then the decision is out of my hands, and I'm forced to bid $5. If I'm really lucky, I'll get Inge for $5. If not, someone else will bid $6, and then I'll quickly say "$7" before anyone else.

When the auctioneer says "going twice . . ." there's only going to be a second or two before he says "Sold!" Therefore, I can't hesitate to see if anyone else will bid. I'm forced to act immediately.

There are situations where I want to act immediately. For example, if someone brings up Miguel Cabrera, I immediately want to bid $34 as quickly as I can get the words out of my mouth.

But there are other situations where I may want to sit back and wait. If I have a clear plan as to what I want to do about Inge, then I will bid quickly. But if I'm uncertain whether to try for the $6, or take the safe $7—or I'm thinking there's even a chance I could get him for $5—then I may just sit back and wait until the auctioneer is saying "going once . . . going twice . . ." And that will dictate what I do.

What About Pitchers?

My biggest target is Felix Hernandez because I have him valued at $36.3, which is significantly more than the next guy, Justin Verlander, at $30.8. If I were to get a $4 discount on either of these, it wouldn't really matter whom I get. But Felix is my #1 target because many fantasy players have a limit as to how much they will spend for a pitcher. Some won't even consider spending more than $20. Some won't get past $25. And very few will go to $30 or above. It doesn't matter that the pitcher might actually be worth $35 or $40. They just don't want that much money tied up in one pitcher. So I have a better chance at a good discount with the higher-priced pitcher. While most will be reluctant to go to $30 or beyond for Felix, there will be more people willing to approach $30 for Verlander.

So with Felix being my top target, I am going to want to get his name brought up first. If I can get him for my maximum bid of $32, or hopefully less, I want to take him. My nightmare scenario is that Verlander goes first for, let's say, $27, and I didn't bid $27 because I'm assuming I can get Felix for $32 or even better . . . and then Felix comes up and someone else bids $33. Then I'm screwed.

So I really want to get Felix nominated early. If someone does go $33, then I'll pass on him and know what to do when Verlander come up. So along with Miguel Cabrera and Ellsbury, Felix is a guy I want to bring up right away.

A little later in the auction I'll be looking to bring up my best candidates for a #2 and #3 starter, but there's no rush. I do know that I want at least a $4 discount. If someone not on my target list is available for a $4 discount, I may very well bid on him. If possible, I would like to get Trevor Cahill out before too long, because he's my top target for the mid-level pitchers, with a projected discount of $5.5. Again, I'd hate to take a $4 discount on someone else and then later not be able to afford Cahill, even though he's available for a $5.5 discount.

I plan to get either six starters and three relievers, or seven starters and two relievers. I think this is the ideal balance. Going with three relievers should help the ERA (earned run average) and WHIP (walks and hits / innings pitched), while going with only two should help wins and strikeouts. For most formats, it's not necessary to try to decide exactly which is better going into an auction. Typically, I'm going to have six starters and two relievers I want to use on a regular basis. My ninth pitcher can be rotated based on matchups and my needs at the time. Some weeks I might go with a seventh starter, and some weeks with a third reliever. (If I buy seven starters at the auction, I'll definitely want to get a reliever on my reserve squad. And vice versa.)

If you use just five starters and four relievers for the bulk of a season, you're going to be overly strong in WHIP and ERA, and weak in wins and strikeouts. If you use eight starters and just one reliever, you'll have the opposite problem.

As I said in chapter 3, my goal for a mono-league is to buy one reliable closer. My top target was Joakim Soria. He was the only reliable closer who looked like a great bet for a $3 discount. I wanted to get him nominated early, hopefully before the other top relievers. As with some of the hitters, I didn't want to have to decide whether to take, let's say, a $2 discount on Mariano Rivera or Chris Perez while Soria was still out there.

Having thought through and mapped out everything, I prepare my list of players to nominate:

2011 Tout Wars Nomination List

1.   Miggy (open at $34)

2.   Felix

3.   Ellsbury (open at $29)

4.   Soria

›   If don't get Ellsbury, Gardner (before Pierre)

›   If don't get Soria, Rivera (before Perez)

›   Cahill (if miss him, Romero)

›   Big Papi (if miss him, Thome, Hafner)

> Inge

> Gutierrez

> DeJesus

> Francouer

The 2011 Tout Wars Auction

The auction took place at the offices of MLB Advanced Media in Manhattan.

Jason Gray, the defending champion, began by nominating Mariano Rivera. (So much for my getting Soria out first!) He went for $24, more than I had expected. Next was Jose Bautista, 3B, who sold for $27. Then Carl Crawford, OF, sold for $38.

Felix Hernandez was next. This was good for me, because I wanted him out before the other starters, and it saved me the trouble of having to do it myself. When I bid $29, I was thinking, "When someone bids $30, should I immediately bid $31 and take a shot at getting him for that price . . . or should I wait and see if someone else bids $31, and then go to $32?" While I was debating this with myself, to my surprise nobody bid $30, and King Felix was mine for the surprisingly low price of $29. A $7.3 discount. "Wow!" I thought.

Next Justin Verlander sold for $25. This is exactly why the order in which players are brought up is so critical. If Verlander had been before Felix and was sitting there at $25, I would have bid $26. Perhaps the person who bid $25 would have gone to $27, and then I'd have passed. But quite possibly I would have bought him for $26. I'd have been happy with the $4.8 discount, which was $1 less than my max bid. But later Felix would have been bought by someone else for $29 (or perhaps even $28), and then I would have been unhappy. The $4.8 discount for Verlander pales in comparison to $7.3 for Felix.

It was now my turn, and sticking to my plan, I bid $34 on Miguel Cabrera. He went for $35.

Kendrys Morales, 1B, was next. He was a special case. In 2009 he produced $30 value. In 2010 he was doing just fine, until one of the most bizarre and unfortunate injuries in the history of the game. After hitting a walk-off grand slam, his teammates mobbed him and he broke his leg, missing the rest of the year. At the start of spring training, they said he'd be ready for opening day, but by the Tout Wars auction, he was still having trouble running and was expected to miss opening day. They thought—or at least hoped—that he'd be ready a couple of weeks later. I always like to be conservative, so I projected him to miss a full month. This reduced him to a $20 value. And I had a max bid of $18.

When Mike Siano, from MLB.com, bid $17, I thought, "*Okay, Larry, make the $18 bid . . .*", but I just couldn't do it. Even as the auctioneer said, "Going twice . . . sold!" I couldn't make the bid. Although I had downgraded him to missing a full month, which seemed conservative enough, I just didn't feel comfortable the way his outlook kept getting worse. But when he was sold, I wasn't at all sure I had done the right thing.

For my second nomination, I bid $29 on Ellsbury. Silence. Just what I wanted to hear. I nervously waited to see if everyone would stay silent through the "going once . . . going twice . . . sold!" They did. At last, I owned Ellsbury.

A bit later, Colby Lewis, SP, worth $21, was sold for $16. My listed max bid was $17, but I decided to pass, because it was only the third round, and at this point I was hoping to do even better than a $4 discount for my next couple of starters.

Joakim Soria was brought up and I was in on the bidding, but he went for $24. I was not happy about this. My best closer target was gone. And that left only Chris Perez as a likely alternative.

Not surprisingly, the prices on hitters were consistently too high. Many of the top hitters were gone, including two more from my target list: Pedroia (sold for $28) and Adam Jones ($21). While happy to land the high-priced Ellsbury, I was getting a little nervous about landing another top hitter, especially a power hitter, for a decent price.

By my third turn, the first four players on my nomination list were gone. And since I *had* landed Ellsbury, I crossed Gardner and Pierre off my nomination and target lists. I decided I'd try one of the few remaining high-price hitters on my target list, Paul Konerko. His projected 31 home runs looked very appealing.

Although I've said that I'm looking to get discounts for everyone except possibly catchers and very-high-priced hitters, in this case I was willing to go full price for Konerko. I had three more slots for $20+ hitters—the prices had been high, and the number of $20+ value hitters was starting to dwindle—especially those with a lot of power—and those I might be able to get for a decent price.

If I have to pay full price for a couple of top hitters, that's not going to kill me. But if I hold out for discounts that never happen, and there are no more $20 hitters left, then I am going to have a big problem.

There's a balance that must be struck between being patient, but not overly patient. I don't want to panic too soon, and I definitely don't want to overpay for anyone. On the other hand, I don't want to be too patient and totally miss out.

Once more, I didn't want to beat around the bush, and I nominated Konerko for the full price of $22. No sooner did I get the words out of my mouth than Dean Peterson, from Stats LLC, bid $23. And that was that.

Once again, I was second-guessing my decision not to bid $18 on Morales.

As it got close to my next turn, I was looking at the two high-value guys left on my target list, Shin-Soo Choo ($28) and Alex Rios ($27). I was thinking I would bring up Choo, because I preferred his better batting average and fewer stolen bases compared to Rios. I was still thinking average was going to be a concern, while good buying opportunities for stolen bases would be plentiful.

Just before my turn, Rios was nominated. When the bidding got to $25, I should have bid $26 (my max bid), but I hesitated because I was thinking how I'd prefer Choo and could probably get Choo. My hesitation allowed someone else to bid $26. I then thought that perhaps I should go the extra dollar, to full price, just as I'd done with Konerko. But again, I thought how Choo would be better, and I didn't do it. Rios was sold for $26.

Now it was my turn, and I was determined to get Choo. Aside from him, there was only one other guy—Bobby Abreu—still on my target list with a value above $20, yet I still had three slots available for $20+ hitters. So I *had* to get Choo. His price had been $27 at CR and $28 at LABR. I wasn't going to mess around and hope $27 would be good enough. I made an opening bid of $28.

Someone bid $29 and as I thought "oh, no," someone else went to $30.

Now I was in trouble. I was really kicking myself for not bidding on Rios. Once again, this shows how critical the order in which players are nominated can be. If Choo had been before Rios, I certainly would have been willing to go to $27 on Rios.

I was going to have to adjust immediately and be willing to go full price for any decent higher-value (non-stolen-base) hitter.

Or else I was going to get stuck with a lot of unused money. I also could see that I wouldn't be filling my remaining three $20+ hitter spots. I'd have to take the $27 slot and a $2 slot and convert them to a $16 and a $13, or something along those lines.

Adam Lind, OF, was brought up next. He fit the profile of what I needed: a fairly high-value ($17.8) power hitter. I knew I needed to be willing to go full-price for him. I bought him for $17. Getting Lind, with his $17.8 value and 26 homers, secured on my roster, and for a $1 discount, made me feel a little better. However, I still had three $20+ hitter slots open.

When the bid was $16 on Lind, I bid $17 and got him. This worked out fine but was a situation where I could have considered making a jump bid to $18. Had someone trumped my $17 bid with an $18 bid, I would have missed out. Considering that I was willing to pay $18 and was getting a little desperate to land a somewhat high-value power hitter, it would have been a safer option to jump the bid to $18.

When Michael Cuddyer, a $17.5 value, was nominated, he was one of the last few remaining hitters on my target list valued in the mid-to-high teens. Even if I got Abreu, which was no sure thing, I still would have two slots for $20+ hitters and nobody on my target list in the twenties. So I needed to be willing to go full price for Cuddyer, or, in this case, actually 50 cents more than full price. After someone bid $15, I went to $16, knowing that I'd go to $18 if necessary. It wasn't necessary, though, and I landed him for $16.

On my player pages, I wrote "yay!" next to his name. I was happy to get the discount despite being willing to go full price if needed. You'll note that my first three hitter purchases were all from my target list and I did get a discount on each of them.

For my next turn, it was now time for Chris Perez ($19.5).

Looking at the remaining closers, it looked very bleak after him. As for everyone else remaining, I probably wouldn't get a discount and wasn't thrilled about owning any of them anyway. So I realized I needed to be willing to go to $18 or even $19 for Perez.

I opened with a $10 bid, and then sat back. When the bid got to $16, I jumped in with $17. It wasn't enough. After the $18 bid, I immediately said $19. Any hesitation could lead to someone else getting in the $19 bid before me, so in a situation like that I pretty much say "$19" virtually the split second after the "$18" has come out of the other person's mouth. I got Perez for $19.

Soon after, Delmon Young was bought for $19. I made a mistake not bidding on him. He was sold for my max bid, at a time when I still would have been willing to go an extra dollar for the right person. He fit the profile of what I needed . . . worth $21, with a good batting average and some power. My hesitation was that I still had several outfielders I really liked on my target list. But when he was sold, I was kicking myself for passing on him.

This is just another example of the snap decisions that must be made at an auction. There really is little time to think about things. I do as much as possible to prepare in advance, but there are still always many tough decisions that must be made in a matter of seconds or less.

Next up was Derrek Lee, 1B. He went for $18 at CR and $17 at LABR, so when I had the bid at $14 I wasn't expecting it to be the final bid, but it was. A very nice surprise!

Already having Cuddyer at first base, I put Lee at my corner spot. On my player page of first baseman, I put a sticky note that said "only DH." This was to remind me that I could buy another first baseman, but would have to use my DH spot. Since I was expecting to probably get a good bargain on a DH-only hitter,

I didn't want to buy another first baseman unless the price was irresistible.

Mark Reynolds, 3B, came up during the next round. His $20 value and 33 home runs fit what I needed, but it came with a .229 batting average. As I've said, I was concerned that average could be a problem. But my overriding concern was that I still needed a few higher-value players, and there were very few left. I bought Reynolds for $19. Having added Reynolds, I was definitely going to need to pay attention to batting average from now on.

A little later, one of my favorite targets, Franklin Gutierrez, was nominated. I projected him for $17.6. I bought him for $14.

At this point, my template looked like this:

Plan	Actual	+/−	
32	Ellsbury 29	−3	|
27			|
22	Reynolds 19	−3	|
20	Cuddyer 16	−4	|
17	Lind 17	E	|
15	D Lee 14	−1	|
12	Gutierrez 14	+2	|
8			|
6			|
4			|
2			|
2			|
2			|
1			|
$170	Total 109	−9	

My first six hitters had cost $109. I was hoping to get Abreu, or at least a high-teens hitter, to fill the $27 slot. Even then, I wasn't going to spend anywhere near $27 and would have money left over from that spot . . . plus the $9 I already had left over. So I knew that I could easily afford a second hitter worth mid-to-high teens. Besides Abreu, I still had Guerrero, Kubel, and Big Papi on my target list.

Looking at it another way, I had $61 left for eight spots. So if I didn't buy a high-priced hitter or two, I could buy a lot of hitters averaging around $8 each. However, it's best to spend on the one or two higher-dollar hitters rather than to have to get so many in the $8 range. The point, though, is that I wouldn't have to panic if I couldn't land a couple of higher-price hitters for a decent price.

So far, I had a total projected value of $120.7 for my $109 spent, an average of just about $2 discount per hitter. I was happy with that. My projected team stats were a .2653 average, with 477 runs, 118 homers, 457 RBIs, and 95 stolen bases. I needed 55 more homers and 21 steals to get to the team projected averages. So I needed to go after homers more than steals.

The .2653 batting average stuck out like a sore thumb. My projected mean team average was .269. Considering that so far I had bought my best, most expensive hitters, my batting average should be above the mean, not below it. It definitely tends to drop when you start buying the less-expensive hitters, not to mention possibly a cheap catcher or two. I was extremely concerned about this.

Had I bought Delmon Young and his .293 average instead of Mark Reynolds, my team average now would be .2757, which would be just fine. There's no guarantee that I would have gotten

Young if I'd been the one to bid $19, or if I'd gone to $20, but it was surely looking like a mistake that I didn't try.

For my next turn, I went for Abreu. I was confident I could get him for $20, but Jason Collette bid $21. I considered going full price at $22, but opted against it because I still had a few targets in the upper teens, and Abreu's .268 average and 21 steals weren't the ideal match for my team.

After a few more picks, it was time for a quick break. Since I'd gotten good prices on Cuddyer and Lee, I wasn't second-guessing myself anymore about Morales. But on my way to the bathroom, I saw Mike Siano and out of curiosity asked him, "If I'd bid $18 on Morales, would you have gone $19?" Mike said he probably would have. So I most likely wasn't going to have gotten him, anyway.

John Danks, SP, a $19.6 value, was brought up and I bought him for $15. A $4.6 discount on Danks was worth taking. I couldn't expect to do better than that, except possibly for Cahill, and even with Danks, I still had room for Cahill.

When it was my turn I wanted to get Cahill out, but I also still needed a couple of good hitters. I brought out Big Papi ($17.6). He went for just $13 at CR and LABR. I would have been very happy to get him for $13 or even $14. Surprisingly, he went for $17.

I was getting nervous again. I had missed on Abreu and Big Papi, and the number of high-value hitters was dwindling. And I really needed to buy a couple of them in the teens or I was going to be in real danger of wasting money . . . or having to shift money from hitting to pitching. Shifting money is not the disaster that wasting money is, but at a planned $90 for pitching I'm already at the high end. If I spent more than that, I'd enter the season knowing I'd have to look to trade a pitcher for a hitter.

There were several outfielders remaining with values more than $10, but other than that, there was only one second baseman, Ryan Raburn, and two shortstops, Erick Aybar and Reid Brignac. Brignac was on my target list, but hopefully I wouldn't even need to pay in the double digits to get him.

So when Hideki Matsui, OF ($12.8), was nominated, I knew I'd better try to get him. I especially liked that he was one of the few remaining outfielders with a bit of power (18 homers). I had to go to $12, but I got him.

A bit later, Raburn, a $14.2 value, was sold for $17. And then Aybar, a $12.9 value, went for $14.

I was happy to hear Trevor Cahill's name next. And I was even happier when I heard the words "Sold to Schechter for $11." A $7.4 discount!

I had now spent $74 for four pitchers, so I only had $16 left for five more. I couldn't spend more than about $10 on a pitcher unless I was to take money from my hitters.

For my next turn, I went with my best remaining higher-value hitter, Jason Kubel, OF ($16.2). I was able to get him for just $14. My purchases of Matsui and Kubel barely helped my team average, but did bring my home runs and stolen bases into a good balance. I now had 157 homers and 95 steals, compared to the mean of 173 and 116. My outfield was also now filled.

Catcher J. P. Arencibia was brought up. He had gone for $10 at both CR and LABR, so it was surprising when the bidding was slowing down at $4. I bid $5. It was even more of a surprise when that was the final bid and I owned him for $5. What had changed in the two weeks since CR and LABR was that Arencibia had a terrible first couple of weeks of spring training, and there was some talk that Jose Molina could share the starting job with him. But I only had Arencibia projected for 375 at bats, which he should be able to attain even if he was only a slight #1 over Molina. For $5, I thought he was a fine purchase.

And then came Jeff Francoeur. I only had one hitting spot left for a non-catcher—second baseman or shortstop—so I had to choose very carefully, but he looked like the prime target. There were a handful of outfielders remaining worth a little more, and I did want to spend as much money as possible, but Francoeur was on my target list as a potentially huge bargain. I bought him for $6. I was very happy to get a $4.6 discount.

I had $24 left to spend on four spots. This was a lot more money than what, according to my template, I should have at this point. I had planned to have approximately three $2 slots and one $1 slot, for a total of $7.

I looked at the remaining catchers and middle infielders to see if there was a path to spending my $24. At catcher there was Olivo ($7.3) and Jaso ($6.5). There were five middle infielders worth between $6.8 and $8.6. So it was possible, but I had little margin for error. I needed to land one of the two catchers, and three of the five infielders. After these players, the value dropped off significantly.

The question here is do I go the extra dollar or two to get these guys, or do I hold out for a discount and if necessary switch money to my pitching budget? My decision was that I'd better go the extra dollar or two on at least a couple of these guys, or else I might get stuck filling these hitting slots with $1 and $2 players, in which case I'd end up spending something like $107 on pitching, which would be massively too much. Or worse, the valuable pitchers might also dry up, leaving me with unspent money.

Lawr Michaels nominated Craig Breslow. I had blown my chance to bring him up myself and get him for $1. It was only the 14th round of bidding, so I had thought I'd be safe waiting a little longer. I was not going to bid $2. I had only wanted him if I could get the full $3.5 discount. As it turned out, I wouldn't have gotten him anyway, because Jeff Erickson, from RotoWire, bid $2.

Marco Scutaro, one of the five middle infielders I needed to try to get, was brought up. I valued him at $6.8, and he went for $12.

It was my turn now. Since I needed to buy three middle infielders, but only one catcher, I brought up my best catcher target, Miguel Olivo. My max bid was listed at $6, but due to my dire need to spend money, I was willing to go to $8. I opened at $4, planning to then go to $6 and $8, if necessary. I got him for $4.

I was very happy to get that price on Olivo, but it meant it was even more unlikely I'd be able to spend my entire hitting budget. I now had $20 left for three middle infielders. If I could get Orlando Cabrera ($7) at shortstop, and two of Maicer Izturis ($8.6), Mark Ellis ($7.9), and Chris Getz ($6.8) for second base and middle infielder, then I might spend all of the $20. But if I didn't get three of them and/or got a really good deal on one or more, then I would have to shift money to pitching. After those guys, the next most valuable middle infielder was Brendan Ryan ($4.4), whom I expected to be able to buy for just a dollar or two, anyway.

I now had 193 home runs (20 above the mean) and 105 stolen bases (11 below the mean). So I did need to get more steals. Looking at the projected stolen bases for the middle infielders I was considering, it was apparent that I'd probably get at least 25 more, so I'd be fine.

I had 745 runs (60 below the mean) and 781 RBIs (22 above the mean). With three more hitters I'd be nicely above the average in both categories.

I didn't even want to look at my batting average. I knew it

was awful and I couldn't do much about it at this point. It was .2623, almost .007 below the mean. Buying three lower-value middle infielders wasn't going to help. I'd just have to evaluate after the auction what to do about this. Trying to trade would certainly be a possibility.

When Orlando Cabrera ($7) was nominated, I had the bid at $6 and was very hopeful that would be enough, but it wasn't. After the bid went to $7, I knew I could really get stuck with unspent hitting dollars, so I did something I absolutely hate to ever do . . . I went to $8 . . . a dollar more than he was worth. It's not a terrible thing to have to do that once in a while for a high-value hitter, but to pay more than someone's worth for a lower-level hitter is disgusting to me. Yet it's still much better than wasting money altogether, or ending up spending more than $100 on pitching. I did land him for $8.

When it was my turn, I wanted to stick with the hitters so that I would know how much, if any, money I'd need to shift to pitching. It was encouraging that the three second basemen I was targeting—of which I hoped to get two—were all on my original target list. So hopefully I could get two of them at a good price. I brought up Mark Ellis, 2B ($7.9). I went to $6 but was outbid at $7. For some reason, I couldn't bring myself to go to full price at $8. I'm not sure why, but perhaps I still had the bitter taste in my mouth of having overspent on Cabrera. I let Ellis go at $7.

When it was my turn for round 16, I really needed to get both Izturis and Getz. I expected that if I was willing to go to $8 that should be enough to get Izturis. And hopefully I'd get him for less than that. I did have to go to $8, and to my surprise and displeasure, I was then outbid at $9. As the auctioneer was saying "going once . . . going twice . . ." I held my nose and bid $10. I knew I just had to spend this money, and now I was wondering why the heck I hadn't just gone to $8 on Ellis. Then the bid went to $11 and I didn't get Izturis.

There's no guarantee I would have gotten Ellis if I'd gone to $8, but now I was kicking myself for not trying. As you can see, I find auctions fairly excruciating at times, as I'm constantly second-guessing myself.

At this point, I was looking at hopefully getting Getz for $6 or less and Ryan for a buck or two, so now I knew that I should plan on shifting about $4 to pitching.

Jeff Niemann, SP ($10.8), was nominated and I bought him for $6. Next was Dallas Braden, SP ($13.5). I got him for $7. His $6.5 discount was even better than the $4.8 I'd just gotten on Niemann.

These purchases left me with just $10 remaining for four slots. Under the theory that I had shifted $4 to pitching, I had $8 to spend on my two hitters and $2 for two more pitchers. Obviously, it wasn't necessarily going to work out that way, but I did want to spend as much on hitting as possible.

For my turn I brought up my highest-value remaining middle infielder, Chris Getz, 2B ($6.8). I was hoping to buy Getz for just $3 or $4 but was prepared to go full price, under the circumstances. I opened with a $1 bid, then quickly went to $3 and then $5 when others bid. I got him for $5.

When you get to the late stages of an auction, many people are running low on money, and some don't have open slots left at various positions. Therefore big bargains are possible. That's why I opened at just $1 for Getz. It was now the 17th round of the auction. So it was possible he could have gone dirt cheap.

When it got to me again, I brought up my highest-value remaining middle infielder, Brendan Ryan, SS ($4.4). I got him for $1. This completed my hitters. Although I only spent $164, while everyone else was undoubtedly spending around $180, I had hitting value of $194. I had $25 more than the average projected team value of $169. Despite my overspending for Cabrera, I averaged a $2 discount per hitter.

Once again, everyone took a turn and I didn't buy anyone. When it was back to me, I had $4 left for two pitchers. My best target was Doug Fister ($7.6) whom I thought I might be able to get for $2. I decided to hold off on him for the time being. My thinking was that I'd start by trying to get as much pitching value as I could. There were a few pitchers on my target list who were more valuable than Fister, and as I just said, this late in the auction you never know when you just might run into a humongous bargain. So I went with Jeremy Guthrie, a $10.1 pitcher. I opened at $1, went to $3, but he sold for $6.

For my 20th turn, I went with the highest-value pitcher remaining, Jason Vargas ($8.4). He was also a member of my original target list. Again, I opened at $1, someone bid $2, and I quickly said $3 before anyone could beat me to the punch. I got him for $3.

This left me with $1 for my final pitcher. It also meant that I was out of the bidding for everyone else brought up by the other owners, since they all had to open the bidding for at least $1, and I couldn't go to $2. My pitching staff to this point had an ERA of 3.57 and WHIP of 1.23, which were both well below the projected averages of 3.94 and 1.295. My projected wins, 79, were seven more than the mean, and my strikeouts, 969, were 22 above the mean. So I had no doubt that I'd like to get another starter, rather than a reliever. My ERA and WHIP would still be terrific, my wins total would become dominant, and my strikeouts would be nicely above the norm. (Not to mention that the highest-value remaining relief pitcher, Jason Frasor, was worth only $3.5. There were several starters worth more than that, so by getting a starter, I'd also get a more-valuable pitcher.)

When it got to my turn, my best hope to get a great deal for my last $1 was clearly Doug Fister. Although I valued him at $7.6, he went for only $2 at CR and $1 at LABR, so there was a chance I could get him for a buck. I said "Doug Fister, $1" and waited with bated breath—trying to look cool and inconspicuous—as there was silence until the "going once . . . going twice . . . sold to Schechter."

That completed my team in round 22. I was the second team to finish. Once again, my target lists proved to be very useful. Fifteen of the 23 players I bought were on my target lists.

Reserve Draft

My goal for the reserve draft is always to get an even split between hitters and pitchers. I want to get a backup for as many hitting positions as possible, especially those where I have an injury risk. And I want to get at least one starting pitcher and one reliever, so that I've got options. However, getting good value is still of utmost importance.

Tout Wars has four reserve spots per team. The available players who stood out were:

2B —   Adam Rosales $1.5
OF —   Ryan Sweeney $3.3
        Corey Patterson $1.7
        Trevor Crowe $1.1
        Darnell McDonald $0.9

SP — Bruce Chen $4.3
Nick Blackburn $3.8
Mitch Talbot $1.8
Kevin Millwood $1.2
Rich Harden $1.0 (when healthy 170IP = $8.4)
Josh Outman <$0.7> (chance FT = $5)
Josh Tomlin <$0.8> (chance FT = $4.7)
David Pauley <$1.6> (chance FT = $3.0)
Freddy Garcia <$2.0> (chance FT = $2.4)

RP — Jason Frasor $3.5
Ryan Perry $3.1
Tony Sipp $1.9
H Takahashi $1.9
Mike Gonzalez $1.8
Darren Oliver $1.6
Robinson Tejada $1.5

As you can see, because of others' differences of opinion with me, many players with a positive value were not bought during the auction.

I projected Rich Harden for 85 innings pitched and a value of $1 because he stays off the DL as often as Lindsay Lohan stays out of trouble, but when he's healthy and pitching full-time, he's worth $8.4. Therefore, he's a good guy to gamble on.

Josh Outman, Josh Tomlin, David Pauley, and Freddy Garcia were all battling for a rotation spot. Their projected values were negative, but if at any point during the year they are in the rotation, they would have a positive value. This makes them worth considering after better options are exhausted.

The reserve picks are done by a snake draft, and the order is determined by a random draw. Unfortunately, I got the 11th pick.

By the time it got to me, my best choice was Nick Blackburn, SP ($3.8). Next I took Jason Frasor, RP ($3.5), then Tony Sipp, RP ($1.9), and Hisanori Takahashi, RP ($1.9).

This did not go as I'd hoped. I had missed out on Ryan Sweeney, Corey Patterson, and Adam Rosales, and there was never another hitter really worth taking. If I ever had an injury, a similar-caliber hitter to what I could have taken would probably be available as a free agent.

Some people like to use a reserve pick to speculate on a minor league prospect. Unless a player has a very realistic chance of making a contribution this year, I ignore him. I'd much rather have a guy who I know will be worth $1 or more starting from day one. And the really great prospects are usually already bought during the auction. Those remaining are likely to only be worth a few dollars anyway, if and when they are ever called up.

Final Results

The final auction results were this:

	$ Value	Avg.	RUN	HR	RBI	SB
Average team	$169	.269	805	173	759	116
My team	$193.9	.2607	883	199	890	142

	$ Value	ERA	WHIP	Win	Save	K
Average team	$ 91	3.94	1.295	72	37	947
My team	$144.2	3.64	1.238	87.7	53	1073

I wasn't happy that I'd spent just $164 on hitting and $96 on pitching, and I was horrified by my projected batting average, more than .008 worse than the average team. I don't always end up with the exact balance I want, but I couldn't remember ever having a category as pathetic as this.

But otherwise, everything looked excellent. For my $260, I got $338.1 value. Except for batting average, I was very strong in all other categories. I would have to examine trade possibilities to see if I could improve the batting average, but overall I was pleased with the outcome.

Since I used a 65/35% money split in my value formula, the value is actually skewed toward pitching. Had I used a more conventional 67/33% split, I would have ended up with the same team, but the $ *Value* column in the table would be different. It would show a better balance, approximately $200 for hitting and $138 for pitching.

I learned after the auction that some people both at the auction, and following it on the Tout Wars website live blog, thought I was punting batting average intentionally. That was funny. They had no idea I was actually trying like heck to do better and was horrified to see how bad it turned out.

Walking a Fine Line

I want to emphasize one point. The prices paid for many of the best hitters at auctions are excessively high. Typically several of them will be bought for $2–5 more than I think they're worth. Sometimes this is just a legitimate difference of opinion between my projected value for a player and someone else's. In other words, the buyer doesn't agree that they have overpaid for the player.

However, in many cases people do willingly overpay. Some think they must land their share of studs even if it costs them a premium. Some think "the talent falls off the table at first base after the top handful" and they must get one of the best. Some pay a premium due to a false notion of scarcity for middle infielders. Some use draft software that tracks the amount of money spent compared to remaining talent and tells them "draft inflation" now justifies paying more for a player than was justified at the beginning of the auction.

But a player is really only worth the value of what his projected stats will produce, as determined by a logically sound value formula. When you pay more than this price, you're losing value. You're on track to get less than $260 of value for the $260 you spend. Therefore the key is to not overspend and to get as many bargains as possible at all levels.

However, there's a fine line that must be drawn between holding out for good prices and being too patient, which can result in disaster. If you don't buy enough higher-value hitters, you may end up with too much money remaining for not enough talent. This will result in your having to grossly overspend to buy some of the scarce remaining hitters or, just as wasteful, you'll leave money on the table.

This is why I am often willing to pay full price, or perhaps even a dollar more, to land a top hitter or two. I need to make sure I spend enough money. And then I'm freed up to be patient and get great discounts on my other hitters.

It's easy to panic and get caught up in the spending frenzy. Sometimes I feel like since everyone else seems to be doing it, and the studs are disappearing, I'd better pay whatever it takes so that I get a stud as well. But I resist this and try to stick with only $1 more than full price at the most.

I use my target list to identify potential good buys, and I try to get them nominated as early as possible. As you saw, I did buy Ellsbury, a $31 value, for just $29. But then the other top hitters kept getting bought for more than full price, except for a couple, such as Rios, when I was too stubbornly still holding out for a discount and declined to go full price. At this point, I was in panic mode and willing to go essentially full price on most any higher-value hitter. But it didn't work out, and other than Ells-bury, I never spent more than $19 for another hitter. Fortunately, I was able to get good discounts on more hitters than planned in the $5–17 range and I bought less than planned for under $5. So I still got great overall value and avoided a disaster, although I did have to shift $6 to pitching.

I mentioned earlier that, starting in 2012, I changed my planned spending split from $170/$90 to $180/$80. This makes it even more important to buy three or four $20+ hitters.

Therefore, I've come to the conclusion that unless there are several $20+ hitters on my target list that I think I can get for a discount, I shouldn't wait for the better hitters to start disap-pearing and the panic to set in. I should plan to buy pretty much anyone I can get for full price or even a dollar more right from the start. Once I've landed one or two, then I can start holding out for the discounts.

Prior to the 2013 Tout Wars auction, based on my others' value prices and the actual prices paid at LABR, I could see that there was probably only one $20+ hitter I could expect to get a discount on. Other than that, I'd be doing well to get another couple for full price or $1 over full price. So I went to that auction prepared right from the start to pay up to a $1 premium.

I had five hitters valued at $30 or above, and Mike Trout ($39) was the only one that I thought I had even a small chance of landing for just a $1 premium. He had gone for $42 at LABR, and I expected a $41–43 price at Tout Wars. But I figured that if

I could get him for $40 that would be smart, because my likely options were approximately these:

Player	Value	Price	Player	Value	Price
Trout	$39	$40	Other	$25	$26
Other	$12	$10	Other	$25	$25
Total:	$51	$50		$50	$51
Gain:		+$ 1	Gain:		<-$ 1>

If I bought Trout, that would essentially fill two of my $20+ slots and allow me to get a $2 (or perhaps better) discount on a lower-value hitter, for a net gain. Without Trout, I'd undoubtedly have to pay full price or $1 more on a couple of mid- to upper-$20 hitters, which would give me a net of even at best, and more likely a loss.

Based on the above, I could even justify spending $41 on Trout, but I decided to stick with $40. As defending champion, I got the first nomination. Since I was expecting $40 probably wouldn't be enough, there was no need to open with a lower bid and risk that someone else might beat me to $40. So I opened the 2013 auction with "Mike Trout . . . $40." To my pleasant surprise, I got him. And that allowed me to wait for good prices for the rest of the hitters, even the $20+ hitters.

CHAPTER 8

Mixed-League Auctions

In March 2005, I was invited to join the Tout Wars experts league (ToutWars.com). They traditionally had an AL-only and an NL-only auction league, but for 2005 they added a 12-team mixed auction.

I had never been in a mixed auction—and I only had one week to prepare—so this was very problematic. But I wasn't going to pass up the chance to join the renowned Tout Wars, so I said yes.

I only had a week to try to figure out the differences between a mixed auction and a mono-league auction. I searched the Internet but found pretty much no useful strategy information. And for dollar values, most websites and magazines provided dollar values only for mono-leagues, but not mixed leagues. And I quickly figured out that the mixed-league dollar values that were provided actually made little sense, anyway.

So I was really left to my own devices. Apparently, I did a good job, because I won the league, and won again in 2006 and 2007.

Had someone else written this chapter before March 2005 and I could have just read it, that would have made things a lot easier. So here you go . . . here's everything you need to know about a mixed auction . . .

Mixed-League Prices

In a typical mono-league auction, you have $260 to spend to acquire as much value as possible. In a typical mixed league, you still have a budget of $260, but since you can select players from both the AL and NL, you will be able to acquire a lot more value than in a mono-league.

Here's where some people would debate me. They would say, "Yes, in a mixed league your team would acquire more *stats* than a mono-league. But when you use the word *value*, it's all relative."

This is correct. When you convert players' stats into a dollar value, the formula should be structured such that the total value of all players adds up to the total amount of auction money available. For a 12-team league, this means $3,120 (12 × $260). Also, the value of your 168th-best hitter and 108th-best pitcher—the last hitter and pitcher to be included in your player pool—should be exactly $1.

Therefore, your value formula for a mixed-league auction should be structured in the same way. This means that while your team would have better stats than a mono-league team, in terms of dollar value, each team would still average $260 of value, just as in a mono-league.

While this is technically correct, I've always preferred to approach mixed-league bidding by thinking in terms of mono-league prices. Why? Because dollar values generated for mixed leagues are not very useful.

To illustrate this, I'm going to use my 2012 projected values to identify the player pool for a 12-team mixed league. This means finding the 168 best hitters (with at least 24 catchers, 60 outfielders, etc.) and the best 108 pitchers. Based on my mono-league values, this pool has a total value of $5,180, which means each team would average $432 worth of value for their $260 budget. On average, to buy each player would only cost 60% of the players' value ($260/432 = 60%).

So, you might wonder, does that mean we should just spend about 60% per player? Since Prince Fielder is worth $30 for an AL-only league, should we make him an $18 player for the mixed league? And a $15 player would go for $9? And a $2 player would go for $1?

The answer is no. And the reason is clear when you consider the worst players who've made my player pool at each position:

Pos	Last Player
C	$ 6.0
1B/3B	$13.2
2B/SS	$13.0
OF	$13.4
DH	N/A
Pitcher	$ 8.8

In a mono-league, the players at the bottom of the pool, whom you can snap up for $1 at the end of the auction, are mostly worth only $1. But in this mixed league, the players at the bottom are worth at least $13 at every hitting position except catcher, where they are worth at least $6. And the pitchers are worth at least $8.8.

Therefore, there's no sense in spending more than $1 for a catcher worth $6, nor for any other hitter worth $13, nor a pitcher worth $8.8. You're automatically going to be able to get someone worth at least that much at the end for a dollar.

Since there will be so many good players available at the end for $1—and you can buy them for a fraction of their value—that means the best players will still go for full price, or perhaps even more than full price. Some people take a "stars-and-scrubs approach," which means they plan to buy a lot of studs as well as many $1–2 players. Since they can spend just $1–2 and get players at a fraction of their true value, they want to invest those saved dollars into getting their fair share—or actually more than their fair share—of the studs.

Overall, the mono-league values will be bought for just 60 cents on the dollar. But that savings of 40 cents per dollar ranges from pretty much nothing for the studs down to about 90 cents per dollar for the very worst players—and everything in between.

Why Mixed-League Value Formulas Are Mostly Useless

I'm going to show you some various published 12-team mixed-league values. The *Mono* column is what the source valued the player at for a mono-league. The next columns show what the same source valued the player at for a mixed league.

HITTERS					PITCHERS				
	Sources					Sources			
Mono	#1	#2	#3	#4	Mono	#1	#2	#3	#4
$40	$38	$34	$37	$40					
$35	$34	$28	$31	$34	$35	$33	$25	$34	$28
$30	$28	$23	$27	$27	$30	$28	$21	$29	$22
$25	$23	$18	$22	$19	$25	$24	$16	$20	$18
$20	$19	$12	$14	$14	$20	$19	$13	$17	$14
$15	$13	$ 6	$ 8	$ 8	$15	$13	$ 6	$10	$ 8
$10	$ 8	$ 2	$ 2	$ 2	$10	$ 8	$ 2	$ 2	$ 2
$ 5	$ 5	$ 0	$ 0	$ 0	$ 5	$ 5	$ 0	$ 0	$ 0

These are typical values that you'll find in magazines and websites. In fact, if I use my own value formula, I also get similar results. What this shows, for example, is that for a hitter where all four sources agreed he is worth $40 for a mono-league, when they run the numbers for a mixed league, he is now worth $34, $37, $38, or $40. And a $35 pitcher becomes worth anywhere from $25 to $34.

A small part of the discrepancies is simply because a properly done value formula has to consider the total stats generated by the player pool. So even with the same stats, a player's dollar value would usually be a little different if he's in an AL-only pool, an NL-only pool, or a mixed league. However, most of the discrepancies are due to the simple fact that overall players should be worth about 60% of their mono-league values, and these four sources adjust for that in differing ways.

Also, when compiling this chart, I didn't simply just find one $20 value per source and then write down his mixed-league value. I looked at several players at each value level and recorded the average, or most common, mixed-league value. (I didn't include catcher values in this chart, because they are treated differently. And it's not necessary to include them for me to make my points right now.)

Looking at these sources individually, we see that #1 has simply deducted $1–2 at every level, except the very lowest, where they deduct nothing. This is just flat-out stupid. Among other things, it means they are saying you should pay $5 for a hitter worth $5, even though the reality is that you can get a much more valuable hitter for just $1. Also, their total player-pool salary adds up to much more than the $3,120 it's supposed to.

The biggest problem with source #2 is with the high-value players. This may actually be a well-thought-out value formula, but the reality is that the $31+ hitters will mostly be sold for full value, not the $6–7 discounts as they show. And the $31+ pitchers will mostly be sold for a small discount, not the $7–8 that they show.

Sources #3 and #4, overall, do a better job. Yet they still don't show what really happens at many levels of bidding. Therefore, as I've said, most of this information is essentially useless. It's not that these aren't well-thought-out formulas (except for #1), it's just the nature of the beast. There is *no* way to create a mixed-league formula that will accurately reflect what will happen.

You need to know how much you should *actually* be bidding for players!

Based on my five years in the Tout Wars mixed league, as well as some other leagues I've been in—and examined—this is what actually happens:

HITTERS

	Sources				
Mono	**#1**	**#2**	**#3**	**#4**	**Reality**
$40	$38	$34	$37	$40	$40
$35	$34	$28	$31	$34	$35
$30	$28	$23	$27	$27	$25
$25	$23	$18	$22	$19	$15
$20	$19	$12	$14	$14	$ 7
$15	$13	$ 6	$ 8	$ 8	$ 2
$10	$ 8	$ 2	$ 2	$ 2	$ 1
$ 5	$ 5	$ 0	$ 0	$ 0	$ 0

PITCHERS

	Sources				
Mono	**#1**	**#2**	**#3**	**#4**	**Reality**
$35	$33	$25	$34	$28	$32
$30	$28	$21	$29	$22	$26
$25	$24	$16	$20	$18	$21
$20	$19	$13	$17	$14	$14
$15	$13	$ 6	$10	$ 8	$ 9
$10	$ 8	$ 2	$ 2	$ 2	$ 4
$ 5	$ 5	$ 0	$ 0	$ 0	$ 0

The *Reality* column shows the average actual sales price. In this case, it is correlated to my opinion of what the mono-league value was. So if the average price paid for a $35 pitcher was $32, in some cases the person buying the pitcher may have thought he was buying a $37 value, a $33, or whatever. Since my dollar values tend to be in line with others, this gives an accurate idea of the real prices paid.

In the case of a $10 pitcher, it doesn't make much sense to spend $4 in a 12-team league. Sometimes people who spent $4 had a different opinion than me and thought the pitcher was worth more than $10. But in many cases, I'm quite sure it's just because they didn't know any better. They didn't realize they could wait and get a $10 pitcher for a buck or two later.

I'm not suggesting the *Reality* column is what you should plan to pay at an auction. These are the average prices. Therefore, if you pay these prices, you'll buy an average team. You want to pay less than these prices in order to acquire a superior team. In order to accomplish this, you need to know the range of average prices:

EXPECTED PRICES (12-TEAM LEAGUE, 67/33% SPLIT)

Hitters' Value	Avg. Price Range	Larry's Target Minimum Discount
$31+	$2 discount to overpay by $2	$ 2
$26–30	$2–8 discount	$ 8
$21–25	$6–12 discount	$12
$17–20	$11–15 discount	$15
$13–16	$11–15 discount	$15

When you make dollar values for a 12-team league, they need to add up to $3,120 (12 teams × $260 budget). However, you have a choice of how you split that money between hitting and pitching. For this chart, I have used a 67/33% split, because I think it's the most commonly used. If you use a different split, you'll need to adjust this chart accordingly. Details on how to make the adjustment are in chapter 3.

Also, this chart is for a 12-team league. Average prices for a 15-team league are slightly different. I'll show you that later.

Average Price Range means that most of the $31+ hitters, for example, will be bought for somewhere between $2 less than their value and $2 more. This is solely from my perspective. If I think someone overpaid by $2, they may simply disagree with my price and think the player really is worth more than what I think. Or they may have knowingly paid more than fair value because they have some notion of position scarcity and/or they have adopted the stars-and-scrubs approach and feel justified in overspending to make sure they get some stars. Either way, it doesn't matter to me. I'm not going to be buying a player for more than I think he's worth.

If you use values that are fairly mainstream, this chart will work for you. If you are in the habit of valuing hitters a couple of dollars more—or less—than most people, then you'll have to adjust accordingly.

The column showing my target minimum discount is always the high end of the average-discount spectrum. For example, while most $26–30 hitters will fall in the range of a $2–8 discount, there are outliers. So in addition to a few $8 discounts, there will also be a few even greater than $8. That's why I make it my goal to get at least an $8 discount.

The value of the worst player available is always slightly different, and may also be different by position. So each year I note the worst player at each position and know where my cutoff point is to not spend more than $1. For 2012, Ryan Roberts is the worst middle infielder at $13. While this means that I wouldn't spend more than $1 for him, it also means that theoretically I should be willing to spend $2 for a $14 middle infielder. But actually, I wouldn't. I know that due to differences of opinion in values, there's a very good chance that someone a little better than Roberts will be available at the end. I'll likely be able to get the 33rd to 34th-best middle infielder rather than Roberts (who is 36th).

So rather than buying a $14 player for $2 and thus locking in a $12 bargain, it's better to wait and take a shot that I can get a $14 player—or even better—for just $1. Worst case, I get Roberts and still have a $12 bargain.

The discounts can get nuts near the end of a mixed auction. I've gotten $23 players for $4, $18 players for $1, and lots of other great deals.

Catchers

I showed before that for 2012 the last player at each position was worth about $13, except for catchers, who were worth $6. This is typical of the values every year. There is rarely any scarcity for middle infielders or any position other than catchers. But many people do pay extra believing in scarcity for middle infielders. That's fine with me. If everyone else wants to waste their money, I have no problem waiting until the late rounds to buy my second baseman, shortstop, and middle infielder all for a buck or two.

Catchers, however, are scarce in the sense that if you wait until the end, you'll get much less value for $1 than with other positions. Also, there are typically only a couple of catchers worth $20 or more, and not a whole lot even worth more than $10. Therefore, many people do pay a premium for catchers, and the average discounts are much less than for other hitters.

Catchers' Value	Avg. Price Range	Larry's Target Minimum Discount
$17+	$2 discount to overpay by $2	$2
$11–16	$1–5 discount	$5
$6–10	$2–6 discount	$6
$5 or less	Don't pay more than $1	

Pitchers

And the expected discount for pitchers is this:

Value	Avg. Price Range	Larry's Target Minimum Discount
$31+	$2–6 discount	$6
$21–30	$3–7 discount	$7
$9–20	$4–8 discount	$8
$8 or less	Don't pay more than $1	

As with hitters, I'll adjust my cutoff point for spending just $1 based on the worst pitcher available that year. For 2012, the 108th pitcher is worth $8.8, so I would ignore all pitchers worth less than $8.8 and spend only $1 for anyone worth about $9.

Again, though, based on differences of opinion, I would expect to do much better than my 108th pitcher at the end. It's quite likely I'd be able to get my 90th- to 95th-best pitcher, which for 2012 would be worth $10–11. So actually, I wouldn't even pay a dollar for a $9 pitcher. I'd hope to get at least a $10–11 pitcher for a buck.

Disclaimer

Besides the decision of how to split the $3,120 (or $3,900 for a 15-team league), value formulas are all a little different, so your results may not match up exactly with my chart. But the results should be pretty close.

Also, all auctions are somewhat different. Depending on the philosophy of the other owners in the league, you never know exactly where the discounts will be, or for how much. In some auctions there's a higher premium put on hitting than pitching, in which case the average discounts will be a couple of dollars less for hitters and greater for pitchers. In some leagues, closers are discounted more.

Remember, though, that if something is going for more than usual, something else has to go for less than usual. The overall discounts have got to end up in the 40-cents-on-the-dollar range.

There are two important things to realize about these average prices. First, you should *never* do things such as pay full price for a $28 player, pay $17 for a $21 player, pay $5 for an $11 player, etc.

Second, to get a superior team, you must do *better* than the average. For example, the average discount for a $21–25 player is $9. At many 2012 auctions, someone will buy Adam Jones (worth $23) for $14 and will be very happy with the discount he got. "Great buy," he'll think to himself.

But this is actually only an *average* discount. Purchases like this will lead to having an average team and finishing in the middle of the pack.

In order to have a superior team, you need to get discounts that are at the far end of—or better than—the averages shown above.

And there *will* be many buying opportunities at the far end of the discount spectrum, and even better. I know from experience that this will happen. So I will be patient and wait for my opportunities.

The best way to maximize your team's overall value is by getting the best possible discounts at every step of the auction.

The Flaw

As I said, there really is no perfect way to create values for a mixed league. And my system is not perfect, either. There are *price-break points* that aren't smooth and don't make sense. For example, consider these second basemen:

Player	Value	Max Bid
Robinson Cano	$36.2	$34
Dustin Pedroia	$33.0	$31
Ian Kinsler	$27.1	$19
Ben Zobrist	$24.9	$13
Brandon Phillips	$24.7	$13

According to my chart, I want to get at least a $2 discount for a $31+ hitter, at least an $8 discount for a $26–30 hitter, and at least a $12 discount for a $21–25 hitter. That leads to the figures in the *Max Bid* column.

So why would I say that you should pay $12 more to get Pedroia rather than Kinsler, for a gain of only $5.9 value? Why pay $6 extra for Kinsler instead of Zobrist for only a $2.2 value gain? This obviously makes no sense.

In some cases, it's even more nonsensical. For example, according to my chart, the best you'd probably do for a $31 hitter is a $2 discount, while you might get an $8 discount for a $30 hitter. This means you'd spend $29 for a $31 hitter, as opposed to spending only $22 for a $30 hitter.

While I'll admit that this is a flaw in my system, it's even more so just a natural quirk of the mechanics of the mixed-league auction. There really are going to be break points like this. They won't be as exact as my chart, but close enough. There will be an occasional $31+ hitter who will go for a $6 discount, and there will be many $26–30 hitters who go for just a $2–3 discount, or even less.

The important thing is to be aware of this phenomenon as the auction unfolds. I most likely wouldn't actually bid $19 for Kinsler if I see that Zobrist (and Phillips) are still available. I would know that by being patient I will do better than Kinsler later on.

My system gives me a guideline to make good decisions. For the highest-value players, and the lower value, it's a clear-cut, easy to follow plan. And it makes total sense. For the middle range—that is, $20–30 players—it's more unscientific, and a bit more of a crapshoot. However, by knowing the types of discounts I should be able to get, I'm prepared to make good decisions during the auction.

The Other Flaw

Back in 2008, I had a conversation with one of my Tout Wars competitors, Todd Zola, about the values and bidding for mixed leagues. I told him that I based my bidding on mono-league values. Todd pointed out that, as I mentioned before, a value formula has to consider the total stats of the player pool. So even with the same stats, a player's value is usually different if he's in a mixed league rather than a mono-league. I knew that Todd was correct, but I also knew that using mixed-league values didn't work. Since the flaw was relatively minor and wouldn't make much difference for most players' values, I ignored it.

Theoretically, back in 2005 I could have decided to use mixed values and worked out a rule of thumb for adjusting those values into actual bidding prices. But I didn't. I started with mono-league values and worked out a rule of thumb. It seems to me that the rule of thumb is easier to deal with from a mono-league standpoint.

But I did come up with a plan to correct the flaw that Todd mentions. If you don't have any interest in using your own value formula—that is, you just want to use dollar values that you see published by others—then I suggest you just ignore this flaw. It's not going to make a huge difference. Most players will be less than 50 cents different.

But if you do want to adjust for this, you can identify your mixed-league pool of players and determine the denominators based on your SGP (Standings Gain Points)-based or PVM (Percentage Value Method)-based formula. Then use those mixed-league denominators for your mono-league pools. This will give you values for a mono-league that used mixed-league denominators. (If you have no idea what I'm talking about, this is all covered in chapter 6.)

Another way of looking at this is that most mixed-league formulas identify the best 168 mixed-league hitters and best 108 pitchers, and create values within the framework such that the 168th hitter and 108th pitcher must have a value of $1 and the total for all 276 players must equal $3,120.

In order to use the proper denominators for a mixed-league pool of players but put them in a framework of mono-league values, here's what I do. Using my mono-league values, I select the top 168 mixed-league hitters and 108 pitchers. I add up their values. The value will be much greater than $3,120. For 2012, the value is $5,180. I also note that the 168th hitter is worth $6 and the 108th pitcher is worth $8.8.

I then use the proper mixed-league denominators and create values within a framework that the 168th hitter must have a value of $6, the 108th pitcher must be worth $8.8, and the total for all players must equal $5,180. This gives me mono-league values while using the proper denominators for a mixed-league pool.

Having done this, I need to double-check and see if there have been any changes to who the best 168 hitters and 108 pitchers are. For example, the 110th-best pitcher might have moved up to be 107th.

And finally, I need to adjust the values to make sure I have a 67/33% split. (Although I started out with mono-league values that were based on a 67/33% split, combining them into a mixed pool may have shifted the split.)

Adjusting for 15-Team Leagues

The more teams in your league, the lower the discounts will be. One reason is that the worst players will have less value. For 2012 the 168th hitter is worth $6 and the 108th pitcher $8.8. For a 15-team league, the 210th-best hitter is worth only $2.5 and the 135th-best pitcher is worth $6.1. The worst non-catching hitter goes from $13 to $10.

The other reason is that most people want to get their fair share of stars, and now you have more teams bidding for the same limited number of stars. And even for lesser-value players, more teams are competing. Everyone has to spend their $260.

Here's how a 15-team auction compares to 12-teams:

EXPECTED PRICES (67/33% SPLIT)

Hitters' Value	12-Team League Avg. Price Range	15-Team League Avg. Price Range
$31+	$2 discount to overpay by $2	Full price to overpay by $5
$26–30	$2–8 discount	$3 discount to overpay by $3
$21–25	$6–12 discount	$2–8 discount
$17–20	$11–15 discount	$3–9 discount
$13–16	$11–15 discount (Don't pay more than $2)	$5–11 discount
$12 or less	Don't pay more than $1	Don't pay more than $1–2

Catchers

$17+	$2 discount to overpay by $2	Full price to overpay by $4
$11–16	$1–5 discount	$3 discount to overpay by $1
$ 6–10	$2–6 discount	$1–5 discount
$ 5 or less	Don't pay more than $1	Don't pay more than $1–2

Pitchers

$31+	$2–6 discount	$4 discount to full price
$21–30	$3–7 discount	$1–5 discount
$ 9–20	$4–8 discount	$3–7 discount
$ 8 or less	Don't pay more than $1	Don't pay more than $1

If you're in a league with fewer than 12 teams or more than 15, you can use this chart to make a good guess about what kinds of discounts you can expect. For example, in a 17-team league, the discounts will be $2–3 less than for a 15-team league at all levels.

Identifying Potential Bargains

As I explained in chapter 4, prior to the auction, I attempt to identify potential bargains by comparing my values to those published in various magazines and websites.

For 2012, I have Ben Zobrist valued at $24.9. If every source I look at shows him at $23 or less, then he would make my target list. For a mono-league, I'd be happy to buy him for $23. But for a mixed league, that's obviously not the case. According to my chart, a $24.9 value like Zobrist should go for a $6–12 discount. And I want to buy players at the high end ($12) of that spectrum. So a $1.9 discount does me no good. But the fact that I value a player such as Zobrist more than most other people does mean that he's more likely than others to be available for that

$12 discount. If everyone else pretty much agreed with my value of $24.9, then it's more likely Zobrist would be sold for an average discount ($9).

As also explained in chapter 4, when I get to the auction, I will nominate players from my target list. As much as possible, I want my best targets to be put up for bid before I have to make decisions on other potential buys.

LOL

Next I want to look at the bottom of the middle-infielder pool:

Player	Value
Yunel Escobar	$15.4
Jose Altuve	$14.8
Aaron Hill	$14.4
Daniel Murphy	$13.4
Cliff Pennington	$13.3
Ryan Roberts	$13.0
JJ Hardy	$12.5
Zack Cozart	$12.4
Alcides Escobar	$12.3
Omar Infante	$11.7

There are a total of 36 second basemen and shortstops that will fill each team's second base, shortstop, and middle infield spots. Well, actually, if the auction had 11 Larry Schechter clones that would happen. But since other people will disagree with my values, there will undoubtedly be at least a couple of players not in my pool who will be bought.

I mentioned before that Ryan Roberts is the 36th-best middle infielder. The 37th best, JJ Hardy, is not part of my player pool. I considered him as a designated hitter option, but there were enough $13+ hitters left over at other positions to fill the DH pool.

In my opinion, Hardy, Zack Cozart, and Alcides Escobar are all within $0.7 of Roberts. That's so close that it would be no surprise if most of my competitors would prefer one or two of those guys over Roberts. Some might even prefer Infante over Roberts. Some might prefer a player below my cut line over Pennington, or perhaps even Murphy or Hill.

Some of the middle infielders are eligible at other positions, so it is hypothetically possible that Roberts could be bought and put at third base; Daniel Murphy could be put at first base; or nobody below my cut line could be bought, and thus when it gets to the end of the auction I could be stuck having to buy Cozart rather than Roberts. However, the chances of this are next to nothing. If a player is eligible at middle infield, it's rare that he would be used elsewhere. And aside from that, it's almost a certainty that due to differences of opinion at least one or two—if not more—players below my cut line will be bought.

So the bottom line is that I start by knowing I'll be able to get at least Roberts for $1. If someone buys a player not in my pool, such as Hardy or Cozart, then I know I'll be able to get at least Pennington. If someone then buys another player below the cut line—or buys Roberts or Pennington—then I know I can get at least Daniel Murphy. If one more player gets taken, it bumps me up to Aaron Hill, which is a nice jump because my guaranteed minimum value jumps a full dollar, from $13.4 to $14.4.

Before the auction, I will examine the middle-infield pool, the corner-infield pool, and the outfielders, to see where I have the chance to reap the biggest gains when this happens. For 2012, it's the corner pool. The last player is Mitch Moreland, a $13.2

value. Next to last is Danny Valencia, at $14.4. So if just one player below the cut line—or Moreland—is bought, then I am guaranteed to get at least an extra $1.2 value at the end. If two more players are taken, it would jump to $15.8.

To help this process along, I will often nominate a couple of players myself, very early. Near the end of the auction, all of these guys will be sold for $1 or $2, because nobody has much money left. And as I've explained, they really should never go for more than $1, anyway. But not everyone knows that. So when it's relatively early in the auction, and I announce "Mitch Moreland, $1," there are several competitors looking at their cheat sheets and thinking "Moreland? He's worth a lot more than $1." Someone will bid $2 . . . then $3 . . . and perhaps even more. I just sit back and try not to laugh out loud. But I am laughing on the inside.

Then a turn or two later, I'll bring up Valencia for $1, and the fun happens again. Next thing you know, it's the late stages of the auction and I buy that $15.8 player for a buck. Mission accomplished.

I've never tried to do this and had it not work. Even if it didn't work, there's not much risk. It wouldn't have been a disaster to get stuck with Moreland or Valencia for a dollar. The only caution is that you need to do it by the middle rounds, not any later. Also, I guess now that I've written this, you might want to make sure that everyone else in your league hasn't also read my book.

Be Prepared

As I mentioned in chapter 3, the bidding at an auction happens very fast, and you must make snap decisions often in a split second.

That's why I prepare as much as possible before the auction. In addition to having a target list, and deciding which players are a priority to nominate, I also decide in advance my maximum bid for players. This process isn't as tedious and time-consuming as it might sound. I simply go through my list of players and, using my chart of expected discounts, arrive at a maximum bid. As the auction unfolds, I might make slight adjustments as developments warrant. For example, if the high-value hitters seem to be going for unusually high prices and I'm getting concerned I might miss out, then I may increase my max bid by a dollar or two.

Here's what my 2012 max bids look like for second basemen:

Player	Value	Max Bid
Robinson Cano	$36.2	$34
Dustin Pedroia	$33.0	$31
Ian Kinsler	$27.1	$19
Ben Zobrist	$24.9	$13
Brandon Phillips	$24.7	$13
Dan Uggla	$23.2	$11
Howie Kendrick	$20.7	$ 8
Neil Walker	$20.1	$ 5
Jason Kipnis	$17.7	$ 3
Rickie Weeks	$17.6	$ 3
Jemile Weeks	$17.2	$ 2
Danny Espinosa	$16.9	$ 2
Kelly Johnson	$16.8	$ 2
Dustin Ackley	$15.6	$ 1
Jose Altuve	$14.8	$ 1
Aaron Hill	$14.4	$ 1
Daniel Murphy	$13.4	$ 1
Ryan Roberts	$13.0	$ 1

Being prepared like this is invaluable, especially for a mixed league, where the gap between a player's value and what you should actually spend for him is so drastically different. For example, if someone nominates Kelly Johnson for $2 and I look at my list and see that he's worth $16.8, I might shout out "$3!" if I didn't have a column on my sheet telling me the max bid is $2. It is completely odd and confusing to think that I should let a $16.8 player get bought by someone else for $2, but that's the way it is.

Distributing the Hitting Dollars

I plan to spend $180 on hitting and $80 for pitching. I use the following template to acquire my 14 hitters:

Plan	Actual	+/−	
35			
28			
26			
23			
21			
17			
13			
11			
1			
1			
1			
1			
1			
1			

$180

At the auction, when I buy a player, I write the amount in the *Actual* column and adjust my future buys accordingly. As you can see, I have six spots allotted for $1 players. This is quite different than my template for a mono-league, where I usually have only one spot for a $1 player and a few spots for a $2 player. This is because there are so many good buys available at the end for a mixed league. Since I only have eight slots for someone worth more than a dollar, it helps me be patient and wait for really great buys.

As the auction unfolds, I can easily adjust this as needed. If it turns out that I don't spend more than $30 for a player, I can take the $35 slot and the $11 slot and turn them into two $23 slots, or whatever.

Is Stars-and-Scrubs the Best Strategy?

I've said that some people think a stars-and-scrubs strategy is optimal. Here's a comparison between getting a star and a scrub vs. two mid-level players:

COMPARISON #1

	Value	Price		Value	Price		Value	Price
	$33	$31		$27	$19		$29	$21
	$15	$ 1		$25	$13		$23	$11
Total:	$48	$32		$52	$32		$52	$32
Gain:		**+$16**			**+$20**			**+$20**

COMPARISON #2

	Value	Price		Value	Price		Value	Price
	$41	$39		$30	$22		$28	$20
	$15	$ 1		$26	$18		$28	$20
Total:	$56	$40		$56	$40		$56	$40
Gain:		**+$16**			**+$16**			**+$16**

For these comparisons, I've assumed that I can get my projected target discounts for all levels of hitters, and that—helped by differences of opinion—I can get players worth at least $15 at the end for $1.

You can see that in comparison #1 I'm better off not getting a star and a scrub. In comparison #2 it's a toss-up.

You could infer from this that it's best to actually avoid buying stars. However, I have allotted one slot for a $30+ hitter and will buy one if I can get a $2 discount or better. One reason is that I do want to make sure I spend some money—the worst thing you can possibly do at an auction is to leave money on the table. A second reason is that if I add more slots in the $20 range, it becomes more difficult to be selective and hold out for the minimum discounts that I want to get. However, I am not so desperate to land a star that I'm willing to overpay for one.

Catchers

What to spend for catchers requires its own separate analysis. If I wait until the end and buy catchers for $1, for 2012 I expect to get values in the $6–8 range. If I instead buy other positions for $1, I'll be getting $15 values. Therefore, at first glance, it would appear that I should not wait until the end for my catchers. But exactly what happens if I spend more than $1 for catchers?

CATCHER COMPARISON #1

Position	Value	Price	Value	Price
Catcher	$22	$20	$ 7	$ 1
Other	$15	$ 1	$28	$20
Total:	$37	$21	$35	$21
Gain:		+$16		+$14

If I were to buy a very-high-value catcher, I'd be better off than if I were to buy a $1 catcher, provided that I hold out for my $2 discount. If I pay full price for the expensive catcher, I've defeated the purpose.

CATCHER COMPARISON #2

Position	Value	Price	Value	Price
Catcher	$15	$10	$ 7	$ 1
Other	$15	$ 1	$22	$10
Total:	$30	$11	$29	$11
Gain:		**+$19**		**+$18**

Again, it's very close. If I don't hold out for the $5 discount on a $15 catcher, I've defeated the purpose.

CATCHER COMPARISON #3

Position	Value	Price	Value	Price
Catcher	$ 9	$ 3	$ 7	$ 1
Other	$15	$ 1	$18	$ 3
Total:	$24	$ 4	$25	$ 4
Gain:		**+$20**		**+$21**

In general, it's very close, but I'll probably do slightly better if I can buy an $11+ catcher. Actually, I should say if I can buy *two* $11+ catchers. Since there aren't usually a whole lot of $11+ catchers, this can be easier said than done. If I can't get the minimum discounts I want, I'll pass and just go with the cheap catchers.

Distributing the Pitching Dollars

My pitching template looks like this:

Plan	Actual	+/–	
22(SP)			
18(RP)			
16(SP)			
13(RP)			
5			
3			
1			
1			
1			
$80			

As you know, the pitching discounts are much more consistent from top to bottom:

Value	Avg. Price Range	Target Discount
$31+	$2–6 discount	$6
$21–30	$3–7 discount	$7
$ 9–20	$4–8 discount	$8
$ 8 or less	Don't pay more than $1	

According to this, it might be wise to make a template where I only buy pitchers worth $20 or less. I could reap an $8 discount on every pitcher and still spend my $80. The problem with this is that, again, if I have too many slots in the same price range, it will be difficult to maintain selectivity. I would most likely be forced to accept some $6–7 discounts, defeating the purpose.

Therefore, if I can get a $6 discount on a $31+ pitcher, or a $7 discount on a $21–30 pitcher, I'll take it. Let's look at a comparison:

	Value	Price	Value	Price	Value	Price
	$35	$29	$22	$15	$27	$20
	$ 9	$ 1	$22	$15	$18	$10
Total:	$44	$30	$44	$30	$45	$30
Gain:		+$14		+$14		+$15

It's basically a wash. For 2012, the 108th pitcher is worth $8.8, so there's actually a great chance I'd end up getting a pitcher worth $10–11 or more for a dollar. The stars-and-scrubs approach is acceptable but not necessarily any better than avoiding a star. The key, as always, is getting the acceptable minimum discount.

You Just Never Know

As I've said, some mixed-league auction prices can just be nuts. At the 2008 Tout Wars auction, as the defending champion, I had the honor of the first nomination. There were a few possibilities for my landing a top stud. The best option looked like Chone Figgins. I had him projected as a $32 value, whereas other sources I checked had him in the $28–30 range.

I decided I'd nominate Figgins for $20 and have a $30 limit. I began the auction with my $20 bid. Someone else said "$21." I said "$22." Silence. More silence. Then the auctioneer: "Going once, going twice . . . sold! Chone Figgins, $22, to Schechter."

Suggested Reading

If you haven't already done so, you should definitely read chapters 3 and 4, which contain strategy information that applies to all auctions and drafts. And even if you aren't interested in mono-leagues, I suggest you read chapter 7, or at least skim through it. I go into more depth about some of my strategies, such as target lists and bidding tactics, which you'll find helpful for a mixed-league auction.

CHAPTER 9

Snake Drafts

A snake draft—also called a *serpentine* or *straight* draft—is one in which each participant selects a player one at a time. If there are 15 teams, the teams will select in order from #1 through #15, and then in reverse order for the second round, whereby team #15 picks first and team #1 picks last. Then the draft snakes back: The order for round three is the same as the first round; round four is the same as round two, etc.

Some people say, "A snake draft is simple, just take the best player available, keeping in mind what positions and stat categories you need."

This is totally wrong! It is not that simple.

Many people would agree with me, and say, "Yes, Larry, it isn't that simple . . . you need to account for position scarcity."

These people will draft a catcher, second baseman, or short-stop earlier than others would, to allow for the scarcity. But how do they decide? If a second baseman is worth $27, would you draft him before a $30 outfielder? Before a $32 first baseman?

Some people use a system in which they group players by position into tiers. But in my opinion, this is too vague and imprecise. How do you decide if you should take a shortstop from tier one and an outfielder from tier three, or vice versa? What if a player is at the low end of a tier or the high end? And how do you decide in the first place what tier a player belongs in? The cutoff points are arbitrary, and some tiers have a bigger spread from top to bottom than others.

I've said before that I think position scarcity is mostly a myth. For a snake draft, I wouldn't say that it's completely a myth, nor would I say there is scarcity. What I would say is that there is an analysis that needs to be done—and an adjustment to be made—to allow for different positions. I call this analysis and adjustment my *draft curve*. This will tell you *exactly* the relationship between positions, and at what point—if any—you should choose that $27 second baseman instead of a more valuable outfielder or first base-man. Or at what point you should ever choose any player who is less valuable than someone else.

There certainly could be a point in a draft where you might take a $19 player who will get 30 stolen bases rather than a $20 home-run hitter, because you need speed. But for this discussion, we're ignoring stat categories. We're simply talking about maxi-mizing the sheer value.

Before I explain my draft curve, I want to address one question . . .

Is Picking First an Advantage?

For this chapter, I'm going to use as an example a 15-team mixed league, but the logic will apply equally to a 12-team mixed league, a mono-league, and even a football, basketball, or any other snake draft.

I'm going to use my 2010 projected values. It doesn't matter if you agree or disagree with my specific values. The logic will still apply no matter what values we use.

As explained in chapter 6, for an auction I convert the players' projected stats into a *dollar value*, but for a draft or salary-cap game I just call it a *value*. So you'll see, for example, Albert Pujols with a projected value of 424. I could use his dollar value, which would be approximately $38–40, but for me it's just easier to use the value without the "$" associated with it, especially since I like to use fractions for my dollar values.

I have made the values such that there is a 67/33% hitter-to-pitcher ratio. This keeps my values in line with the norm. If I were to use, let's say, a 62/38% ratio, my pitcher values would be much too high compared with everyone else and my hitters much too low. Also unlike an auction, it's not necessary to make the 210th hitter and 135th pitcher worth one unit.

If I were selecting for each team and simply taking the best player available, the first four rounds would look as demonstrated in the following chart:

Order	Pick #1	Pick #2	#1+2 Total	Pick #3	Pick #4	#3+4 Total	Grand Total
1.	Pujols 424	Werth 308	732	Felix H 307	Morneau 281	588	**1320**
2.	Hanley 403	Rollins 308	711	Bay 306	McCutchen 282	588	1299
3.	A Rod 397	Choo 309	706	Haren 305	Wainwright 282	587	1293
4.	Braun 391	Abreu 309	700	Markakis 304	Pierre 283	587	1287
5.	Howard 379	Votto 310	689	Youkilis 304	A Hill 283	587	1276
6.	Kemp 376	Adrian G 310	686	Cruz 303	Verlander 284	587	1273
7.	Ellsbury 374	Greinke 312	686	Ichiro 302	Bourn 285	587	1273
8.	Lincecum 369	Kinsler 315	684	Z'man 302	D Lee 286	588	1272
9.	Crawford 360	Sizemore 315	675	T Hunter 299	Granderson 287	586	1261
10.	Teixeira 360	Tulowitzki 317	677	Phillips 299	Cano 288	587	1264
11.	Fielder 360	Pedroia 317	677	Lind 299	Jeter 291	590	1267
12.	M Cabrera 352	Reynolds 324	676	Mauer 298	BJ Upton 291	589	1265
13.	Utley 351	Halladay 330	681	Morales 293	Sabathia 291	584	1265
14.	Longoria 340	J Upton 331	671	Ethier 293	Sandoval 292	585	1256
15.	Wright 335	Holliday 334	669	B Roberts 292	Zobrist 292	584	**1253**

As you can see, there is an advantage. The total value descends from team #1 through team #15 almost perfectly. Team #1 gets a total of 1,320, which is 67 points more value than team #15 with 1,253. (In terms of *dollar value*, 67 points would be about $5–6.)

It makes sense to think there would be an advantage to picking early, because there are usually a handful of players with superior values, and then as you get lower the values bunch up. For example, the team with the #1 pick gets Albert Pujols, who is 21 points better than the #2 pick and 89 points better than the #15 pick. By picking first in the second round, the #15 team gets Matt Holliday, who is only 26 points better than Jason Werth, whom the #1 team gets. So by virtue of picking first, the #1 team starts with a 63-point edge over the #15 team.

By the third round, the values get bunched even more closely. There's only a 15-point gap from top to bottom, and only an 11-point gap in round four. The total value obtained by teams in rounds three and four varies only from 584 to 590. If we were to carry this analysis out further, we would see the gaps getting even closer as we get into lower rounds.

So it is clear that picking early is an advantage. If I use my projections for 2011, 2012, or any other year—or if you take projections from a magazine from 2008 or 1998—you'll find the same thing. There's always going to be a handful at the top with superior values, and then the gaps get smaller and smaller.

Why did I bring this topic up first? I did so because when doing the analysis and comparisons that I'm going to do next, we want to keep in mind that the earlier drafters have an edge to begin with.

I will also mention that while most leagues determine draft order randomly, some leagues give you the option of requesting specific draft spots and then randomly drawing. This analysis shows that there is no reason to ever request a lower draft spot. The earlier you pick the better.

Also, in reality, everyone has a different opinion, especially after the first few picks. Therefore, if you have the #1 pick, when you get your next turn at #30, it's almost guaranteed you'll be able to select someone you think is actually better than #30. You might even get someone you think should have been in the top 15 or top 20.

When you have a top pick, you're securing a good advantage in round one, and you probably won't lose as much in round two as shown above because of the differences of opinion.

My Draft Curve

The first step in creating my curve is to identify the player pool. This is comprised of the players who, based on my values, should be selected to fill out the starting lineups for all of the teams. If I was drafting all 15 teams, this would actually happen. However, since the other owners will have different opinions than I have, undoubtedly some players not included in my pool will be drafted. This is fine. In fact, the more players outside of my pool that are taken, the better, because it leaves me with more valuable players to scoop up at the end.

We'll use a roster of 14 hitters and 9 pitchers. This means there will be 210 hitters (15 teams × 14) and 135 pitchers (15 teams × 9) in the pool.

There are always players who qualify at more than one position. I slot each player where he will typically be the most valuable. I put Ramon Hernandez at catcher rather than first base, because the talent at the bottom of the catcher pool is always worse than other positions. Anyone who qualifies at shortstop or second base—and another position—I put at shortstop or second base. And I give first and third base priority over the outfield.

I identify the 30 most valuable catchers (15 teams × 2). Then I find the top-15 first basemen and third basemen, and the next 15 most valuable first basemen *or* third basemen, who would occupy the corner spot. I do the same for second basemen, shortstops, and the middle infielder. There will be five outfielders needed per team, so I identify the 75 most-valuable outfielders.

The designated hitter can play any position, so I identify the next 15 highest values not already included in my player pool.

Most leagues have no requirement to take a certain number of starting pitchers as opposed to relievers, so I simply need to identify the 135 most valuable pitchers.

The next step is to examine the last players who will be available at each position:

Pos	#	Worst
C	30	67
1B	25	169
2B	24	151
SS	22	162
3B	23	157
OF	83	152
DH only	3	186
Total	210	
Pitchers	135	107

For this discussion, we will assume that all teams fill their starting lineups in the first 23 rounds. In reality, some drafts have reserve rounds, and you don't need to necessarily fill all 23 spots in the first 23 rounds, but it doesn't matter. It also doesn't matter if we were to use a league with 13 hitters and 10 pitchers. This analysis will still apply correctly to those variations.

So if you wait until round 23 for your second catcher, you're guaranteed to get someone with a value of at least 67. If you wait until round 23 to select your fifth outfielder, you're guaranteed to get someone worth at least 152.

If you wait until round 23 for your shortstop, you're guaranteed to get someone worth at least 162. Oops, wait a minute, that's actually not true! If you wait, that shortstop worth 162 might have already been taken to fill someone's middle spot. Therefore, the second base and shortstop pools must be combined. We need to identify the top 45 (which must include at least 15 second basemen and 15 shortstops). Similarly, the first-base and third-base pools must be combined to account for the corner slot.

The next step is to curve everyone off the most valuable last player, which in this case is the corner spot. The curve is as follows:

Pos	Worst	Curve
C	67	+90
1B/3B	157	E
2B/SS	151	+6
OF	152	+5
DH	186	N/A
P	107	+50

A second baseman worth 184 (+6 = 190) and a first baseman worth 190 are actually identical values. A catcher worth 110 (+90 = 200) is a superior selection.

For the DH position, you can select any hitter, so the curve doesn't apply. If there is a second baseman available worth 205, and your second base and middle spots are already occupied, you don't add the +6 when considering the 205 second baseman to be your DH.

Adding the curve, Tim Lincecum becomes the #2 draft pick and Joe Mauer, the highest-value catcher, goes from #42 to #6.

You might wonder why I don't curve everyone off the DH slot, since the last DH (186) is worth more than the last corner infielder (157). It's because there are only three players eligible only at DH, and thus the DH spot includes nine players from other various positions, with the lowest value being 151.

Another question you might have is that since any player can be selected for the DH spot, how can I be assured of getting a corner worth at least 157? If I wait until round 23, isn't it possible another team might have taken that 157 hitter as their DH? This is a very good question, and the answer is yes, it is possible. I'm going to examine this in detail shortly.

Position Scarcity?

This analysis disproves much of the scarcity nonsense. Yes, a valuable catcher is scarce. But what about middle infielders? If you wait until the end, you'll get a middle infielder worth 151, which is virtually as good as an outfielder (152). So everyone who is drafting a middle infielder over a more valuable player from another position because of *scarcity* is making a big mistake!

Here's a typical example of what happens:

	Team A		Team B	
Round #1	2B	350	OF	370
Round #23	OF	152	2B	151
	Total	502	Total	521

Team A takes the second baseman early thinking there is scarcity, or that the talent drops off the table after the top few, and he has lost 19 points in value.

Remember I was using my 2010 values as an example. Let's look at my 2011 player pool:

Pos	Worst	Curve
1B/3B	145	+4
2B/SS	148	+1
OF	149	E

In this case, first and third basemen are actually scarcer than middle infielders. Essentially, it's a tie, because if we convert these values into a dollar value, the difference between the 145 and 148 is only about 25 cents.

If you learn nothing else from this chapter, please take away that except for catchers, there is virtually no scarcity for other positions! And even when there is a small scarcity for other positions, it isn't always the middle infielders who are scarce!

The catcher scarcity that does exist—and the slight scarcity that exists with other positions—is measured by my curve, which gives you an exact measurement of the discrepancy between positions.

Effect of Multi-Position Players

I mentioned that I assign multi-position players to where most people would consider them more valuable. In reality, though, it's almost guaranteed that at least a few players will be drafted and placed at a different position. Theoretically, this could cause havoc with my curve.

When you analyze it, though, it will rarely affect the curve. If I switch some players from first base to the outfield, or first base to third base, or whatever, it will only affect the curve if a player moved happened to be the worst player in that category (C, CI, MI, or OF)—or if moving a player gives me less than 45 MI, 45 CI, or 75 OF, in which case I would need to add a new player to the pool and drop someone. These possibilities won't happen very often.

What *is* likely to happen, though, is that because of differences of opinion, some players not in my pool will be selected. Theoretically, when you're at a draft and a player not in your pool is chosen, you could change your curve on the spot. This would be quite confusing, and since it won't start happening until fairly late in your draft, it's not necessary.

However, you can pay attention. For example, if you're deciding between a first baseman and a shortstop—and it's a close call—and you know that two first basemen outside your pool were already taken—then it'd be wise to take the shortstop, because you will do better than expected at first base for the last player.

Proving My Draft Curve

When I started playing in draft leagues years ago, I came up with a few theories as to what might be a better way to draft rather than just taking the best player available. I tested those theories and arrived at my draft curve. I no longer have those tests, so for this book, I did some new testing.

I'm going to show you these tests. I'm not going to bore you with every round-by-round pick. I'm simply going to explain the test and show you the results. If you want to take a set of player projections, determine the curve, and do your own tests, you're welcome to do so.

For the first test, I used my 2010 player pool. I conducted a 23-round, 15-team draft. The stipulations were that each team must fill its 23 positions, and whenever two players are tied in value (adding in my curve), I choose the player with the highest raw value.

Initially I am not going to worry about stat category balance, but rather just sheer value. The goal is to prove whether or not this curve works. I'll worry about balance later.

For 13 teams, I simply took the best player available to fill any open position. For two teams, I used my curve. I used draft picks #4 and #11 to test the curve. The results were:

Picks	Avg. Team Value
#1–3	4,762
#4 (curve)	4,839
#5–10	4,740
#11 (curve)	4,790
#12–15	4,706

The teams using my curve finished with the most value. Despite being at a little disadvantage against the teams drafting #1–3 (according to the above section "Is Picking First an Advantage?"), team #4 had 77 points more value than the average of teams #1–3. Team #11, despite a bad draft spot, beat everyone else except my other curve team.

This, to me, proves the validity of the curve. Perhaps one test could be a fluke, but I have done many similar tests in the past, always showing that the curve is better than just taking the best available player.

Effect of the DH Spot

This brings me to the question I raised earlier. Since anyone can potentially be used as a DH, can I really be guaranteed anything at the end? Shouldn't the hitters maybe just all be lumped together in one category?

First, it's obvious that a catcher will never be part of the DH pool. You could play fantasy baseball for 100 years, and the 31st-most-valuable catcher will never be one of the top-15 values you identify to fill the DH spot. (Once in a blue moon someone might draft a third catcher and place him at DH, but that would not affect your predraft player pool.)

Therefore, the hitters should not be lumped into one category. But perhaps they should only be split up between catchers and non-catchers?

In some years, there may not be any middle infielders included in your DH pool. For 2010, as shown above, there were a total of 46 middle infielders in my pool. This means that one of them was allotted as a DH. But when there are only 45 in the pool, you could justify making them a separate category. This would give you catchers, MI, and 1B/3B/OF as three categories.

I never really considered this question until the fall of 2012, when I started writing this chapter. In order to test it, I realized it would be a lot less time-consuming to do tests using only hitters. For the purposes of this test, pitchers were irrelevant. So I ran tests using a 14-round draft, with no pitching. My curve adjustment for the new test was this:

Standard Curve			Catcher/Non-Catcher		
Pos	Worst	Curve	Pos	Worst	Curve
C	67	+90	C	67	+84
1B/3B	157	E	Non-Catcher	151	E
2B/SS	151	+6			
OF	152	+5			

Once again, I drafted for teams #4 and #11. Since one year could be a fluke, I also tested with my 2011 and 2012 player pools. And the results were:

Year	Standard Curve	Catcher/Non-Catcher
2010 (avg #4+#11)	3,106	3,107
2011	3,040	3,042
2012	3,434	3,434
Total Average	3,193	3,194

The results were virtually identical. In fact, for 2012 both teams #4 and #11 drafted the same 14 players with both curves.

These tests were all using my own values, and things can be quite different against actual competition, given everyone's differences of opinion. So I also tested against the real world. For several years, I've participated in the National Fantasy Baseball Championship (NFBC), at www.nfbc.stats.com. They have a variety of draft and auction leagues, both in-person drafts and online. I highly recommend them. I used the actual draft order from my NFBC leagues in 2010–2012 to conduct a test. For teams #4 and #11 I used my curves, and for everyone else I simply went down the list in order and chose players for each team, provided that every team had to fill all 14 hitting spots. The results were:

NFBC	Standard Curve	Catcher/Non-Catcher
2010 (avg #4+#11)	3,383	3,401
2011	3,297	3,304
2012	3,701	3,701
Total Average	3,460	3,469

The Catcher/Non-Catcher was slightly better, but in terms of dollar value, it's less than a dollar difference, so essentially it's a tie. Based on this evidence, it appears fine to use either method. If I had 50 or 100 years of data to examine, perhaps I could arrive at a more definitive conclusion. For now, I'm going to continue using my Standard Curve, because it will be easier to demonstrate some other points.

You'll notice that the test against the NFBC resulted in my teams averaging about 270 points more in value than when testing against my own values. This is because of my difference of opinion with other owners. Since I was using my own values, I naturally came out way ahead of everyone else.

If you're wondering why my 2012 values were so much greater than 2010 and 2011, it's because I had made some adjustments to my value formula, which resulted in all hitters (and pitchers) having an increased value. So in relative terms, nothing had changed.

48 Hours of Panic

Prior to the fall of 2012, I had never done any testing without including pitchers. And when I eliminated pitchers, something very surprising happened. I've added another column to the previous table:

Year	Standard Curve	Catcher/ Non-Catcher	Avg. Other Teams
2010 (avg #4+#11)	3,106	3,107	3,150
2011	3,040	3,042	3,074
2012	3,434	3,434	3,472
Total Average	3,193	3,194	3,232

For the first time ever, the teams with my curve did worse than the teams that simply took the best available player!

I was shocked and dumbfounded. Had I been wrong about all of this all these years? Was my curve useful for pitching but actually counterproductive for hitters? What the heck was happening here?

It took me two days to figure this out. What was happening was that in some of the early rounds, a catcher would be a better deal (with the curve added) than another hitter. Thus, I would select the catcher. In the middle and later rounds, I would ignore all catchers because my slots were filled. When I selected the catchers early, their edge on the non-catchers was by a small margin, such as 10–20 value points. When I was ignoring them in the middle and later rounds, I was passing up opportunities where they had a margin of 40–75 points.

This is because my two teams using the curve were the only teams placing a premium on catchers (or any positions). In the real world, this doesn't happen. But in my laboratory experiment, it did. My conclusion was that the goal of my curve is to have a system where I do better than just taking the best available player. If the real world actually had nobody else adding a premium for catchers, then I would simply add a rule of thumb that said, "Don't take a catcher unless the margin is at least 50 points more than the non-catcher." With this rule of thumb, my teams in the above test would have gotten approximately 100 points more and would have kicked the butts of the other teams.

Having figured this out, my panic disappeared, and I was reassured that I was doing the correct thing.

The only reason I'm even bothering to mention this is in case you decide to try some tests on your own. If you use the same set of values for all teams drafting, and only draft for hitters, you'll probably find that your best available teams do better than your curved teams, for the same reason I did. So I want you to understand what's happening and not think this curve theory is all completely wrong! (For those not planning to do your own tests, you can forget I said this, and I apologize for wasting the last two minutes of your life.)

Adjusting for Differences of Opinion

The goal of the curve is to identify the value of the players I should be able to get at the end of the draft. Since I know that some players outside my pool will be selected by others, perhaps I should allow for this.

I took a look at how many hitters outside my pool were selected by other teams to fill their 14 hitters' slots in my NFBC drafts:

Year	C	1B	2B	SS	3B	OF	Total
2010	5	1	2	2	5	5	20
2011	2	1	3	2	2	8	18
2012	4	6	2	1	0	6	19
Average	3.7	2.7	2.3	1.7	2.3	6.3	19

Unfortunately, I don't have the NFBC draft records from prior to 2010, and even then, it would probably require 25 or more years to get something definitive. So with only three years of data, this is hardly conclusive but does give us a clue.

I think the fact that first base averages 2.7 while shortstops average only 1.7 is probably a fluke. So I prefer to lump the infielders all together. Their combined average is 2.25. It appears that it is probably safe to assume that, on average, two players from each infield spot not in my pool will be taken, as well as three or four catchers and six outfielders.

Another useful thing to examine is the breakdown of my player pools. For this, I do have two more years of data, as shown in the next chart.

	2008	2009	2010	2011	2012	5-yr avg.
C –	30	30	30	30	30	30
1B –	25	25	25	29	30	27
2B –	25	22	24	21	22	23
SS –	22	23	23	24	23	23
3B –	23	26	23	24	25	24
OF –	78	82	82	77	77	79
DH –	7	2	3	5	3	4
Total –	210	210	210	210	210	210

It's logical to think that the number of players taken outside my pool by position would correlate to the sheer number of players in my pool. There are 79 outfielders and approximately 24 at each infield spot; that's 3.3 (79/24) times more outfielders than infielders. Since I don't place any multi-position players in the outfield, I could estimate that if I put a few of them in the outfield the ratio might change to approximately 82/23 = 3.6.

The ratio of the actual NFBC results is 6.3 outfielders to 2.25 infielders, which is a 2.8 ratio. This is fairly close to my player-pool ratio. I think the player-pool data is more reliable than the three years of actual NFBC results. My player pool isn't going to vary much from year to year from the above table.

Therefore, for the *ratio* I'm going to use my player pool data, and for the *quantity* I'm going to use the NFBC data. I'm going to assume two from each infield position will be taken and multiply by a ratio of 3.3–3.6 to assume seven outfielders will be taken. For catchers, my player-pool ratio is 30/23 = 1.3. So that means an average of 2.6 catchers will be taken.

So I can "bump up" each infield spot by two players—in other words, remove the worst two at each infield position from my player pool. This is based on the assumption that, on average, two players not in my pool will be selected, and thus the value of the worst player I can get at the end will be increased by two spots. Similarly, I can "bump up" seven outfielders and 2.6 catchers. Since I always like to be conservative I'll round down to two catchers. Also, it would make sense to combine the 1B/3B and 2B/SS into their corner and middle pools. So rather than remove the worst two first basemen and worst two third basemen, I'll remove the worst four from the corner spot, and similarly the worst four middle infielders.

Making these adjustments, my curve changes to:

	Standard		Bump Up (2–4–4–7)	
Pos	Worst	Curve	Worst	Curve
C	67	+90	78 (2 spots)	+94
1B/3B	157	E	169 (4 spots)	+3
2B/SS	151	+6	172 (4 spots)	E
OF	152	+5	159 (7 spots)	+13

This may be a good idea, but it makes me a little nervous. All of a sudden, I'm counting on getting a middle infielder worth 172 rather than 151, which is a big difference. And since my assumption of two infielders from each position is an average of all four infield positions, for any given position, in any given year, the actual number could certainly be only one, or even zero. Certainly others will disagree with my values, but if there's that big a gap—even though it's only my opinion—between the worst middle in these two different curves—then it seems logical to assume this could be a situation where the actual number taken outside my pool would most likely be less than four middle infielders.

There is another way of making the adjustment to account for the differences of opinion. I can take the averages of 2–2–2–2–2–7 per position and say that I want to be conservative about counting on which worst players will safely be available. Therefore, I won't "bump up" the catchers and infielders at all, and will subtract the baseline of two from each position. This leaves me with 0–0–0–0–0–5.

	Standard		Bump Up (2–4–4–7)		Bump Up (0–0–0–5)	
Pos	Worst	Curve	Worst	Curve	Worst	Curve
C	67	+90	78 (2 spots)	+94	67	+90
1B/3B	157	E	169 (4 spots)	+3	157	E
2B/SS	151	+6	172 (4 spots)	E	151	+6
OF	152	+5	159 (7 spots)	+13	156 (5 spots)	+1

This curve is close to the standard one, as it only changes the value of outfielders by four points. However, this isn't always the case. Look at the 2012 numbers:

	2012 Standard		Bump Up (2–4–4–7)		Bump Up (0–0–0–5)	
Pos	Worst	Curve	Worst	Curve	Worst	Curve
C	109	+72	127 (2 spots)	+79	109	+94
1B/3B	179	+2	182 (4 spots)	+24	179	+24
2B/SS	181	E	189 (4 spots)	+17	181	+22
OF	180	+1	206 (7 spots)	E	203 (5 spots)	E

In this case, there is a huge change in the value of outfielders. If this plan backfires and I get stuck with a 180 outfielder rather than at least a 203, that would hurt. But I know from experience and the averages I've shown above that there will always be at least a few outfielders outside my pool who will be taken. Plus, the actual NFBC average is 6.3, and with this curve I'm only counting on five.

Intuitively, I feel better about the 0–0–0–5, but let's test these two and see what happens. I tested both curves against my actual NFBC leagues:

NFBC	Standard	Bump Up (2–4–4–7)	Bump Up (0–0–0–5)
2010 (avg #4+#11)	3,383	3,380	3,402
2011	3,297	3,337	3,347
2012	3,701	3,715	3,726
Total average	3,460	3,477	3,492

The 2–4–4–7 curve is better than the standard, and the 0–0–0–5 curve is even better than that.

Three years of testing isn't enough to say that this is 100% concrete evidence of which is best, but I am comfortable declaring the 0–0–0–5 curve the winner, because not only does it have the best results, but it also makes logical sense. The goal is to identify what value I should safely be able to get at the end for each position against the real world. I think the 0–0–0–5 is the most logical and safest.

What I've taken you through so far may seem a bit complicated, but the bottom line is pretty simple. Identify the 210 players in your pool. Find the worst catcher, middle infielder, corner infielder, and *sixth*-worst outfielder, and then curve everyone off of the position with the highest worst-player value.

Rather than continuing to call this the *Bump Up (0–0–0–5)*

curve, I'll refer to it as the *Bump 5* curve, because all I'm doing is eliminating the worst five outfielders.

Having declared the Bump 5 a better curve than my standard one, I wanted to take another look at the question of splitting the hitters into only catcher and non-catcher. This time, though, with the caveat of bumping up the outfielders by five spots. So I created three categories—catchers, infielders, and outfielders. The results were an average of 3,493—one point better than the regular Bump 5—so it was essentially a tie.

Thus, using either one would be fine. But I'll stick with the regular Bump 5, just because I prefer making a distinction between the MI and CI infielders.

Competing Against Myself

I've used two teams (#4 and #11) in these tests to get a more accurate result than if I'd just used one team, where there's a chance a result could be a little fluky. The average of two teams is safer than just one.

However, it also means that I've been competing against myself. If I think Michael Bourn is better than most others think, then Bourn will likely end up on team #4 or team #11, but he can't be on both. So in a sense, I've got teams #4 and #11 both using my values and competing against each other.

Let's see what happens if I draft just one team, from the #8 spot.

NFBC	#4 + #11 Standard	#4 + #11 Bump 5	#8 Standard	#8 Bump 5
2010	3,383	3,402	3,409	3,430
2011	3,297	3,347	3,385	3,405
2012	3,701	3,726	3,770	3,815
Total Avg	3,460	3,492	3,521	3,550

I've again confirmed that the Bump 5 is better than the standard curve, and by drafting just one team, I've averaged 58 points more value.

Differences of Opinion on the Catcher Adjustment

I also want to take a look at what actually happens with catchers. I realized in the "48 Hours of Panic" section that if nobody else uses a scarcity adjustment for catchers, then using my curve would mean I'd take catchers too early.

In reality, most people do make an adjustment for catchers. But not everyone does it, and those who do are using various systems and forms of logic—or even guessing—as to when to take a catcher. Therefore, if the average adjustment of what everyone else is doing is not as great as my curve's adjustment, then I could be reaching for catchers too soon by simply taking a catcher whenever he was even one point better than another hitter.

I did some analysis with my actual NFBC drafts and tested some possible rules of thumb. It turned out that there is no rule of thumb that helps improve my overall results. So it is fine to take a catcher even when he is only one point better than another hitter.

Getting a Balanced Team

So far, we've just been trying to achieve maximum value. In a real draft, you're going to need to pay attention to category balance. For a league like the NFBC, it's especially critical, because trades aren't allowed. This means that if you have excess home runs and need stolen bases—or whatever—you're stuck. So in a real draft, there will be times when you may need to sacrifice a little value to get a category you need.

Back to Pitching

This finally brings us back to pitching.

As with hitters, many pitchers—usually at least 15—outside my pool will be selected by others. Using the Bump 5 curve, it is therefore very conservative to also bump up ten pitchers.

As you'll remember, the first test I showed in this chapter was this:

Picks	Avg. Team Value
#1–3	4,762
#4 (curve)	**4,839**
#5–10	4,740
#11 (curve)	**4,790**
#12–15	4,706

This demonstrated that the teams using my curve did better than the other teams. But I didn't show you the hitting and pitching breakdown:

Picks	Avg. Value	Hitting	Pitching
#4	4,839	2,499	2,340
#11	4,790	2,488	2,302
Others	4,735	3,251	1,484

While my teams got more overall value, they are extremely pitching-heavy. In fact, both teams #4 and #11 actually took all nine pitchers (and two catchers) with their first 11 picks. They both have more than 800 pitching points more than the average team, and both are more than 750 points weak in hitting. This is not going to lead to a championship!

Does this mean my curve is flawed or useless? No, but it does mean that I must adjust for what happens in the real world. I must find a way of spacing out my pitching selections. This means I'll have to pass on taking a pitcher many times even when their curved value is greater than the hitter. So ideally I want to find a rule of thumb as to when to select a pitcher.

To begin this exploration, I did a test using the actual NFBC draft from 2010. The results were:

Picks	Avg. Value	Hitting	Pitching
#4	5,215	2,753	2,462
#11	5,176	3,051	2,125
Others	4,541	3,145	1,396

Against the real world, the hitting is closer to the average, but still weak. And the pitching still has massive overkill. Team #4 took their nine pitchers in the first ten rounds.

During this test, I documented my choice in every round between a pitcher and a hitter. The round-by-round comparison follows. Players shown in boldface were taken by teams #4 and #11.

The comparison makes it clear that by simply taking a pitcher even when he was just a point or two more valuable than the hitter, not only did I get overkill on pitching, but I also had to pass up some better deals later. So if I would simply hold off on taking a pitcher every time he was even just one point better than the hitter, not only would I get better balance, but I wouldn't be losing any overall value. I'd still find pitchers later on who had the edge over the hitter.

Round	Hitter	Team #4 Pitcher	Hitter	Team #11 Pitcher
1.	A Rod 397	**Lincecum 419 + 22**	**Mauer 388 + 8**	Halladay 380
2.	V Martinez 350	**Greinke 362 + 12**	Ellsbury 375	**Halladay 380 + 5**
3.	V Martinez 350	**Felix H 357 + 7**	Abreu 310	**Haren 355 + 45**
4.	Abreu 310	**Wainwrght 332 + 22**	Abreu 310	**Verlander 334 + 24**
5.	Abreu 310	**Broxton 314 + 4**	D Lee 286	**J Johnson 306 + 20**
6.	Bourn 286	**C Lee 293 + 7**	Bourn 286	**Hanson 301 + 15**
7.	Bourn 286	**Nolasco 289 + 3**	**Bourn 286 + 3**	Bell 283
8.	**K Suzuki 284 + 1**	Bell 283	**Pierre 284 + 1**	Bell 283
9.	Napoli 278	**A Bailey 279 + 1**	**Napoli 278 + 9**	Baker 269
10.	Martin 267	**Jurrjens 268 + 1**	**McLouth 269 + 1**	Jurrjens 268
11.	**Ibanez 266 + 16**	(Aardsma 250)	**Gutierrez 251 + 1**	Aardsma 250
12.	**Pierznysk 249 + 3**	(Danks 246)	Hawpe 238	**Aardsma 250 + 12**
13.	**Hawpe 238 – 8**	(Danks 246)	**Coghlan 233 + 7**	Hughes 226
14.	**Wells 224 + 5**	(Lilly 221)	Wells 224	**Hughes 226 + 2**
15.	**Ross 224 + 3**	(Lilly 221)	**J Rivera 221 E**	Lilly 221
16.	**Theriot 208 – 1**	(Wolf 209)	Theriot 208	**Lilly 221 + 13**
17.	**DeJesus 207 – 2**	(Wolf 209)	**O Cabrera 206 + 4**	Kuroda 202
18.	**Francoeur 197 – 3**	(W Davis 200)	Blake 199	**Kuroda 202 + 3**
19.	**Huff 184 – 16**	(W Davis 200)	**Teahen 184 – 16**	(W Davis 200)
20.	**Castillo 178 – 11**	(Saunders 189)	**S Sizemore 181 – 8**	(Saunders 189)
21.	**Branyan 176 – 13**	(Saunders 189)	**Izturis 168 – 16**	(Correia 184)
22.	**M Ellis 162 – 18**	(Meche 180)	**Rolen 162 – 22**	(Correia 184)
23.	**Inge 158 – 22**	(Meche 180)	**Overbay 143 – 37**	(Meche 180)

I could make a rule such as only take a pitcher with a 10-point or more edge, or a 15-point or more edge, or whatever. But I would still risk overkill. For example, look at team #11. What if my rule of thumb is to take a 10-point edge? Four out of my first six picks would still be pitchers. And if I wasn't competing against myself with team #4, it's possible I would also take Lincecum and/ or Greinke in rounds #1 and #2.

On the contrary, if for some reason I set my goal too high and the bargains didn't materialize, I might end up not taking any pitchers in the first several rounds. In that case, I'd potentially be looking at getting too *little* pitching.

Therefore, I simply want to make a rule of thumb for how often I should be taking pitchers at various stages of the draft.

On a side note, you may have noticed that the last first baseman in my pool was Chris Davis, with a 169 value, but yet team #11 got stuck with Lyle Overbay (143) as their last pick. Had I not been drafting for two teams, this wouldn't have happened. With only one team, I would have gotten Russell Branyan (176), as team #4 did.

Also, pitcher Gil Meche, who was still available in round 23, was my 95th-ranked out of 135 pitchers. This is a great example of what happens with the difference of opinion. Also not taken were my #101, #104–105, #107–108, and several more in my top 135.

Ideal Balance

I should define exactly what the ideal balance between my hitting and pitching should be. In the test I just did, taking the average of teams #4 and #11 shows this:

Pick	Hitting	Pitching	Total Value
Avg. teams #4+#11	2,902	2,293	5,195
Others	3,145	1,396	4,541
Difference	– 243	+ 897	+ 654

Since I have a total edge of 654, it could be argued that an ideal balance would be to have a 327-point edge in both hitting and pitching:

	Hitting	Pitching	Total Value
Ideal balance	3,434	1,761	5,195
Others	3,107	1,434	4,541
Difference	+ 327	+ 327	+ 654

(You'll note that in this equation my hitting gain and pitching loss results in a hitting loss and pitching gain for the other teams.)

It could also be argued that you should calculate the ideal balance on a percentage basis. If we do this, 5,195 is 14.4% better than 4,541, so getting the hitting and pitching to also have a 14.4% edge would lead to this:

	Hitting	Pitching	Total Value
Ideal balance	3,546	1,649	5,195
Others	3,099	1,442	4,541
Difference	+ 447	+ 207	+ 654

I think theoretically the ideal balance would be on a percentage basis, but having a 327-point advantage in both would be fine as well. That would not lead to pitching overkill. So my goal would be to get something between these two:

Hitting goal: 3,434–3,546
Pitching goal: 1,649–1,761

The Pitching Template

Most teams will take their #1 starting pitcher somewhere between rounds #1 and #4. Very few teams will take two pitchers in the first four rounds. So let's see if I can work out a template for when to take my pitchers.

If I plan to take just one pitcher in the first four rounds, my choices from the above chart would be Lincecum, Halladay, Greinke, Felix Hernandez, Haren, Wainwright, and Verlander. The average of these pitchers' value, not including the curve, is 313.

If I planned to take one more pitcher during rounds #5–7, my choices would be Broxton, Josh Johnson, Hanson, Lee, Nolasco, and Bell. Their average value is 248.

Continuing in this fashion throughout the draft leads to this template:

Pitcher	Rounds	Average Value
1.	# 1–4	313
2.	# 5–7	248
3.	# 8–10	224
4.	#11–13	191
5.	#14–15	174
6.	#16–17	161
7.	#18–19	151
8.	#20–21	136
9.	#22–23	132
Total:		1,730

Since my pitching goal is 1,649–1,761, this template works.

I've used this template since 2009, and it works well. It allows me to get a good balance between hitting and pitching. You don't necessarily need to calculate the figures for the *Average Value* column. In fact, it can be difficult to do this. What I've done here is a mock draft after the fact. To estimate what choices you might have for an upcoming draft is more difficult.

You should, however, pay attention to the rounds in which you're taking your pitchers. For example, if you take pitchers in rounds #1, #5, #8, and #11, you're probably getting too much value and better start holding off a little.

If my overall draft goes better or worse than expected—that is, I get a total value edge of +750 or only +550, as opposed to the targeted +654—this template will still give me a good balance between hitting and pitching.

This template also works well for a 12-team draft. The average value numbers would be a bit higher, but so would my target total value of 1,730.

In this example, I've based my ideal balance and expected edge on other teams by taking the averages of team #4 and #11. In reality, since I would only be drafting one team, I'd expect to do better than +654.

Recapping the Entire Curve Strategy

Summing this all up, here's what you do:

1. Determine the 210 hitters and 135 pitchers who comprise your player pool.

    (Note: If there's a tie for the last DH spot between two hitters from different positions—for example, a shortstop worth 179 and an outfielder worth 179—then include both of them for the purposes of calculating your curve.)

2. Record the value of the worst catcher, corner, middle, *sixth*-worst outfielder and *eleventh*-worst pitcher. Curve every position off the highest-valued player of all of those worst players.

3. Use my pitching template to space out your pitching selections for proper balance.

    For a 12-team draft, the only difference is that your player pool will consist of 168 hitters and 108 pitchers. And you should use the *fifth*-worst outfielder and *ninth*-worst pitcher.

    Once you've identified your player pool, you can calculate the projected average team stats. For example, your average team may be expected to hit 230 homers and steal 145 bases. Knowing this will allow you to track your team during the draft and try to get it relatively balanced. You don't want a team that's going to hit 330 homers and steal 50 bases.

Add a Little Common Sense

Suppose it's late in your draft and you still need a second baseman and an outfielder. Your list of best available is this:

Second Base (curve +11)		Outfielders (curve Even)	
Sizemore	175	Ordonez	188
Ellis	156	Sweeney	186
Iwamura	153	LaPorta	186
Callaspo	148	Stubbs	185

According to your curve, Ordonez at 188 is a better choice than Sizemore at 175 + 11 = 186. However, if you pass on

Sizemore—and he gets taken by someone else before your next turn—you'll be left with Ellis (at best) for 156 + 11 = 167. Meanwhile, there are several outfielders close to the value of Ordonez. So in this case, it would be wise to take Sizemore.

So when you get to the later rounds of your draft, keep an eye on where there may be a big gap or drop-off in value at a position.

Average Draft Position

There are some sources for *average draft position* (ADP) information. This is data collected from mock or real drafts that shows the average draft pick used to select each player. This data can be very useful.

For example, suppose it's your turn in round three, pick #40 of the entire draft. Your top two choices are Alex Gordon, curved value of 300, and Dan Uggla, curved value of 297. Ordinarily, you would choose Gordon. But what if the ADP for Uggla is 38 and for Gordon it's 55? You can take Uggla and gamble that Gordon will still be there for your next pick at #51.

I suggest gambling only when it's a close call. Remember that if an *average* draft position is 55, there are times when that player is being taken at #50, #45, and occasionally even sooner.

Also, you must be using *reliable* ADP data. Some sources collect samples only from mock drafts. And many participants don't even bother completing the entire draft. When people drop out, the source uses its own default rankings for the remainder of the draft. So what you end up with is mostly just the opinion of one source, not a good sampling of the public.

And ADP info may be from a slightly different scoring system or roster requirement than your league uses. And some of the data may be outdated. If you have a draft on March 28 and have ADP that includes drafts that took place as early as February, it won't accurately reflect the results of position battles, injuries, etc. that happened more recently.

But even unreliable data is better than no data. If I have a total toss-up decision, and one player's ADP suggests he has a better chance of being available later, I will use that to make my decision. But if it's not a toss-up, I won't gamble based on unreliable ADP.

Reliable ADP, on the other hand, is collected from actual drafts and isn't too old. In the NFBC, for example, they have various leagues that start in early March and they collect all the data. So by the time I draft my league in late March, I have a pretty reliable ADP report. It is from real drafts, with the same scoring system, and not very outdated.

The Flow Chart

Having reliable ADP data allows me to map out an idea of what will occur during my NFBC drafts. I create a flow chart that shows who my choices are likely to be in each round. Below is my flow chart from the 2012 NFBC draft. I'm just showing the first seven rounds, but my entire chart covers 23 rounds. The values shown include my curve.

2012 NFBC FLOW CHART

Round	SP	Catcher	Hitters
1. #5			Kemp 459
			Pujols 455
			Braun 446
			Miggy 446
			Cargo 434
2. #26	Halladay 401?	Napoli 366	Wright 359
	C Lee 369?	Santana 359	Beltre 348?
3. #35	J Weaver 350	Napoli 366?	Wright 359?
	Felix 349?	Santana 359??	Pence 345?
	Sabathia 346		Bourn 344
4. #56	Greinke 343??	McCann 341?	Bourn 344?
	Price 328??		Konerko 342?
	Haren 324?		Zobrist 329?
	Cain 323		

	SP	RP	Catcher	Hitters
5. #65	Cain 323	Kimbrel 337?	Mauer 329	Konerko 342??
	Kennedy 321		Posey 326?	M Young 336?
	Lester 318?		Wieters 323	
6. #86	Adam W 312?	Axford 309	Mauer 329??	D Gordon 329?
	D Hudson 302	Rivera 303	Wieters 323??	Cuddyer 328?
	Bumgrnr 298?	Papelbon 301	Avila 323	Gardner 311?
7. #95	Adam W 312??	Axford 309?	Avila 323?	Cuddyer 328??
	D Hudson 302	Rivera 303?		Ichiro 306?
	Latos 291?	Papelbon 301?		Stubbs 302?

I had the #5 pick for this draft. So for round #1, I've listed my top five choices, in order of preference. Matt Kemp and Albert Pujols were #1 and #2, respectively, on the ADP list, so it was unlikely I'd get either of them, but I had them listed, just in case. I also didn't just automatically write down the top five values. I did consider, for example, if it might be better to take Miguel Cabrera, or even Carlos Gonzalez, ahead of Ryan Braun, based on considerations of what categories and positional players it might be easier—or more difficult—to get later on.

After round #1, I'm listing the best players who might be available, based on their ADP. For example, there are several hitters with a better curved value than Mike Napoli, but based on the ADP report, none were likely to still be available for my second pick, which was the 26th overall pick. I will obviously pay attention to who is actually being drafted, and if one of the better hitters surprisingly is still available at #26, I would select him instead of Napoli.

Napoli's ADP is 37. Not only should he certainly be available for me in round #2, but there's a decent chance he'll still be there in round #3, when I have the 35th pick. For round #3, I've put a question mark next to his value, which means there's about a 50-50 chance that he will be available. Two question marks next to a player mean it's unlikely—but possible—the player will still be available.

Roy Halladay's ADP is 24. I am definitely hoping he will be available for me in round #2, because he has a 35-point edge over Napoli. If I miss out on Halladay, it looks like my other pitching choices in rounds #2–4 won't have much of an edge over the hitting choices.

Good ADP information is extremely helpful. Making a flow chart for all 23 rounds allows me to analyze choices I may have.

For example, I can see if there are a lot of stolen-base options—or a lack of stolen-base options—who are on my chart. If it gets to round #3 and my top two choices are Pence (345 value with 10 SB) or Bourn (344 value with 58 SB), then if there's a scarcity of stolen-base guys, I'll take Bourn, or vice versa.

Or suppose in round #3 I'm deciding between Napoli (366) and Wright (359). I can see on my chart how often it looks like there'll be good catching options as opposed to good third-base options.

When I get to round 13 or so, I assume I'll have taken my two closers by then, so I eliminate the *Relief Pitcher* column. I also start listing all hitters by position—first base, second base, etc.—rather than just lumping them all into "hitters." I want to start paying more attention to the choices I'll have for each specific position.

As it actually turned out, my first seven picks were Cabrera, Halladay, Napoli, Bourn, Kimbrel, Posey, and Axford. This was all very predictable based on my flow chart. The only surprise was that Posey (ADP 68) was still available in round #6 (pick #86).

It's funny looking at this list after the fact. Cabrera was the first player to win the Triple Crown since 1967, but Halladay, Napoli, and Axford were all disasters. My team finished in ninth place.

More Uses for the Flow Chart

When I make player projections, I like to take a second look at as many as possible. After making my flow chart, I definitely want to take a second look at anyone I haven't already done, or even a third look. I want to make sure people aren't showing up on my flow chart only because I've been too optimistic.

Some people like to prepare by participating in mock drafts. They get to experience various options and choices that may occur. Personally, I never bother. In less time than it takes for a mock draft, I can make my flow chart. The flow chart will show me lots of various options and choices that are likely to occur, not just based on one mock draft, but based on lots of actual drafts.

After making my flow chart, I look at the pitching choices I'm likely to have in various rounds, and I revise the *Average Value* column of my pitching template. Then, as the draft happens, I keep a log of whom I actually take and a running tally of how far ahead—or behind—my target I am. This helps me make choices as the draft goes on, and know if I should be getting a little more aggressive—or hold off—on getting pitching.

Similarly, I can make a template for hitting. For 2012, my NFBC templates were these:

Hitter	Rounds	Avg. Value With Curve	Actual	+/– Total	
1.	#1	445			
2.	#2–4	344			
3.	#2–4	344			
4.	#5–7	305			
5.	#5–7	305			
6.	#8–10	286			
7.	#8–10	286			
8.	#11–13	266			
9.	#11–13	266			
10.	#14–15	257			
11.	#16–17	247			
12.	#18–19	230			
13.	#20–21	223			
14.	#22–23	210			
Total:		4,014			

Pitcher	Rounds	Avg. Value Without Curve	Actual	+/- Total
1.	#1–4	286		
2.	#5–7	255		
3.	#8–10	235		
4.	#11–13	210		
5.	#14–15	195		
6.	#16–17	182		
7.	#18–19	169		
8.	#20–21	168		
9.	#22–23	151		
Total:		1,851		

Based on my player pool, the average team would have a 3,500 hitting value and a 1,725 pitching value. If I met the above targets, I would have 3,743 hitting value (after deducting the curve) and 1,851 pitching value, which are both 7% more than the average team. So this would be good balance.

As it turned out, I got 3,750 hitting value and 1,952 pitching.

ADP Trumps Picking First?

The NFBC allows you to request your draft spot, and then people are randomly awarded a spot based on their preferences. I showed earlier that picking first is always an advantage. However, with reliable ADP, there are exceptions. For example, if you think Giancarlo Stanton is the fourth-best pick, and only 15 points worse than your #1 pick, and Stanton's ADP is #12, then you can examine what benefit you're likely to get in round two if you drop down in the first round and take Stanton at, let's say, the ninth pick. If you think that, based on the ADPs of other players, this will allow you to gain more than 15 points in round 2, it may be worth requesting the #9 spot.

However, this can be dangerous. If someone surprises you and takes Stanton at #8—or the player(s) you thought you'd be able to get in round two are surprisingly gone—then you've blown it. Also, dropping down in round one will affect whom you get in rounds three, four, and later.

How Not to Use ADP

I was in an NFBC draft where there were two co-managers sitting next to me. They were talking in code, so that nobody would know what they were thinking. They would have conversations such as, "What do you think of #18?" followed by "I like him, but I like #22 better."

It didn't take long to figure out their code was the NFBC ADP list. So when it got to a point where I was choosing between two players, I knew which one they were thinking about taking. I took that player before they could. And when it was my pick again, the other guy I wanted was still available. Had they been using a better code, such as speaking in Latin, I might have only gotten one of those two players.

Also, at one later point in the. draft, it was my turn and I announced, "I'll take Jason Kubel."

One of the guys next to me then announced, "We'll take #207! Oops, I mean Alfonso Soriano."

CHAPTER 10

Salary-Cap Games

Salary cap is a form of fantasy baseball in which every player is assigned a salary by the game operator. You must compile your roster of players such that the starting lineup each week does not exceed a total salary cap. The scoring can be either standard Rotisserie, where teams are ranked from first to last in various categories, or it can be Points style, where you are awarded something like one point for a single, two points for a double, ten points for a win, etc.

For this chapter, I will discuss the CDM Sports Diamond Challenge Rotisserie-style game (www.cdmsports.com). However, the principles I outline can be applied to other forms, such as Points style, and some even apply to football or salary-cap games based on other sports.

CDM started in 1992 and is considered the granddaddy of fantasy baseball, because it was the first national contest. The starting lineup each week consists of two catchers, two from each infield position, six outfielders, and two designated hitters. You also have six starting pitchers, three relief pitchers, and one swing pitcher who can be either a starter or a reliever. You have 12 spots on the bench. The total roster, therefore, is 18 hitters, 10 pitchers, and 12 bench players, for a total of 40. The starting 28 players must not exceed a total salary of $30,000,000.

You may change your lineup once a week. During the season, you're allowed 16 purchases, where you can drop a player from your roster and add a new player. The salaries and players' position eligibility are set by CDM before the season starts and don't change. The scoring is standard 5×5 Rotisserie categories.

One of the drawbacks of salary-cap style is that unlike auction and draft leagues, you don't exclusively own a player. Anybody who wants Albert Pujols can take him. If 80% of the teams have him, he can become somewhat irrelevant (unless you're in the 20% who don't have him, in which case he's extremely relevant for you).

But the big advantage of salary-cap games is that if you own Albert Pujols and he tears his ACL on April 15, it does not ruin your team. You simply use one of your allotted player changes, and replace him with Miguel Cabrera, Joey Votto, etc. Instead of a crushing blow to your season, it's not a big deal.

This makes salary-cap games potentially less aggravating than other formats. In my opinion, this is the fairest style of game. It removes some of the luck by eliminating the potential for a couple of key injuries to ruin your season.

Selecting Your Team

The first thing you need to do is determine each player's value. You project the player's raw stats for the year (discussed in chapter 5), and then convert those stats into a specific value (see chapter 6). For an auction league, you would use a *dollar* value. For a salary-cap game, you can think in terms of an auction dollar value, but you don't need to.

For a salary-cap game, I convert the player's value into a number, such as 150, 375, or 428, simply because it's easier to deal with than a dollar value that may range from $1 to $40 or so. (I'll demonstrate shortly why it's easier to deal with.)

So the question is how do you decide which players to choose? As I say throughout the book, it's all about value. You need to get the most value possible for your $30,000,000 lineup.

I'm going to use the 2012 season as an example. Each position must be examined separately, because the idea is to get the best players—for the salary—at each position. So you can't compare shortstops to first basemen, or second basemen to outfielders, etc., until you are filling the designated hitter slots.

Typically, I want to have an even distribution by position, which looks like this:

Position	Players	Pitchers	Players
C	3	Starters	10
1B	3	Relievers	5
2B	3	Total	15
SS	3		
3B	3		
OF	9		
Total	24		

This gives me one backup at catcher and each infield spot, three outfielders to back up six starting outfielders, and a similar ratio of approximately 50% backups at pitcher. The above totals 39 players, so there is still one spot left for an extra player.

Starting with the shortstops, following is a list of all the starters in the major leagues, along with my projected 2012 value and their salary assigned by CDM.

Analyzing this list, some things are obvious. Dee Gordon stands out as a great value. He is worth 306, which is essentially tied with Jose Reyes (307) for the second-most-valuable shortstop. And Gordon's salary ($740,000) is much less than Reyes's ($1,360,000) and less than everyone else's in the higher-value range. You have to go all the way down to Alcides Escobar at a 214 value to find someone less expensive. I can pretty safely pencil in Dee Gordon as one of my three shortstops.

Whether or not you agree with my player values doesn't matter. If you think I was crazy to value Dee Gordon so highly, no problem. You can use your own values. I'm explaining here the process of how best to compare players and make your choices.

Another obvious comparison is that Ian Desmond is a better deal than Jhonny Peralta. He is worth one value point more, for $210,000 less cost. So it would be stupid to take Peralta rather than Desmond. Similarly, Asdrubal Cabrera is worth 21 more points than Jimmy Rollins but costs $110,000 less.

But much is not obvious. Is it worth the extra $220,000 to get Cabrera and his 291 value instead of Desmond's 235 value? Is it worth paying $1,440,000 for Troy Tulowitzki and his 367 value? That's a lot more value than both Cabrera and Desmond, but also a lot more expensive.

Player	Value	Salary
T Tulowitzki	367	$1,440,000
J Reyes	307	$1,360,000
D Gordon	306	$ 740,000
S Castro	302	$1,200,000
E Andrus	298	$1,180,000
A Cabrera	291	$1,020,000
J Rollins	270	$1,130,000
A Ramirez	264	$1,080,000
E Aybar	263	$1,100,000
D Jeter	257	$1,030,000
I Desmond	235	$ 800,000
J Peralta	234	$1,010,000
Y Escobar	230	$ 940,000
A Escobar	214	$ 690,000
C Pennington	207	$ 760,000
J Hardy	205	$ 900,000
Z Cozart	202	$ 600,000
R Furcal	189	$ 710,000
J Lowrie	185	$ 580,000
J Bartlett	183	$ 960,000
A Gonzalez	177	$ 760,000
T Pastornicky	176	$ 400,000
S Drew	175	$ 770,000
R Tejada	168	$ 490,000
S Rodriguez	167	$ 500,000
J Carroll	162	$ 590,000
E Nunez	160	$ 500,000
C Barmes	156	$ 660,000
M Aviles	155	$ 530,000
B Ryan	154	$ 630,000

The answer lies in the *marginal* value. You need to compare how much extra value you get, compared to the extra cost, and then take the best deals.

For example, if you take Tulowitzki over Cabrera, you spend an extra $420,000 to get an extra 76 value. Each extra point of value costs you $420,000/76 = $5,526.

Tulowitzki rather than Desmond costs $640,000/132 = $4,848.

Taking Cabrera rather than Desmond costs $220,000/56 = $3,929.

So looking at these options, it would appear Cabrera is the best deal. He only costs $3,929 per point more than Desmond, and if you were to substitute Tulowitzki for him, it would cost you $5,526 per point.

But it isn't quite this simple. First, we need to compare all 30 shortstops on the list. Second, we need to have their average salaries fit within a certain range. With a $30,000,000 salary cap and 28 starters, that means an average salary of $1,071,000. So we can't just take all the most-expensive players, and if we take too many cheap players, we'll be too far under the cap and be missing out on value.

You can see now why I prefer to use a value number like 367, rather than a dollar amount, such as $30. With a dollar value, the Tulowitzki and Cabrera equation would be something like $420,000/8 = $52,500. It's hard enough dealing with the $5,526 number, so I'd rather not get into five-figure numbers. Not to mention that I use decimal points for auction dollar values, which would make things even more confusing.

To also make these comparisons easier, I'm going to ignore the last three zeros on the salaries. In other words, taking Tulowitzki over Cabrera would be $420/76 = $5.53. This may just be a matter of my own taste, but I think it's easier to compare $5.53 and $4.85 than $5,526 and $4,848. (And it makes no difference for the analysis. We're still comparing which ratio is a better deal than the other.)

Comparing 30 players with one another will be very time-consuming if you take every combination of two players and then figure out who the best three players are. To shorten this process, I add a column in my database called *Dollar Value*. This is *the ratio of a player's value to his salary*. For example, Tulowitzki is 367/$1,440 = .255. Cabrera is 291/$1,020 = .285. Just to make it simpler to compare numbers, I multiply this ratio by four. Again, I find it easier to compare the resulting 1.02 and 1.14, rather than comparing .255 and .285.

To complete the list, there's one more extremely important thing to do. When it comes to injury-prone players, they must be considered differently for a salary-cap league. For example, Tulowitzki is a guy who can't seem to make it through a year without spending time on the DL. Therefore, my projected value for him of 367 is based on an expected 515 at bats. For an auction or draft league, this is all I can justify paying for. However, for a salary-cap league, I need to consider how valuable he'll be when healthy. I add him again in my database, but this time with 595 at bats and correspondingly better statistics. This gives him a "full-time" value of 415.

I make a similar entry for all players whom I had downgraded as being injury risks. I deemed Asdrubal Cabrera a small risk and accordingly gave him 560 at bats. When he's healthy, I'm expecting he'll also play at a pace of about 595 at bats. I give Jose Reyes, another big risk, a full-time pace of 625 at bats, because he's a leadoff hitter.

So the idea is that when one of these players is healthy, if they are producing a value that is superior to others relative to the salaries, they need to be seriously considered for my team. If they produce a value that is not really better than other, safer choices, then there's no reason to take them and the risk.

Sometimes there are players who are going to start out full-time but are at risk of being supplanted by a top prospect from AAA. These are other players that I may give an "FT" value to. Again, their value must be superior to safer options, because if they do lose their full-time job, they become useless.

My complete list, with the full-time players and dollar value looks like this:

Player	Value	Salary	Dollar Value
T TulowitzkiFT	415	$1,440,000	$1.15
T Tulowitzki	367	$1,440,000	$1.02
J ReyesFT	363	$1,360,000	$1.07
J Reyes	307	$1,360,000	$ .90
D Gordon	306	$ 740,000	$1.65
A CabreraFT	305	$1,020,000	$1.20
S Castro	302	$1,200,000	$1.01
E Andrus	298	$1,180,000	$1.01
J RollinsFT	296	$1,130,000	$1.05
A Cabrera	291	$1,020,000	$1.14
J Rollins	270	$1,130,000	$ .96
A Ramirez	264	$1,080,000	$ .98
E Aybar	263	$1,100,000	$ .96
D Jeter	257	$1,030,000	$1.00
J HardyFT	243	$ 900,000	$1.08
R FurcalFT	241	$ 710,000	$1.36
I Desmond	235	$ 800,000	$1.18
J Peralta	234	$1,010,000	$ .93
Y Escobar	230	$ 940,000	$ .98
A Escobar	214	$ 690,000	$1.24

Player	Value	Salary	Dollar Value
J LowrieFT	209	$ 580,000	$1.44
C Pennington	207	$ 760,000	$1.09
J Hardy	205	$ 900,000	$ .91
Z Cozart	202	$ 600,000	$1.35
R Furcal	189	$ 710,000	$1.06
J Lowrie	185	$ 580,000	$1.28
J Bartlett	183	$ 960,000	$ .76
A Gonzalez	177	$ 760,000	$ .93
T Pastornicky	176	$ 400,000	$1.76
S Drew	175	$ 770,000	$ .91
R Tejada	168	$ 490,000	$1.37
S Rodriguez	167	$ 500,000	$1.34
J Carroll	162	$ 590,000	$1.10
E Nunez	160	$ 500,000	$1.28
C Barmes	156	$ 660,000	$ .95
M Aviles	155	$ 530,000	$1.17
B Ryan	154	$ 630,000	$ .98

The higher the dollar value is, the better it is. Not surprisingly, Dee Gordon jumps out at a $1.65 dollar value. This is superior to everyone on the list except Tyler Pastornicky at $1.76.

To show how the *dollar value* helps, let's first compare some players by just using their value and salary. For players where I've given an "FT" projection, I can ignore their non-FT projection. Some examples follow.

If I take Tulowitzki instead of Reyes, it only costs me $1.54 per extra value point. (Remember, the actual figure is $1,540 per extra value point, but I'm eliminating the last three zeros to make it easier.) If I take Tulowitzki rather than Gordon, it costs $6.42.

So the question is, where's the cutoff point of what is an acceptable figure to pay for extra value?

Take Player	Rather Than	Extra Cost
TulowitzkiFT	ReyesFT	$1.54 ($80/52)
TulowitzkiFT	Gordon	$6.42 ($700/109)
TulowitzkiFT	CabreraFT	$3.82 ($420/110)
TulowitzkiFT	Castro	$2.12 ($240/113)
TulowitzkiFT	Andrus	$2.22 ($260/117)
TulowitzkiFT	RollinsFT	$2.61 ($310/119)
TulowitzkiFT	Ramirez	$2.38 ($360/151)
TulowitzkiFT	FurcalFT	$4.20 ($730/174)
TulowitzkiFT	Desmond	$3.56 ($640/180)
TulowitzkiFT	LowrieFT	$4.17 ($860/206)
TulowitzkiFT	Cozart	$3.94 ($840/213)
TulowitzkiFT	Pastornicky	$4.35 ($1,040/239)

If I just take the three best dollar values, they would be Gordon, Pastornicky, and Furcal. The problem is that the total salary of those three is $1,850,000, for an average of $616,667. If I do this for each position, I would be massively under the average of $1,071,000 per player and missing out on value. Obviously, I can afford to spend more.

If I just take the three highest-value players—Tulowitzki, Reyes, and Gordon—that's an average salary of $1,180,000 per player. That's a bit too much. If I do this for each position, my average weekly lineup would total $33,040,000. That's $3,040,000 over the cap, which would make it extremely difficult to field a lineup each week.

The answer lies in comparing the marginal values of lots of players, then choosing the best deals and adjusting based on my team's average salary. For example, if I arrive at an average salary of $1,050,000 per player, I can look for the best deal available to increase value somewhere.

By using my *Dollar Value* column, I've learned some rules of thumb that greatly reduce the number of comparisons I need to make. First, if two players have the same dollar value, the one with the most value points will be a better deal. Therefore, for a less-valuable player to be a better deal than a more-valuable player, the dollar value has to be superior.

The second rule of thumb is that the cutoff point for someone being a good deal is typically around $5.50–$6.00. In other words, if the marginal cost of a player is greater than $6, it's usually not a good deal. If it's under $5.50, it usually is. The exact figure will vary from year to year, but it's usually in this range.

If you set up your own comparison system, you will learn your own rules of thumb, so that you don't need to spend countless hours comparing everyone.

Looking at the above comparisons, I know that Tulowitzki is a better deal than everyone else on the list, other than Gordon. Even Pastornicky, with his $1.76 dollar value, can be replaced by Tulowitzki for just $4.35.

Because of this knowledge, when I first glance at my printout of shortstops, I can quickly eliminate several, just by looking at the *Dollar Value* column. For example, with TulowitzkiFT, Gordon, and CabreraFT, I have three high-value players with a dollar value of $1.15 or more. This means that everyone below them who doesn't have a dollar value of greater than $1.15 can be wiped off the list.

I said before that the injury risks need to be a *superior* value. In this case, they are. Of the players I've crossed off my list, the best dollar values were Castro, Andrus, Pennington, and Carroll. Here's how they compare:

Take Player	Rather Than	Extra Cost
TulowitzkiFT	Castro	$2.12 ($240/113)
TulowitzkiFT	Andrus	$2.22 ($260/117)
TulowitzkiFT	Pennington	$3.27 ($680/208)
TulowitzkiFT	Carroll	$3.36 ($850/253)
CabreraFT	Castro	$0 (<$180>/3)
CabreraFT	Andrus	$0 (<$160>/7)
CabreraFT	Pennington	$2.65 ($260/98)
CabreraFT	Carroll	$3.01 ($430/143)

Since my typical cutoff point for a good deal is $5.50–$6.00, I consider these all superior values. If the extra cost were $5.50–$6.00, then it wouldn't be worth taking the injury risk. If the cost were $4.50–$5.00, it's debatable.

Having eliminated all of those with less than a $1.15 dollar value, I can see that the bottom three remaining—Tejada, Rodriguez, and Nunez—can probably also be eliminated. All I need to do is identify three players above them with a better dollar value. Gordon, Pastornicky, and Cozart fulfill that requirement to eliminate Rodriguez and Nunez. Cozart has a $1.35 dollar value and Tejada $1.37, so I can't automatically eliminate Tejada. But doing the math quickly reveals that Cozart costs just $3.24 ($110/34) more than Tejada, so I can safely eliminate Tejada.

I've now whittled my list down to ten possibilities:

Player	Value	Salary	Dollar Value
T TulowitzkiFT	415	$1,440,000	$1.15
J ReyesFT	363	$1,360,000	$1.07
D Gordon	306	$ 740,000	$1.65
A CabreraFT	305	$1,020,000	$1.20
R FurcalFT	241	$ 710,000	$1.36
I Desmond	235	$ 800,000	$1.18

Player	Value	Salary	Dollar Value
A Escobar	214	$ 690,000	$1.24
J LowrieFT	209	$ 580,000	$1.44
Z Cozart	202	$ 600,000	$1.35
T Pastornicky	176	$ 400,000	$1.76

I need to find the best three. I suspected earlier that Gordon would be one of them. I can now try to confirm this. Tulowitzki costs $6.42 more than Gordon, and Reyes costs $9.25 more than Gordon. Both are above my acceptable threshold. Gordon has a higher dollar value than everyone with less value, except Pastornicky. Comparing Gordon for Pastornicky, the cost is just $2.62, which is a bargain. Therefore, not only has Gordon made my roster, but he should be in the starting lineup virtually all the time, because he's the best value of all shortstops.

Next I'll compare Tulowitzki to everyone remaining:

Take Player	Rather Than	Extra Cost	
TulowitzkiFT	ReyesFT	$1.54	($80/52)
TulowitzkiFT	CabreraFT	$3.82	($420/110)
TulowitzkiFT	FurcalFT	$4.20	($730/174)
TulowitzkiFT	Desmond	$3.56	($640/180)
TulowitzkiFT	Escobar	$3.73	($750/201)
TulowitzkiFT	LowrieFT	$4.17	($860/206)
TulowitzkiFT	Cozart	$3.94	($840/213)
TulowitzkiFT	Pastornicky	$4.35	($1,040/239)

Tulowitzki is a superior value to everyone else. So Tulowitzki is being penciled onto my roster. The only question remaining will be if I can afford his high salary. I'll determine that later.

Next I'll compare Reyes with everyone else remaining:

Take Player	Rather Than	Extra Cost
ReyesFT	CabreraFT	$5.86 ($340/58)
ReyesFT	FurcalFT	$5.33 ($650/122)
ReyesFT	Desmond	$4.38 ($560/128)
ReyesFT	Escobar	$4.50 ($670/149)
ReyesFT	LowrieFT	$5.06 ($780/154)
ReyesFT	Cozart	$4.72 ($760/161)
ReyesFT	Pastornicky	$5.13 ($960/187)

Reyes compared to Cabrera is basically even. With my rule of thumb being $5.50–$6.00 for a good deal, he's right in that range at $5.86. Since Furcal and Lowrie are also injury risks, Reyes is a better deal. Desmond, Escobar, and Cozart are safer options but are inferior values when Reyes is healthy. If I want to go with a safer option, Pastornicky would be the choice.

So my options are Reyes, Cabrera, or Pastornicky. The cost of Cabrera over Pastornicky is $4.81 ($620/129). Since Cabrera is not a huge injury risk, I would be inclined to take him for just a $4.81 cost over Pastornicky. In fact, using Cabrera's non-FT value of 291, he still costs just $5.39 ($620/115).

Therefore, I will eliminate Pastornicky. Later on, when I've compiled the rest of my roster, if I need to cut back on salary somewhere, Pastornicky would be an option.

If I take Tulowitzki, Gordon, and Reyes, that would be a total salary of $3,540,000 for an average of $1,180,000. This is a little more than the goal of $1,071,000, but there may be other positions that will be lower than $1,071,000 and balance it out. (If I take Cabrera rather than Reyes, my average salary would be $1,067,000.)

So I'm going to definitely take Tulowitzki and Gordon, and once I see what the rest of my roster looks like, I will decide between Reyes and Cabrera (or even Pastornicky if necessary). Aside from the salary question, when making that final decision I will also look at my stat category balance. For example, Reyes provides a better batting average and more stolen bases, but Cabrera has more power and RBIs.

If you're a real tech wizard, you can actually set up Excel (or other software) to make these comparisons for you. The software can be designed to automatically give you the ideal roster with the most value.

I compare players at every position, just as I did with the shortstops, and arrive at a preliminary roster:

Pos	Must Take	Next Best	Options
C	Napoli $890		
3–$2,300	Santana $740		
($767 avg)	Avila $670		
1B	Goldschmidt $600	Votto $1,490	Pujols $1,700
3–$3,050		Hosmer $960	Freeman $760
($1,017 avg)			LaHairFT $400
2B	KinslerFT $1,150		Pedroia $1,270
3–$2,540	R WeeksFT $930		J WeeksFT $760
($847 avg)	Kipnis $460		
SS	TulowitzkiFT $1,440	ReyesFT $1,360	A CabreraFT $1,020
3–$3,540	D Gordon $740		Pastornicky $400
($1,180 avg)			
3B	H RamirezFT $1,250	WrightFT $1,230	A RodriguezFT $1,150
3–$3,310	Lawrie $830		YoukilisFT $1,130
($1,103 avg)			FreeseFT $840

OF	Ellsbury $1,350	Kemp $1,610	A Gordon $860
9–$10,320	C GonzalezFT $1,230	Braun $1,590	L CainFT $400
($1,147 avg)	N CruzFT $1,030	HamiltonFT $1,370	
	CrispFT $900	JD Martinez $420	
	Jennings $820		

The really superior values are in the *Must Take* column. If I need to increase or decrease my total salary, I'll consider replacing players in the *Next Best* column with one of the *Options*.

The catcher spot is all set. Compared to my three choices above, there's nobody else even close to being a good value.

The total average salary for my roster is $25,060,000 for 24 hitters, an average of $1,044,000 each. This means I need to add salary to get to the average of $1,071,000 per player. If anything, I like to be a little above the average, because during the season lower-priced values tend to emerge. There may be a lower-priced setup guy who gets to close because of an injury, a part-time player who gets to play full-time due to an injury, or similar developments.

So now I've got to look at my options for adding salary:

1B	Pujols for Votto	$ 7.78
	Pujols for Hosmer	$ 6.17
	Pujols for Goldschmidt	$ 6.51
	Freeman for Goldschmidt	$17.78
2B	Pedroia for Kinsler	$ 9.23
	Pedroia for R Weeks	$ 6.94
	Pedroia for Kipnis	$ 6.38
	J Weeks for Kipnis	$ 8.57
SS	A Cabrera for D Gordon	N/A (less value for more salary)
3B	A Rodriguez for Lawrie	$15.24
	Youkilis for Lawrie	$15.00
	Freese for Lawrie	N/A (less value for more salary)

OF	A Gordon for Jennings	N/A (less value for more salary)
	A Gordon for JD Martinez	$ 6.57

The best option is taking Pujols instead of Hosmer at a cost of $6.17. This change puts my average salary at $1,075,000. This is just slightly above $1,071,000, which is fine.

Stat Category Balance

Before I make this my final roster, I need to consider stat category balance. Considering balance for a salary-cap game is quite different than for an auction or draft league, where you can identify the likely pool of players who will be taken—just once per team—and calculate the average expected team stats. You can then assemble your team with those averages in mind.

But for a salary-cap game, some players will be on 30% of the teams, 40%, 50%, etc., and many players won't be taken at all. So it's impossible to predict what stats the average team will produce. Therefore, I simply look to see if my team appears to have a reasonable balance. My projected team total stats are:

AVG	RUN	HR	RBI	SB
.283	2,208	563	2,018	504

There are about 10% more runs than RBIs, which is normal, since not every run scored results in an RBI. So this looks fine.

The ratio of stolen bases to home runs is pretty high. For a typical mixed league, home runs are usually about a 3-to-2 ratio greater than steals. So I am concerned that this roster may be a little too speed-oriented. However, I expect some of the speed players, such as Dee Gordon, Kinsler, and Jennings, to be owned by most teams. So I'm not going to make any changes.

If it does turn out that I have too much speed, it's easy to correct that as the season unfolds. For example, I can leave Crisp and Dee Gordon on my bench more often. If necessary, I could drop a player like Crisp and add a power hitter.

Similarly, if my batting average turns out to be weak (or too strong), I can leave some of the lower averages on my bench more often and/or drop one of them for a high-average hitter (or vice versa).

Choosing Pitchers

As with hitters, I look at the pitchers' dollar value to whittle down the list, and then compare the remaining players. I go through the same steps as with hitters until I arrive at my final roster.

You don't need to specifically try to load up on high-value pitchers, nor specifically make sure you include lower salaries. It's all a question of getting the best values. There have been years where there were so many superior, high-priced pitchers that it was necessary to average more than $1,100,000 per pitcher and cut back a little on hitting, but that's not always the case.

There is a term some of the CDM players use—the *stank pen*. This means a bullpen with all low-priced relief pitchers, which you set up so that you can use the money elsewhere. The theory behind this is similar to what some people do in auction and draft leagues; they don't want to pay a lot for just one category—saves. The problem with this theory, as I've mentioned in other chapters, is that it is a misconception to think closers only contribute saves. They also contribute ERA (earned run average),

WHIP (walks and hits / innings pitched), wins, and strikeouts, albeit at less volume than starting pitchers. A good value formula takes this into account. It credits them the proper amount of value given their ERA and WHIP relative to innings pitched, and it credits them for the wins and strikeouts. Therefore, the value formula determines an accurate value for them, including all five categories.

Then, using this accurate value, you make the comparisons relative to salary, as with the other positions. It may—or may not—be that some of the lower-priced closers are a good value. If they are, then fine, take them and use the extra money elsewhere. If not, spend for the better closing options.

You'll note that I'm only referring to closers. In this format, setup men do you no good. "Holds" aren't a category, and you'll need the saves.

There are always some closers who start the year on a short leash. For example, Javy Guerra began 2012 as the Dodgers closer, but he barely beat out Kenley Jansen. It was quite likely that Guerra would be unable to keep the job all year. Therefore, I gave Guerra an "FT" projection. Typically, I'll do this for several closers and potential closers. As with hitters, if the "FT" value isn't superior to others, there's no reason to take them and the added risk.

40th Player

It sure is nice to have an extra hitter, and it also sure is nice to have an extra pitcher. Some years I've taken a hitter and other years a pitcher. I also may switch during the year and drop a hitter to pick up a pitcher, or vice versa.

At this point, I'd say that I prefer taking the extra pitcher. On a weekly basis, it helps a lot to have an 11th pitcher when choosing which six (or even seven) to start. Approximately every three weeks, a starter will throw two games, which is an advantage. The more starters you have, the more "two-steps" you get. Also, it's not unusual to have one starter out with a minor injury, another with a bad matchup, and another who's underperforming—and all of a sudden my choices are limited.

Multiple Teams

CDM and most other salary-cap games allow you to enter multiple teams. And many people do. Some enter identical teams more than once, and some enter different lineups. It might sound odd that someone would play identical teams, but the reason is that in CDM (and most other games) there are prizes for your league as well as the overall competition. So while your identical teams will finish together in the overall competition, your league results may vary. By the luck of the draw, some leagues are easier and some more difficult.

The logic behind entering different teams is that it gives you more chances to have a good team. Even small differences in your lineups can end up producing very different results.

This gives you a better chance of having at least one good team that will retain your interest throughout the year and give you a chance to win a league, or possibly even compete for the overall title. One downside of entering different lineups is that it's more time-consuming.

Personally, I have always entered multiple different teams. When I won CDM in 2002, I entered six teams. In 2005 I entered four teams. Someone once commented (not about me in particular), "Why would anyone take different lineups? Why not just choose who you think are the absolute best players?"

The reason is simple. I don't know who the absolute best players are. Many of the choices I make are close calls. If I take a player because he's a $5.70 cost over another player, that certainly doesn't mean he's the clear-cut best player to take. I'm not a mathematician, but I think you could call that essentially a statistical tie.

In the example I gave of choosing my 2012 CDM team, I wanted to make it as simple as possible and show you how to compare players. So I wrote it as though I was putting together just one team. However, the truth is that I entered six teams. Therefore, most of the players in the *Next Best* column and some of the *Options* get scattered about my teams.

For example, rather than making a tough call between Reyes and Asdrubal Cabrera, I put them each on three teams. And Alex Rodriguez and Kevin Youkilis were so close in value to David Wright that I put each of them on two teams.

Schedule Considerations

I know some CDM players place a great deal of emphasis on scheduling. They try to find some pretty good values who play at the hitters' parks, and match their schedules as well as possible so that most weeks one of them will be at home.

I think this does more harm than good. First, you need to take the best values—not the second best, nor third best, nor some "pretty good" ones. And you can't mix and match schedules perfectly. Whatever you think on April 1 you're going to be able to do, forget it. Things will change. Players will underperform or get hurt. The bottom line is that you'll end up being forced to use players who aren't the best values many weeks when they don't have an all-home week.

Therefore, I don't totally ignore scheduling and home parks, but I only consider them for close calls. If two players I'm considering are very close in overall value and one of them plays in a good hitting park, then I may pick that player because it will be an advantage to start him for every home week.

However, keep in mind that if two players are very close in value and one will be better when at home, that means he will be worse when away. Therefore, if I don't manage to bench him for many of his away weeks, I've gained little or nothing.

As for taking pitchers who play in great pitching parks, the same is true.

Some CDM players may take—or avoid—a pitcher based on what they perceive as a really good, or really bad, early schedule. When I select my pitchers, I never even look at their schedule. The early schedule isn't going to make enough difference to justify taking an inferior value. And after those early games, you are stuck having to use an inferior value, wasting a roster spot, or using up one of your precious add/drop moves. And that's not even mentioning that a rainout here or there—or a rotation-order change—can turn a perceived great schedule into an average one.

Later in the season—such as when there are only four to six weeks left—if I'm considering adding a new pitcher, I would consider the schedule. The rotation has been set and there are few rainouts.

Weekly Decisions

It's always about getting the best value. And that's something that needs to be looked at player by player, position by position, every week.

David Wright (worth 347) is clearly not as good a deal as Brett Lawrie (worth 308), because he costs $10.26 ($400/39). However, what if Wright is playing seven games and Lawrie only six? In that case, Wright's value, compared to Lawrie, becomes 347 × (7/6) = 405. Now the cost is $400/97 = $4.12, which *is* a good deal.

Clayton Kershaw cost just $4.40 ($550/125) more than Daniel Hudson. What if Kershaw has a neutral matchup and Hudson has a great matchup? I would make my best guess for what stats Hudson would produce if he pitched every game this year with that same matchup and convert that to a value. Suppose Hudson's value goes from 309 to 364. Now the cost for Kershaw is $550/70 = $7.86. Kershaw is no longer a good deal, so I would choose Hudson (assuming I have something better I can do with the $550,000 in salary-cap savings).

Adding and Dropping Players

When a player is exceeding expectations—and he's not on your roster—it's very tempting to want to grab him. If he's on the roster of lots of other teams, it's even more tempting, because you feel as though this guy is killing you.

However, as with players on your roster, unless you have a tangible reason to be confident he will continue to exceed expectations, you should assume he will come back to earth. And if you add him now, you'll have missed the hot streak and have him when he cools off.

Sometimes people are quick to attribute great stats to a

"breakout" or "this guy's finally living up to his potential." This could be true. But more often than not, it's just a hot streak.

In salary-cap games, the add/drop moves are precious. For CDM, 16 sounds like a lot, but it's really not. For me, I tend to take a fair number of "FT" injury (and playing time) risks. And guess what? Sure enough, some of these guys get hurt (or lose their job) and I need to replace them. And guys who weren't injury risks also get hurt. And some players unexpectedly emerge and are tremendous values that must be added to your team. And sometimes you must make moves to address specific category needs. In short, stuff happens. And then, more stuff happens. And when you think it can't possibly keep happening—even more stuff happens.

Moves are precious, and should only be used when it's really going to have a lasting positive effect. It's not sufficient to get a new pitcher because he has a nice two-start week coming up. Unless you think this guy is a good value whom you will use a lot, it's a wasted move.

If your team isn't off to a great start, don't panic. You can still catch up. Here's a chart of where some of my CDM teams were in the overall standings on a weekly basis:

Year	Wk 1	2	3	4	5	6	7	8	9	10	Final
2002	973	142	581	598	269	58	42	20	46	63	1
2005	1700	553	136	409	292	580	348	299	59	97	1
2005	1519	815	1141	1742	1133	1068	774	1110	410	915	26
2007	1101	1918	1336	623	686	897	1382	816	998	469	21
2009	3226	2116	1131	1294	1490	752	810	528	501	291	28

As you can see, my team that won in 2002 was #598 overall after the first four weeks, and in 2005 it was number #580 after six weeks. So it's not necessary to get off to an incredible start.

On the other hand, there is such a thing as being *too* patient. If you have a clear need—such as an injured player who won't be back for two months, or an underperforming player who you have reason to believe will continue underperforming—then don't wait. The longer you have wasted roster spots and the longer you run out an inferior lineup, the harder it will be to do well.

Evaluating Players to Add or Drop

At any point in a season, you can reevaluate your projections for a player. I show in chapter 11 how I will revise a player's final year-end stat projections, subtract what he has already done, and then calculate his "*to go*" value—the projected value he should produce for the rest of the season. I use this process to make add and drop decisions. The question isn't "What has the player produced so far?" It is "What is he likely to produce the rest of the way?"

If you take a fresh look at an underperforming player on your squad, make a revised value, and then calculate his "to go" value, you can make a fair determination as to whether you should release the player. Many times you'll determine that even if the player doesn't reach your original expectations, the "to go" value will still be good enough to justify keeping him.

This is also the analysis you should use to choose players for a *second-half contest*.

When adding players, wait until as close to the weekly deadline as possible to make your move, and check the latest news. There's nothing worse that can happen to your team than to add a player on a Saturday or Sunday morning, and then find out he got hurt before the weekly deadline.

Addressing Category Needs

Early in the year, you want to use a starting lineup that will produce the most overall value. As you start to develop category strengths and weaknesses, I suggest that you address your weaknesses only when you can do so without sacrificing virtually any overall value. Once you start sacrificing value, the gains you make in a category that you need will be more than offset by losses in other categories.

As the season goes along, pay increasing attention to your needs. If you're having a hard time addressing needs without sacrificing much value, consider an add/drop move that does so. If there's a good-value player available who addresses your needs and won't hurt your overall value, then add him.

Later in the year, you may get to a point where certain categories are so strong and others so weak that you may actually be justified in sacrificing a bit of overall value. Again, I caution you about this, because you don't want to suddenly be slipping where you thought you were strong.

As with using purchases, there's a fine line between being too patient and too aggressive addressing needs. If you do too much too soon, you can lose overall value and/or unnecessarily use purchases too quickly. If you wait too long, you can reach a point where it's very difficult to make up ground in your weak areas. It's helpful to look at the league (and overall) standings to see what will happen in various categories. If you gained five home runs, how much would that help? If you lost five home runs, how much would that hurt? If you can make up a significant amount of ground with just five or ten homers, and it's still fairly early in the season, there's no reason to panic.

The Low-Percentage Play

People often want to add a player who is not commonly owned. After all, if your player does great and he's only owned by 5% of the other teams, that'll help you a lot more than if he's owned by 80% of your competition. While this is true, the opposite is also true. If he does poorly, he'll hurt you more. Therefore, I suggest you get the best values. Don't worry if most of your roster is also owned by 50% or more of all teams. Little differences can make a big impact.

You may get to a point in a season where your team isn't doing well and you feel like you need to take some low-percentage gambles to have any shot at all. That's understandable, and I can't blame you for doing so in that situation. On the other hand, though, I can tell you that just by assembling the best roster possible, regardless of percentages, you'll be surprised how much ground you can actually make up.

Put Some Clothes On?

I typically like to have a backup at each position. There is the option of going *naked*, which means taking only two catchers, or two first basemen, etc. This can be a good idea if there are two superior players at a position and the next best guy isn't even close to as good a value. Rather than waste a roster spot with someone you'll only ever use in the event of an injury, you can use that spot for a more useful player.

The downside is that injuries do occur. If a player has a long-term injury, you'll need to replace him anyway. But when a player is only going to miss a week or two, it's a blow to have to use one of your precious moves for this. Also, when you are determining that the third-best player at a position is someone you would never use, consider the schedule. If he had a seven-game week and one of the others had a six-game week, would he still not be a good value? Also, how does he compare to your third-best hitters at other positions? In other words, would he sometimes be an option for designated hitter?

If you do go without a backup and one of your starters has a short-term injury where he may miss just a few days, it is okay to leave him in the lineup rather than using a move just to get a replacement for a few days.

I have seen situations where a CDM team will leave in a low-priced injured player or an underperforming player, simply because they want to get their "stud" in the lineup. This is almost always a mistake. If you compare the expected weekly value of the low-priced player and the stud against the value of two alternative players, you'll almost certainly find that the alternative is better.

The Rush to Beat the Crowd

During the 2012 season, Mariano Rivera suffered a season-ending injury. This left David Robertson and Rafael Soriano as the candidates to close. Robertson appeared to have a clear edge, but it was far from certain. At the next weekly deadline four days later, several CDM teams picked up Robertson, not knowing for sure that he was definitely the new closer.

This, to me, was a terrible move. He hadn't been named the closer yet, and while it was likely, the 16 add/drop moves are too precious to use one on a guy who has an 80–90% chance of being the closer. If it turns out Soriano is the closer or they will share the job, you've totally wasted a move. There's no harm in waiting at least one week to see what happens.

CHAPTER 11

In-Season Management

This chapter will discuss how to manage a team during the year. This includes making trades, picking up free agents, and making weekly lineup decisions. The principles are mostly the same for all formats of play. When there is a difference based on type of league, I will point that out.

General Trade Strategy

I don't make trades for the sake of making trades. I only make a trade if it will improve my team.

Some people have a rule that they won't make a trade until two weeks or a month into the season, because they want to see how their team fares. I don't agree with this. If you know you have a need, there's no reason to wait. In fact, waiting can be harmful.

I've seen people who are constantly fishing for great deals. They have no shame constantly sending their league mates low-ball offers, hoping someone might take the bait. Unfortunately, once in a while some not-very-smart owner does take the bait, and this means the fishers will keep fishing forever.

Personally, I hate getting obviously lowball offers. I find it very aggravating to get an email that says, "Larry, I see you need a third baseman. I'll give you my ($4) third baseman and my ($3) outfielder for your ($20) outfielder."

What I have learned is that there is often a great disagreement over player values. As I've mentioned in other chapters, some value formulas put as much as 69% or more of the money into the hitters' pool, while others use only 65% or less. When you consider this, as well as projecting different expected stats for players and using differing value formulas, there can be a very large disagreement over the value of a player. So sometimes people really are intentionally lowballing, but often it's just an honest disagreement over value.

Suppose you and one of your league mates have identical stat projections for a hitter and a pitcher, but you're using a 65/35% split and she's using a 70/30% split:

	70/30%	65/35%
Hitter	$19	$18
Pitcher	$19	$21

If she offers to trade this hitter for your pitcher, you might think you're being offered an $18 hitter for a $21 pitcher, and therefore it's a bad deal. Meanwhile, she thinks it's a fair $19 for

$19 offer. If you really need a hitter for a pitcher, you might want to just accept the offer. Rather than thinking you're losing $3 of value, you can view it as a situation where you can make a legitimate argument that they are both really worth $19. The average value formula uses about a 67/33% split, so if you use 65/35% you'll tend to think others are not valuing your pitchers highly enough.

Just think of all the times two people have argued about someone's value, without realizing one of them is using a 70/30% split and the other a 65/35% split. Maybe I'll win a Nobel Peace Prize for publishing this and reducing the amount of arguing over trades in fantasy baseball.

I don't intentionally lowball. Since I find it aggravating, I don't want to do it to others. And while I don't lowball, I don't necessarily always make my best offer first. Since opinions vary, you never know what someone might agree to, so it certainly makes sense not to start with your best offer.

I don't always follow that advice, though, because I often make offers I think are fair from the beginning and are my best offer. If I'm trying to alter my category strengths—for example, trading a surplus of stolen bases to get more power—then I'm just looking to make a fair trade. If I happen to also gain a slight edge in total value, that's a bonus. But I'm almost as likely to make a deal where I feel I've lost a dollar or two in value, but it was necessary to get a deal done.

Since throughout this entire book I preach value, value, value, that last sentence may have surprised you. The reason is that one of the biggest mistakes you can possibly make is having excess in a category and never trading it. If you have the most home runs by 50 over the next-best team, that is a colossal waste. So there are some situations where I'm okay with sacrificing a little value to get a deal done.

One year I watched another team finish just one point out of first place, and they had 40 more stolen bases than the next best team. The last three months of the year, I kept waiting to see when they would trade one of their speedsters, but they never did. Even if they had to accept a loss of value in a trade for a power hitter or a starting pitcher, they would have won the league.

Consider Competitor's Point of View

I always look to see what another team needs. Some of the stupidest offers I get are when people don't do this. I'll get an offer to receive a power hitter for a stolen-base guy when my team is first in home runs and near the bottom in steals. Couldn't the other person have glanced at the standings to see who might need power and/or have surplus steals?

Similarly, I don't make an offer without checking to see if the position requirements will work. It's another stupid request when I get offered a third baseman for an outfielder and I either don't have a spot for the third baseman and/or would be short an outfielder.

It's usually good to look at the other teams in your league and try to identify specific trade targets. But also you have nothing to lose by sending a mass email to everyone with a general request, such as "I'm looking to trade a starting pitcher for a power hitter." You never know what other people are thinking. Sometimes my opinion is another team has plenty of power, but then they make a trade to get more.

Once in a while I might want to avoid the mass email because I don't want everyone to know what I'm up to, but typically it doesn't matter.

Some leagues do not allow trading. For these leagues, you

need to be extremely careful at the auction or draft to get a balanced team. If you don't, you're screwed, because you can't trade your surplus for your needs.

You always need to evaluate potential trades from the standpoint of what you will gain in the standings. If a trade will allow you to move up three spots in batting average while losing two spots in homers and two spots in RBIs, then this has a net effect of losing a point in the standings. This wouldn't be a good deal.

However, sometimes—especially early in the year—it's difficult to determine exactly what impact a trade will make in the standings. So many things will change—not only for your team but everyone else—that it can be hard to estimate where everyone will finish in every category. Therefore, if you think you're getting more overall value than you're giving up, making the trade is a good idea.

Example of a Trade

In July 2011, I decided that my Tout Wars AL-only team should make a trade. I sent a group email to everyone, stating "Hitter available for a starting pitcher or closer."

I got an encouraging response from Mike Siano. He wrote, "I think we are a fit. I'm interested in Adam Lind or Michael Cuddyer. Have Ricky Romero, Gio Gonzalez, and Ervin Santana."

This definitely was a good starting point. I calculated the current pace values of these players. What I mean by *current pace value* is based on what the player has actually produced so far, what would his value be if you extrapolate that over a full season?

Cuddyer was at $23.1 and Lind was at $28. (I adjusted Lind's value to reflect that he had missed about 20 games on the DL.) Gio Gonzalez was at $27.8, Romero $23.6, and Santana $15.

Based on these figures, Lind for Gonzalez would be a fair trade, and so would Cuddyer for Romero. However, it's not just a question of what has the player done so far, but—more important— what will he do the rest of the year?

To answer this question, I took a look at my original projections, the current actual pace of each player, their past history, and then estimated where I thought they would end up for the year.

Michael Cuddyer	$ Value	AB	AVG	RUN	HR	RBI	SB
Original Projection	17.5	550	.271	83	17	79	6
Actual pace as of July 15	23.1	565	.296	76	23	77	13
Projected Finish	20.0	560	.280	76	21	77	10

Cuddyer had 588 and 609 at bats in 2009 and 2010, respectively. I had originally projected him for only 550 this year because I thought he would be facing more competition for playing time. His at bats had decreased, but not quite as much as I had expected. So I now projected his final total for 560, almost as much as his current pace, but figured maybe he'd get an extra day or two off during the dog days of summer.

He had hit .276 and .271 in 2009 and 2010, and had only hit above .280 once in his career, back in 2006, when he hit .284. So his current .296 average seemed very likely to regress toward his norm. I put him down for .280.

Cuddyer hits in the middle of the order, and he scored 93 runs in both 2009 and 2010. If you adjust those years downward to reflect only 560 at bats, that would mean 87 runs scored. Therefore, his current pace of 76 seemed a little low. I'd expect it to probably rise by the end of the year, except that since I was expecting his average to tail off some—and therefore his opportunities to be on base would tail off—I kept him at 76.

His power situation was a bit odd. He hit 32 home runs in 2009 and only 14 in 2010. The difference was that in 2010 the Twins moved to Target Field, which was terrible for hitting home runs, and in 2010 Cuddyer played most of the year with a bad knee. So my projection of his hitting 17 this year was mostly a guess, and it was on the conservative side. They had moved the fences in a little this year at Target Field, and Cuddyer's knee was healthy, so it wasn't a big surprise he was on a 23-homer pace. I projected he'd tail off just a bit and finish with 21.

Since he had a better-than-expected average and home runs, his RBI total so far seemed a bit low. As with runs, I might expect them to rise, but since I was also projecting the average and homers to tail off, I kept him at 77 RBIs. He had never stolen more than seven bases in a year for his entire career, but he already had seven this year. I assumed he'd most likely tail off and estimated a final total of ten.

Based on those stats, I projected him to finish with a value of $20. So if Cuddyer had produced $23.1 for the first 90 games and was going to end up at $20, I can calculate what value he will produce for the rest of the year:

$$3,240 \ (\$20 \times 162)$$
$$\underline{- \ 2,079 \ (\$23.1 \times 90)}$$
$$1,161$$

1,161 divided by 72 games remaining = $16.1

My intuition has a hard time accepting that a player who so far is worth $23 will only produce $16 the rest of the season, and if an auction were being held today, undoubtedly someone would pay $20 or more to buy Cuddyer. However, I believe in the law of averages, and there's no compelling reason to think Cuddyer will finish the year at .296 with 23 homers and 13 steals. If my projections are a little too conservative, perhaps he'll end up being worth $17–18 the rest of the way, but I definitely wouldn't bank on $20 or more.

I call the $16.1 figure his *to go* projection. This means the worth of the player for the remaining games to be played, or the rest of the season that's still "to go." (By the way, this is how I suggest you evaluate players if you play a second-half league that starts around the All-Star break. Also, you'll note this is another reason you should use your own value formula. Without your own formula, you'd have to just guess at all of this.)

I went through the same process for the other players and arrived at the following:

Adam Lind		$ Value	AB	AVG	RUN	HR	RBI	SB
Original Projection		17.8	545	.270	72	26	85	0
Actual pace as of July 15		28.0	583	.293	82	39	117	2
Projected Finish		23.9	580	.280	79	33	104	2
"To Go"	18.5							

Gio Gonzalez		$ Value	IP	ERA	WHIP	Win	K
Original Projection		16.5	200	3.75	1.35	12.5	170
Actual pace as of July 15		27.8	201	2.47	1.27	14.2	198
Projected Finish		23.5	200	3.05	1.30	14.0	190
"To Go"	18.0						

Ricky Romero		$ Value	IP	ERA	WHIP	Win	K
Original Projection		17.6	210	3.90	1.31	13.5	170
Actual pace as of July 15		23.5	217	3.09	1.23	12.4	180
Projected Finish		20.5	215	3.55	1.28	13.5	176
"To Go"	16.6						

For starting pitchers, I consider a full season 32 starts. Gonzalez and Romero had already made 18 starts, so I calculated the "to go" value based on their having 14 more starts remaining. (Some top starters get 33 starts, but it wouldn't make any meaningful difference here.)

All of the players I was looking at were over-achieving so far and probably due for a decline. It was possible that any or all of them could continue at their current pace, but I was trying to make my best guess. My objective was to trade a hitter for a starter and to have it be a reasonably fair swap.

Cuddyer had a "to go" value of $16.1, Lind $18.5, Gonzalez $18, and Romero $16.6. Based on this, if I could trade Cuddyer for either pitcher, it would be a good deal. Trading Lind for Gonzalez would be acceptable as well.

I sent Siano an email: "I would do Cuddyer for Gio or Romero."

I could have offered Cuddyer only for Gonzalez, and then reduced my request to Romero if necessary, but I decided not to play hardball to that extent. I assumed Siano would probably want Gonzalez a little more than Romero, and I was happy to take either one for Cuddyer. And I was holding back my best offer, which would be Lind for Gonzalez.

His reply was, "Larry, I'm leaning toward Romero and Morel for Cuddyer and Niemann. Is that a deal you may be willing to make?"

This was a disappointing response. He was making it complicated, and this was a sign that he may have thought Cuddyer wasn't worth as much as Romero. It could be argued that Brent Morel (third baseman for the White Sox) was pretty close to Jeff Niemann (starting pitcher for Tampa Bay) in value, but in my opinion Niemann was worth more, and Morel was currently in danger of losing playing time. So perhaps he thought Cuddyer wasn't a fair offer for Romero, or perhaps he was scared Morel was in danger of losing at bats and was hoping I'd take him, or maybe he was actually willing to trade Romero for Cuddyer and just fishing to see if he could get more.

In any event, adding Morel for Niemann, or any similar options, was completely out of the question. My main objective in making this trade was that I was trying to avoid a pending situation where I'd have to put a valuable hitter on my bench, wasting his value. Getting Morel, or any other hitter, would defeat the purpose.

I replied to Siano with a simple "I wouldn't do that."

He replied, "Replace Niemann with Fister or Vargas?"

He was hoping, or assuming, I would value starting pitchers Doug Fister or Jason Vargas less than Niemann, which wasn't necessarily the case. And, in any event, it was irrelevant. I realized I'd better explain myself to him or else we'd continue going down the wrong path.

I replied, "I want to trade a hitter and get a pitcher. I don't want to also trade an SP, and I don't want another hitter. I think Romero and Cuddyer are pretty even. I could add Frasor, Sipp, or Takahashi if you want."

I was expecting to get a player back from the DL in a week or two, at which point I'd need to release someone. If I added Romero, having two relief pitchers on my bench would be plenty, so I'd release Jason Frasor, Tony Sipp, or Hisanori Takahashi— who are all relief pitchers anyway. Offering one of them now wasn't a big deal. If it was a small carrot that would help Siano make a deal, it was well worth it.

He replied, "Romero for Cuddyer and Takahashi is a deal."

The Perfect Trade Analysis

To do a perfect analysis of every trade you ever consider making, this is what you should do:

1. Analyze each player being discussed, and using every piece of information at your disposal, make your best guess at projecting what stats the player will end the year with. Take that value, and subtract the actual value he's already produced year-to-date to arrive at the "to go" value. If you think the trade is fair or to your advantage, based on the "to go" values, proceed to the next steps in order to see what effect the trade will have on your projected finish.

2. Calculate the current "to go" stats for every other player on your roster. Add these stats to the actual stats your team has already accumulated to date to give you projected final stats in all categories.

3. Calculate the current "to go" stats for every player on every team in your league. Add these stats to the actual

stats already accumulated by each team to arrive at projected final stats for all teams in your league.

4. See where your team will finish in the projected standings, based on these new team projected stats.

5. Change the projected stats for your team, and the team you would be trading with, based on the players that would be traded between the two of you.

6. See where your team will finish in the projected standings if these players are traded. If your projected finish is better with the trade, make the deal. Otherwise, don't make the deal.

7. Explain to your wife, boss, and dog why they haven't seen you for the past 96 hours.

Obviously, nobody has the time to do what I've outlined above. But it does describe the perfect way to analyze a trade. In actual practice, you do want to do as much of this as you can in a relatively easy, timely manner. When you make a trade, and you know you're going to gain something in certain categories, you need to try to estimate exactly how much you will gain. And you need to estimate how much you will lose in other categories.

The Gutsiest Trade I Ever Made

In late August 2011, I was leading the AL Tout Wars when Jon Rauch had an emergency appendectomy. Not that I was glad for Rauch's pain, but this was good news for me because I owned

Frank Francisco, and he would now be the closer for the Blue Jays for at least three weeks and probably the rest of the season.

Unfortunately, I already had a glut of pitching, and this gave me more. I now had four closers and seven pretty good starters, with just nine available spots in my starting lineup. Meanwhile, I had a few offensive holes. So I desperately wanted to trade a pitcher for a useful hitter, because it did me no good having useful pitchers on the bench, and I needed a hitter.

I tried like heck to make a trade. I couldn't find anyone willing to give me a hitter for either of the two pitchers I was mostly trying to deal, Jason Vargas and Trevor Cahill. Even offering someone better didn't help.

After the weekly trade deadline passed, on Sunday, August 29, I was up against the yearly trade deadline, which was August 31. After this, no trades were allowed. I kept trying to swing a deal, but had pretty much exhausted all possibilities by the afternoon of the 31st. I took another look at the possibility of offering one of my better pitchers in a trade. At this late date, besides considering a pitcher's value—or "to go" value—you should also consider his remaining schedule.

I noticed something very interesting about Ricky Romero. After this week, he had just one start for the next two weeks, both times against the Red Sox. The next week he would have two starts, home against the Angels and at Tampa Bay. The following week, which was just a three-day week to close the season, he wouldn't pitch. What was so interesting to me about this was that Romero had historically been horrendous against the Red Sox. Ordinarily, I would never dream of benching a pitcher of Romero's caliber, even with the worst possible matchup. But he had been torched so badly by Boston that it was something to consider. In 2009, he pitched against Boston five times, with a

7.66 ERA and 2.28 WHIP. In four starts during 2010, he had a 7.17 ERA and 1.78 WHIP. So far in 2011, he had made two starts with a 12.38 ERA and 3.12 WHIP. These numbers were almost beyond belief.

Since my team was in first place, there was no reason to risk him getting shellacked again, especially since I was vulnerable in ERA and WHIP. So I realized that I would have to bench Romero for the next two weeks, and the final week he wasn't pitching. That meant that I'd only use him again for one week. With two starts, he would be a really valuable pitcher for that week, but still, I'd only use him once, which meant he was a lot less valuable to me right now than he ordinarily would be.

Since I had acquired him from Mike Siano, he had been terrific, and his current season's pace value was up to $30. For the month of August, he had five wins, a 2.05 ERA and 0.91 WHIP. The thought of benching him seemed absurd, but I couldn't ignore those numbers against Boston.

However, trading him was a great idea. Most people would see the name "Ricky Romero" and just think of an extremely valuable pitcher. They wouldn't consider his remaining schedule. I offered him to Matthew Berry for Ichiro, and I made a couple of similar offers, to no avail.

I noticed that Ron Shandler had Alex Rios on his bench. Rios was an odd case. I originally projected him as a $27 value, and he'd been abysmal. He was currently hitting .214 and on pace for just 63 runs, 10 homers, 40 RBIs, and 12 steals: a $5.8 value. He was possibly the biggest fantasy disaster of the year. I took a look at his game log and noticed he was showing a few signs of life lately. Surely, I could get him for Ricky Romero, especially since Ron wasn't even using him. But surely I could get someone better than Rios for Romero, couldn't I? Well, with time running out, and my having exhausted other possibilities, maybe not.

So Rios it was. I was about to offer a pitcher currently worth $30 for a hitter currently worth $6.

As I wrote the email to Ron, I kept asking myself if I was crazy. I thought, "I'm really making this offer? . . . I can't do better than this? . . . I'll ask him to throw in $3 FAAB . . . What the heck, make it $5 FAAB." (FAAB is free-agent bidding money, explained in the "Free-Agent Strategy" section just below.)

Ron must have been shocked to get the offer. He replied, "Not sure what you're up to, but it's tough to turn this down. Romero for Rios and $5 FAAB is a deal."

In Case You're Wondering How It Turned Out

Surprisingly, or perhaps I should say *not surprisingly*, Romero turned in two fine games against the Red Sox. He pitched 14 2/3 innings, with a 3.68 ERA, 1.02 WHIP, two wins, and 11 strikeouts. I could say that trading him was a mistake, but had I not traded him, I would have benched him for both games anyway. (The following week he pitched two brilliant games. He didn't get a win, but he allowed just three earned runs and 14 hits and walks in 17 innings.)

It wasn't a total loss, though, because Rios did, in fact, heat up. For my team, he went 19 for 68, a .279 average, with 12 runs, 5 homers, 10 RBIs, and one steal. That translates to a year-long pace of $21.

And it all ended up just fine, because I won the league. And at least I got that $5 FAAB from Ron. I would've made the trade straight up.

Free-Agent Strategy

Most competitive leagues use a system of blind bidding to acquire free agents. FAAB stands for Free Agent Acquisition Budget. Typically each team has a budget, such as $100 or $1,000, for the season. Each week teams submit a secret bid on any player(s) they want. The player is awarded to the highest bidder. (Ties are usually awarded to the team currently lowest in the standings.) The amount of the winning bid is deducted from the winning team's remaining budget.

One common question people have is should you spend your money early and often, or wait for something really good to come along?

This is one area where there's a big difference between a mono-league and a mixed league. When a player is traded from the AL to the NL, or vice versa, it has no effect for a mixed league. But under most mono-league rules, he is now a free agent in his new league. After the auction or draft, pretty much every player worth even a dollar is already taken in a mono-league, so the free-agent pool contains mostly worthless players. If a $5, $10, or $20 player gets traded from the AL to the NL, suddenly you have someone with real value available. Each year, there are typically at least a few worthwhile players who change leagues. Mostly this occurs near the MLB trade deadline in July.

Other than trades to a new league, players with much value in the free-agent pool are few and far between. Sometimes a bench player will find a full-time role due to injury, or a setup man will become a closer due to injury, or a top prospect will get promoted to the big leagues, but mostly these players are already owned in a mono-league.

So the question is, should you hoard your FAAB money for

those rare opportunities when someone terrific is available, or should you spend more liberally early on?

My opinion is that it all depends on the circumstances as the year unfolds. If I have needs early, I'll spend as much as I need to. If it works out that I can save my money, that's a bonus.

The goal for someone to save their money is they hope to be in contention for the league title, and then before the trade deadline, a star player worth $20 or more is traded to their league. With the most FAAB, they buy the star player and he puts them over the top for the league championship. This is a nice fantasy, and this can happen. But if you ignore needs early, you probably won't be in contention for the title. The star player will put you over the top . . . to finish seventh instead of ninth.

Also, it is almost certain that at least a $10 or $15 player will get traded at some point to your league, but there's no guarantee any $20 and above player will be. And unless you spend literally none of your FAAB money, there's no guarantee that you'll have the most money available. If you have the third most money at the trade deadline, you may end up only being able to get a $5 player, if that.

Another factor to consider is that most interleague trades take place close to the trade deadline. After you buy a free agent who just got traded, you will reap the benefits for the last eight or nine weeks of the season. This means that if you get a player worth $10 for approximately 33% of the season, you're essentially gaining $3.33. If by hoarding your money you passed on a chance to get a $6 player on May 1, you gave up $6 of value for approximately 5/6 of the season, which would have netted you $5 of value.

You also need to find a good fit for your roster. Suppose you have the most FAAB money at the trade deadline and the best player available is a $22 first baseman. You already have a first baseman worth $20, a corner infielder worth $12, and a designated hitter worth $10. This means that to make room for the new player, you have to bench (or release) the $10 hitter, so you're only gaining $12. Ideally you would then trade one of these hitters before your league's next transaction deadline. But you may not get a fair trade, and you will have lost a week, so you still don't get the full $22 gain from the free agent.

Another possibility is that the only really valuable free agent is a pitcher and you are already dominating pitching, or a slugger and you are already leading in home runs and RBIs. In this case, you would acquire the free agent and then try to make a trade. You have to hope you can make a fair trade, and you lose at least a week before you get help in the categories you need.

So, bottom line, it's very nice to be approaching the trade deadline and have the most—or close to the most—FAAB money in your league, but it's not worth passing up other opportunities and/or filling needs that arise between opening day and the trade deadline.

Mixed-League FAAB

In a mixed league, interleague trades are irrelevant. Thus, the only relevance of the major league trade deadline is if, for example, a team trades its closer and appoints a new closer. This new closer would be very valuable. Similarly, if a full-time hitter gets traded, a bench player or minor leaguer might take his spot and suddenly have value.

In a mono-league, if either of the above occur, it's quite likely the player getting promoted to a more valuable role will already be owned in your league. But in a mixed league, it's quite likely he won't be. In a typical 12- or 15-team mixed league, all major league closers and co-closers will be owned, but not all of the good setup men will be owned.

If a bench player or minor leaguer suddenly has a full-time role, he becomes very valuable for a mono-league, but not necessarily for a mixed league. The talent pool is so abundant in mixed leagues that most teams will have hitters at every position (except catcher) worth at least $7 or more for a 15-team league and probably $10 or more for a 12-team league. So the new full-time hitter may not be worth more than what everybody already has. The same is true when a pitcher is promoted from the bullpen or minor leagues to the starting rotation. He probably won't be worth more than what everyone already owns.

So for a mixed league, there's little reason to hoard your money. When players get traded, injured, called up from AAA, etc., it rarely leads to a tremendous value being available. The only real exception is with closers. Due to injuries, trades, and sometimes ineffectiveness, there will probably be a few opportunities to get a closer during the year. When a closer gets traded, it's usually preceded by rumors and speculation, so the top setup man for that team is probably going to be bought when the rumors and speculation begin. If you need a closer or just want to take a shot to gain a bonanza, go ahead and be the team that buys the setup man when the speculation starts.

For a mixed league, I typically like to have seven starting pitchers and two closers in my lineup. This ratio makes me strong in wins and strikeouts. If it's a 15-team mixed league, every team has an average of two closers, which makes me competitive. If it's a 12-team league, everyone has an average of 2.5 closers. For these leagues, I'll go for the more expensive and reliable closers—who get more than the average number of saves—so that I can be competitive in saves even though several teams have three clos-ers. And as I just said, I know there will probably be a few chances to FAAB a closer, especially in a 12-team league.

Is Pitching Always Available?

Some people say that you can always find pitching on the waiver wire, but it's more difficult to find hitting. I see no evidence of this. All I see is anecdotes about the wonderful pitchers, such as R. A. Dickey, who went undrafted in some mixed leagues in 2012 and ended up winning the Cy Young award. But for every R. A. Dickey, my guess is there are five to ten pitchers who got off to a hot start, were picked up on FAAB, and then struggled the rest of the year. And, again, for every hotshot who gets called up from AAA and picked up on FAAB, I'd guess there are five to ten times as many who are mediocre or bad than good.

This depends a lot on your definition of "useful." If it means you can get a pitcher who will start games and get some strikeouts and occasional wins—albeit with a mediocre ERA and WHIP—then yes, I would agree you can usually find a pitcher like that, especially in a 10- or 12-team mixed league (as opposed to 15 or more teams). And you can try to acquire a *useful* pitcher who has a two-start week or has an apparent good matchup.

But overall, every team has drafted nine pitchers plus another three or so for their reserve squad. Let's say that encompasses all pitchers with a value of $8 or more. Now the waiver wire is full of pitchers worth $7 and less. The same goes for hitters. If all the $10 and up hitters are drafted, the free-agent pool has hitters worth $9 and less. So both free-agent pools are full of guys worth $1 (or more) less than those already on your roster. There is no surplus of pitching talent available.

If there are a few free-agent pitchers in 2014 that turn out to be a huge coup, how do you guarantee that you'll be one of the lucky teams who actually got one of them? Unless you're very sharp or, better yet, clairvoyant, it's more likely you'll get stuck with one of the guys who quickly came back to earth after his hot start. Even if you only want to pick up a useful mediocre pitcher for a week or two, because he has a nice schedule, you will have competition. You have to be the highest bidder.

In 2013, Jose Fernandez of the Marlins had a great spring and then pitched two nice games to start the year. There was lots of hype about him, even though he hadn't previously pitched above A ball. In many leagues, people spent big money to FAAB him. His next three starts, he only lasted a total of 13 innings and gave up 11 earned runs. Not only was this a horrendous result for his owners, but now they're in a quandary. Do they continue to start him or put him on the bench?

So I would never alter my auction or draft strategy based on the idea that during the season it will be easier to acquire good pitchers than hitters. It sometimes can be effective to frequently acquire a pitcher who has two starts or a good matchup and then drop him the following week, but that's different than the notion that there's an abundance of pitching talent available during the year.

How Much to Bid?

What you bid on a free agent is not the same as what you would pay for him at an auction. In a mono-league, if a $5 player is available, there are going to be several teams that could use that $5 player to replace someone worth only a buck or two. And there won't be many chances during the year to upgrade a $1–2 player for a $5 (or more) player. Therefore, he is worth much more than $5.

How much more, and how much to bid, is a subject for great debate. It depends partly on factors such as will this player be worth $5 for just a few weeks while replacing someone on the DL, or is he going to be worth $5 for the rest of the season? For your team, would you be replacing someone worth $1 or someone worth $3? Does he help you in categories you need? Depending on the answers to those questions, I would probably bid anywhere from $3–25 of my $100 FAAB budget.

Some FAAB bids are fairly easy. Suppose your middle infielder goes on the DL and should be back in a few weeks, so you need a temporary replacement. Let's say the three best possible replacements are worth $0.6, $0.4, and $0.3. There's a very small difference in value (you only need the guy for a few weeks) and most likely no other teams will be looking for a crappy middle infielder, so you can safely bid $1. You will most likely get the $0.6 player, and if you don't, you're not going to lose sleep over it.

It's a good idea to be aware of other injuries (or demotions to AAA) that have occurred in major league baseball, so you know if any of your competitors may also be looking for a crappy middle infielder. If there had been a couple of other injuries, and you know that the teams in your league who own those players don't have anyone on the bench to replace them, perhaps you might want to bid $2.

Another obvious situation would be if it's the first week of the season, and in a huge surprise, a $30 outfielder is traded from the AL to the NL. You have an NL-only team with a $1 player in your outfield. You can replace a $1 player with a $30 player, and you get him for the entire season. This is the most value you could ever possibly pick up during this season and probably in your entire lifetime of playing fantasy baseball! You should probably bid your entire $100.

I say "probably" because I don't like the idea of having to play the rest of the season without being able to ever pick up anybody. If injuries strike and I don't have a backup, I might have a hole in my roster. But replacing a $1 hitter with a $30 hitter should more than adequately compensate for that hole. I could bid $97 or $98 or $99 and try to save myself a future move or two, but somebody is almost certainly going to bid their entire $100, so I'd be out of luck.

So while there are some fairly easy decisions, much of FAAB bidding is difficult. You can bid $20 on a player, and when the next highest bid is only $3, you feel like an idiot, and you've wasted $16. On the other hand, if you bid $20, and someone else bid $22, you probably hate that you didn't get the player you wanted. And had you known, you would have gladly bid $23.

So it's constantly a question of guessing how much a player will go for. You want to bid enough to get the player, but you don't want to needlessly waste money. It's not at all an exact science. It's mostly a crapshoot that is guaranteed to piss you off a few times during the season.

There are situations where you don't care so much if you get the player. You might think, "If I can get him for $5, I'll take him . . . if not, I don't care."

So when deciding how much to bid, I always ask myself how much I care. If I really need the player and I'm going to be pissed if I miss him by a little bit, I'll usually bid higher than what I think I need to.

In a mixed league, how much to bid is determined in the same fashion. You are considering the free agents' value above replacement. In other words, if every team in your league has outfielders worth at least $8, then a free agent worth $9 isn't very valuable. A free agent worth $20 is extremely valuable.

Some people try to track what others tend to bid in their leagues. For example, if you notice a lot of people always bidding no more than $7 or $8, you might want to bid $9.

Pre-FAAB Maneuvering

I mentioned earlier that in July 2011, I decided that my Tout Wars team should trade a hitter for a pitcher. This wasn't actually because I had excess hitting and needed pitching but instead was FAAB maneuvering.

I don't plan to hoard my FAAB money, but as it turned out, we got to mid-July and I did have more FAAB than anyone else. So with the MLB trade deadline just two weeks away, at this point I *was* going to save my money and make sure I remained #1.

The two biggest NL players rumored to be on the trading block were Jose Reyes (SS) and Carlos Beltran (OF). Both were worth more than $20. All three of my middle infielders had been producing $7 or more so far. So getting Reyes would be great, but I'd have to bench a $7 player, and then try to work out a trade. If Beltran was the big FAAB prize, I'd have to bench someone worth more than $10. I had room for a pitcher, but based on the rumors it was much more likely the best player traded to the AL would be a hitter.

So in advance of my coming big FAAB acquisition, I wanted to clear a spot for whomever it was going to be. The ideal scenario would be to free up my designated-hitter slot. That way, I could FAAB the best hitter, regardless of position. (I had so many players eligible at multiple positions that if I traded any hitter, except a catcher, that would free up my designated-hitter slot.)

When Do You Give Up on a Player?

This is a very difficult question, and there's no clear answer. I always believe in the law of averages—what goes up must come down—and what goes down must come up. If I projected a player to hit .285 with 20 home runs, and on July 1 he's at .240 with three home runs, I'm expecting a big second half. He may not reach the .285 and 20, but I'm guessing it's more likely he'll have a good second half and get closer to my original projection than it is likely he'll keep hitting .240 with just another three home runs in the second half.

But rather than having complete blind faith in the law of averages, I look to see if there are any apparent reasons for the struggles. An injury is the obvious first thing to consider. If the player is known to be hurt, that may explain everything, and unless he recovers physically, he may well continue to struggle. Unfortunately, more than one player has been known to struggle and not admit to an injury until after the season. It's maddening to own a player, stick with him thinking he'll turn it around, and then after the season he admits he was hurt the whole time.

Aside from injuries, you can look at a player's BABIP (batting average on balls in play) to see if bad luck may be a factor. You can look to see if he has a history of doing poorly in the first half. You can consider if he's on a new team and is having trouble adjusting . . . maybe the team's lineup is worse than expected . . . maybe the team moved the fences out ten feet from the year before, and it's having a bigger negative effect than you had originally estimated . . . maybe Mars is in retrograde . . . and anything else you can think of.

When judging the chances a player will turn it around, I'll also take a look at my original projections: Were they reasonable? Did I miss something? Does this player have a long, solid track record that made my projection fairly safe? Or is this a player without much of a track record and I was guessing to a great extent?

When a player is underperforming, you usually have the option of benching him, rather than giving up completely and releasing him. If the underperforming hitter was originally projected at $12 and so far is only producing at a $3 level, and the best replacement you can come up with is worth $2, then you have to stick with the player. If you can replace him with a $6 value, it might be a good idea to bench him for the time being. However, that's always a risk. Players can turn it around in a day. If I think a player is going to snap out of it sooner or later, I'll typically stick with him. It can drive you crazy trying to determine when someone has snapped out of a slump. You bench him and he has a good week . . . so you start him again and he has a bad week. It can be infuriating.

Exploring the trade market is always a possibility. But at what level do you trade? It's doubtful you'll get back $12 in value, but you certainly want more than $3; otherwise, you might as well just stick with the player and hope he improves. It's going to depend on how confident you are the player will improve—perhaps I should say how panicked you are that he won't improve—and what offer you can get in a trade. It also depends on where you're at in the standings. If you're in first place, you might be happy to get a $7 player in return and not risk continued disappointment. If you're in eighth place, you should probably stick with the player and hope he does have a hot second half.

If a projected $12 player produced only $3 during the first half but does better in the second half and ends the year with an $8 value, then his second-half value would have been $13. If you gave up on him, it would have been a mistake.

On the contrary, when a player starts out very hot, he's due to cool off. If your projected $12 hitter produces at a $25 pace for the first half, it can be very easy to talk yourself into why he's reached a new level and surely will keep it up for the rest of the season. But if there aren't concrete, solid reasons for this surge, he's almost certainly going to cool off. He'll probably finish above the original $12 mark, but even that can make for a rocky second half. If he ends up at $17 for the year, that would have been a $9 second half. If you could have "sold high" in a trade you'd have been better off.

One of the lowlights of my 2011 Tout Wars team was the first two months of John Danks. By the end of May, he had made 11 starts. Projecting these to a full season of 32 starts, we see the pace he was on:

John Danks	$ Value	IP	ERA	WHIP	Win	K
Original Projection	19.6	210	3.75	1.24	14	158
Actual pace as of May 31	–7.5	204	5.25	1.51	0	134

A guy who was supposed to be worth almost $20 was producing negative $7.5. It doesn't get any worse than that. I would have been better off if he'd been on the DL and I'd had to use someone else. Unfortunately, I had kept him in my starting lineup all year. He actually didn't pitch that badly in April, with a 3.92 ERA and 1.33 WHIP. His disastrous month of May—a 6.89 ERA and 1.72 WHIP—included a couple of starts that were decent. Unless you have very good psychic abilities, it's just not a good idea to bench your struggling $19.6 starter in a mono-league. In a mixed league, it's a reasonable thing to consider, because you have much better options than a $1–3 pitcher to bring off the bench.

There was no apparent injury or reason for Danks's struggles. His zero wins were due, in part, to a lack of run support in the games in which he had pitched fairly well. So there was nothing I could do but hope he'd turn it around. After such an awful two months, it was unlikely that he would reach my original projections. Still though, unless it turned out he was hurt, it was very likely he would improve and get closer to the original projections. If I tried to take a guess on June 1 where I thought he would end the year, it would look something like this:

John Danks	$ Value	IP	ERA	WHIP	Win	K
Hypothetical finish #1	7.3	207	4.50	1.38	9	145
Hypothetical finish #2	11.5	207	4.20	1.32	10	150

#1 is a little more conservative and #2 a bit more optimistic. If he did accomplish #1, that would mean his value for the last two-thirds of the season would be $14.7. That's still below my $19.6 expectation, but at least he'd be a valuable pitcher for the rest of the year. With finish #2, his value for the last two-thirds would be $21.

The biggest problem here is that you just never know when a slump will end and someone will turn it around. After his winless April, I expected Danks would get a couple of wins soon. I never dreamt his May would be so awful. And after his awful May, just when I had to start seriously thinking about benching him—and I would have in a mixed league—he suddenly pitched fantastically out of nowhere! He threw a seven-inning shutout and got his first win of the year. Then he gave up just two runs in eight innings and one run in seven innings, to make it three straight wins. He finished the year having produced $8 value.

The point is, you just never know. You can have a hitter in the best hot streak of his life, and the next day he can start a 3–35 stretch.

Weekly Lineup Decisions

In a mono-league, the vast majority of decisions are easy. The players on your bench are mostly worth so little that you're not going to consider replacing one of your starters for them. In a mixed league, you usually have a few close calls to make.

In mono-leagues, sometimes people will keep an injured player in their lineup rather than replace him with someone they perceive will do more harm than good. And if a player's dollar value is negative, that would appear to be the case. However, even most players with a negative dollar value actually make a positive contribution toward gaining points in the standings, so you're better off using them. (This is explained in chapter 6.)

Personally I don't like trying to time hot and cold streaks. As I just said, you never know when a player will suddenly turn around a bad streak or end a good streak. Trying to time this is like day trading stocks. You might get lucky or unlucky. I've never done an analysis of all players' weekly performances, but I suspect you would just find a lot of ups and downs, without much rhyme or reason. Sure, sometimes a player will have an extended hot or cold streak, but mostly the streaks are short and change quickly and without advance notice.

Having just said that, I'm going to contradict myself and say that there are times when a player is obviously struggling and it's probably best to bench him until he figures it out. If someone's mechanics or timing are out of whack, they usually don't just get it back the next day. But again, I could give you a million examples where this approach has backfired. Carlos Gomez began the first two weeks of 2013 hitting 6–37, a .162 average. I then benched him on my CDM teams and he went 11–18 the next week.

As always, you want to get the most value possible. Suppose you're in a salary-cap game, and you have Brandon Phillips valued at 305 and Neil Walker at 284. They have identical salaries, therefore Phillips is the best choice. However, what if Walker is playing seven games and Phillips only six? In that case, Walker's relative value is $7/6 \times 284 = 331$ and he is a better choice than Phillips.

I'm assuming here that Walker will play every game. There's always a chance he'll get a day off, especially in the dog days of summer, so to be more precise you might want to multiply his games by 6.5 or 6.7 or so.

Some people might also take into account what parks Phillips and Walker are playing in and which pitchers they are facing. I usually don't get that complex, unless it's something obvious, such as playing at Coors Field. This doesn't mean I automatically play a hitter just because he'll be at Coors or bench him because he'll be in San Diego. To be precise, you need to project the stats you think the hitter will produce, and the resulting value. For example, my 305 value for Phillips might be lowered to 270 for a week he's playing half his games in San Diego.

Catchers are a little tricky. If they have seven games scheduled, they almost certainly won't catch seven days in a row. For National League catchers, you can assume they'll only play six. For the American League, some of them may still play seven by being used at designated hitter. So you need to try to project this as best you can. Also, keep in mind that for most catchers, all these days off were counted in their original projection. Unlike full-time position players, who will get 550–600 at bats, a full-time catcher would typically be projected for only 475–500 at bats (possibly 525–550 if he'll also be a designated hitter).

Early in the season, I do consider weather. A team may be scheduled for six games but the weather forecast so threatening that a rainout or two is quite possible. The colder weather is also bad for hitters; a guy who typically hits .300 with 25 homers might be a .285 hitter with 18 homers if he always played in 50-degree weather.

For pitchers, taking into account their matchups is, obviously, much more important. Some choices are easy. If a pitcher is a close call with several other pitchers, and he's got one start at Coors Field or at Texas, then bench him. If he's got one start at a good pitchers' park against a weak hitting team, then start him.

I don't think I'm saying anything brilliant here. This is all pretty obvious. My only possible words of wisdom would be to advise you not to overthink and overanalyze matchups. I know some fantasy players who go crazy looking at home and away splits, pitchers' historical records against other teams, etc.

The ideal way to make a weekly lineup decision is to consider the likelihood of all possible outcomes, create projected stats, and convert that to a value.

You could take a lot of time each week analyzing all the pitching matchups and home and away splits, and driving yourself crazy coming up with an exact figure, or you could make this process a little quicker. Here are a few examples . . .

No Designated Hitters at National League Parks

You own David Ortiz, and he's on pace for a $20 season. Ordinarily you wouldn't have to think about possibly benching him, but the Red Sox are going to be playing six games at National League parks, where there will be no designated hitter. The manager has stated that Ortiz will only start one game in each series.

You calculate that if he starts two games, he'll probably get eight at bats. Most likely, he'll get to pinch-hit a couple of times as well. So you take his current pace, but adjust it downward to reflect only ten at bats for a week (which would be approximately 260 for the year).

David Ortiz	$ Value	AB	AVG	RUN	HR	RBI	SB
Current Pace	20.0	520	.285	74	26	92	0
Projected Week	7.7	260	.285	37	13	46	0

For this week his projected value is $7.7. It's interesting to note that the way value formulas work, if a player gets half the playing time and stats, it doesn't mean his value will be cut in half. In this case, his value is less than half. If we want to get more complicated, we can consider how he hits on the road, what ballparks he'll be at, what pitchers he's likely to face, etc., and can further adjust the projections based on all of that. But we'll keep it simple, and just give him the $7.7 projection. If you're in an AL-only league, you're unlikely to have a better replacement. If you're in a mixed league, you might.

Bad Pitching Matchup

You own Jeff Niemann, worth $10.8, and he's at home against the Tigers, which is fine . . . but he's facing Justin Verlander, who's been on a hot streak for the last month. You are concerned it will be tough for Niemann to get a win. You can't just write off Niemann, because there is still a chance he'll get a win, plus he contributes in other categories. You have to ask yourself, "If every game this season Niemann was at home facing a hot Verlander, how many wins would he get?" Make your best guess and plug that number into your value formula and see what you get. For example:

Jeff Niemann	$ Value	IP	ERA	WHIP	Win	K
Current Pace	10.8	175	4.25	1.31	11	128
Vs Hot Verlander	6.9	175	4.25	1.31	6	128

In this case, your guess was six wins, leaving Niemann with a $6.9 projected value for the week. Again, if you're in an AL-only league, you probably don't have a better option. If you're in a mixed league, you might.

If you think Niemann tends to pitch better at home than on the road, you could also adjust his ERA and WHIP downward, and perhaps his IP and strikeouts upward. You can also take into account how good a hitting team Detroit has.

Pitching at Coors Field

You bought Mike Minor, projected for $13, as one of your mixed-league starters. You also have Wade Davis, $7.2, on your bench. This week Minor is pitching at Coors Field, and Davis is pitching at San Diego. Owners often want to avoid pitchers at Coors Field, but you've got to look at the numbers. It's all about the value. The *precise* value.

Minor's original projection is shown here. Starting with that, you take a look at his home and road splits if you care to, and you consider how much better the Rockies' hitters are at home. If you want to spend a fair amount of time analyzing this, you can. If you want to keep it pretty simple, you can just make an educated guess, which is what I'm going to do here. Considering Coors is the best hitters' park in the league, I'll estimate that Minor, if he pitched every game at Coors, would do this:

Mike Minor	$ Value	IP	ERA	WHIP	Win	K
Original Projection	13	190	3.90	1.28	11	156
At Coors Field	3.9	175	4.90	1.43	9.5	142

This is by no means precise. I'm just making a guess.

Since San Diego is typically the best pitchers' park in the league, you can make a similar guess for Davis. His ERA and WHIP will undoubtedly be better than normal. Since you expect his $7.2 value to rise, and Minor has been lowered to $3.9, you don't need to bother estimating Davis's exact numbers, because you've already concluded he's the one you're going to start.

Pitchers Never Have 1.23 Starts

Unfortunately, before we can keep it simple, I've got to make it more complex. There's a problem with the Minor analysis. His 190 innings pitched projection is based on a full season, which covers approximately 32 starts. The season is approximately 26 weeks long. This means that about six times a year, Minor will make two starts in a week.

Therefore, his weekly projection should be based on how many starts he has. Fantasy players are usually aware that when a pitcher has two starts in a week, that's a good thing. But they generally forget that when they have only one start, that's a bad thing. On a weekly basis, Minor is never really a $13 pitcher. He never starts 1.23 (32/26) games in a week.

Dividing 190 innings pitched by 32 starts equals 5.94 IP per start. Therefore, for his one-start weeks, you need to multiply by 26 to gauge the true value. That means 154 IP. His wins and strikeouts need to be similarly adjusted to 8.9 wins and 126 strikeouts. This gives him a value of $8.7 when he has one start. For two-start weeks, his raw stats are doubled, but the dollar value is more than doubled:

Mike Minor	$ Value	IP	ERA	WHIP	Win	K
Projection	13	190	3.90	1.28	11	156
1-Start Week	8.7	154	3.90	1.28	8.9	126
2-Start Week	26.7	309	3.90	1.28	17.9	254

To get back to simplicity, the good news is that when you're comparing two pitchers who are both making just one start, you don't need to bother calculating the actual value of just one start. What I did in the example here, adjusting Minor for starting at Coors, is sufficient. If Davis has more value than the adjusted Minor for the full season, then he will have more value than Minor if they are both making just one start (or if they were both making two starts).

However, if you're comparing a one-start pitcher to a two-start pitcher, then you do need to do the calculations. If you have a $12 pitcher making two starts and a $14 pitcher making just one start, then you don't need to even bother. It's obvious the $12 pitcher will be worth more. His value will be more than $12, and the $14 pitcher will be less than $14. But what if you have a $20 pitcher with one start and a $12 pitcher with two starts? That's not so obvious. And what if one of the $12 pitcher's starts is at Coors Field, or one is in San Diego? You'd want to factor that in as well. Whenever a National League team is playing at an American League park, you'd better add something to the ERA and WHIP because of the DH. On the flip side, when an AL pitcher is in a National League park, you can lower the ERA and WHIP expectation.

And finally, you also have the option of comparing a one-start pitcher to a relief pitcher. For this, you may need to calculate the one-start value. If you have Minor pitching at Coors, and you're in a mixed league, you almost certainly have a pitcher worth more than $3.9 on your bench, whether he is a starter or reliever. But what if you're in an NL-only league and you don't have a starter worth $3.9, but you have a reliever worth $2? Then you'd want to make the calculation for Minor:

Mike Minor	$ Value	IP	ERA	WHIP	Win	K
Original projection	13.0	190	3.90	1.28	11.0	156
At Coors Field	3.9	175	4.90	1.43	9.5	142
1-Start at Coors Field	1.4	142	4.90	1.43	7.7	115

A reliever's value is based on a 162-game season, played over approximately 26 weeks. That's an average of 6.25 games per week. So if you want to be even more precise, you can adjust the reliever's value based on how many games he has scheduled.

Hoarding Starting Pitchers

Some fantasy players love to stash starting pitchers on their bench so that they can maximize two-start weeks and capitalize on extra wins and strikeouts. But they are also capitalizing on crappy ERA and WHIP. And they may be wasting valuable bench spots on pitchers who will only start twice a week six times during the year. Let's look at some examples of pitchers who may be stashed on reserve:

Philip Humber	$ Value	IP	ERA	WHIP	Win	K
Projection	1.2	190	4.80	1.45	8.0	123
1-Start Week	−0.5	154	4.80	1.45	6.5	100
2-Start Week	7.4	309	4.80	1.45	13.0	200

Mike Pelfrey	$ Value	IP	ERA	WHIP	Win	K
Projection	–1.1	180	4.70	1.45	9.0	92
1-Start Week	–2.5	146	4.70	1.45	7.3	75
2-Start Week	3.6	292	4.70	1.45	14.6	149

In a mono-league, you'd be likely to have pitchers of the above caliber on reserve. Philip Humber, only worth $1.2, becomes a $7.4 value when starting twice. Even a pitcher worth negative $1.1, Mike Pelfrey, has a positive $3.6 value for two starts. So there is potentially some wisdom in stashing extra starting pitchers on reserve. The key word in that last sentence is *extra*. It makes sense to have a starting pitcher on your bench no matter what. You've got to have a backup because you almost certainly will have someone land on the DL, you may want to bench a pitcher when he's pitching at Coors, etc. If your reserve squad only has four spots, you may only want to have one starting pitcher on the bench. If your reserve squad has six or seven spots, you're more likely to have two starters.

The question is whether it's worth it to load up with an *extra* starter or two. The trade-off is that you are sacrificing having bench depth at other positions. You can say it doesn't matter to lack depth, because you can always pick up someone as a free agent. But the quality may be worse. You're better off controlling some quality players on your bench. If you pass up a $3 bench hitter to get a $1 bench starting pitcher, you're losing value. Also, if you are intent on loading up with starters, you may pass up a $3 reliever to get a $1 starter. It's better to have the $3 reliever available to use whenever the need arises, rather than waiting for those six weeks a year when the $1 starter has two starts. Not to mention that just when you think your $1 starter is due to start twice in a week, he'll get skipped over in the rotation and only get one start. Why? Because the team had an off day and this guy is their fifth-best starter.

There are some leagues that allow twice-a-week or even daily lineup changes. For these leagues, you are losing more by not having depth at all positions. The National Fantasy Baseball Championship, for example, is a mixed league that allows lineup changes twice a week, but only for hitters. This makes your bench hitters more useful, because sometimes they will have a four-game period when some of your starters only have three games. And if someone gets hurt, you can replace him sooner.

For a mixed league, the quality of your reserve pitchers will be greater. For example:

Wade Davis	$ Value	IP	ERA	WHIP	Win	K
Projection	7.2	190	4.40	1.35	10	120
1-Start Week	4.4	154	4.40	1.35	8.1	97
2-Start Week	16.5	309	4.40	1.35	16.2	195

Note that all of these examples show why it's good to use your own value formula. If you don't have your own formula, you can't make all of these adjustments and comparisons. You have to guess.

Also, it's not necessary every week to make a bunch of calculations for your pitchers. After you first draft your team, you can calculate the value of your pitchers for their one- and two-start weeks and record that value so you can reference it whenever you need it.

Overall, I'm not a fan of hoarding starters. I think it's more important to have quality backup hitters, as well as a good reliever on my bench. Some people like to stream pitchers by constantly acquiring and dropping free agents. For example, if Wade Davis is a free agent in your mixed league and has a two-start week coming up, his two-start value of $16.5 is probably better than one of your other options that have a one-start week. If you try every week to acquire a decent free agent who has a good matchup or two starts, it can be effective. The danger is that this strategy can have the effect of essentially costing you a bench spot, as though you were simply stashing an extra pitcher all along, or you may be forced to drop a pitcher who is generally a good value and worth using, with no guarantee you'll be able to reacquire him later.

Things Always Go Wrong

Every time I've won a league, and even both times I won the CDM challenge competing against thousands of other teams, I have marveled at how many things went wrong during the year, and yet I still won. There are always injuries, players who didn't meet my expectations, start vs. bench decisions that backfired, etc.

So when things go wrong, don't panic. All hope is not lost.

CHAPTER 12

Keeper and Dynasty Leagues

Some fantasy leagues are called *redraft leagues* because you play for one year and then it's over. Some leagues—called *keeper leagues*—allow you to keep all or part of your roster from one year to the next. Players who are not kept by their team are put up for auction or draft.

The main difference between a keeper league and a *dynasty league* is that the keeper league usually involves keeping a smaller portion of your players. Dynasty leagues allow you to keep most or all of your players. There are also hybrid leagues that are somewhere in the middle. In short, there's a great variety of rules for various leagues.

Everything else in this book—advice about projecting player stats, making a value formula, auction and draft strategy, and in-season management—applies to keeper leagues. So you should certainly read all of those chapters. This chapter addresses the areas in which a keeper league differs from a redraft league.

Most keeper leagues have a salary associated with each player. Typically, the price you pay at auction becomes the player's salary. Some leagues allow you to keep a player at his current salary for a year or longer. Some leagues require that if you keep a player, his salary automatically is increased by $3, $5, or whatever. Some leagues allow you to sign a player to a long-term contract.

For a draft league, the salary is the round you selected the player. For example, if you took a player in round #9, and you decide to keep him for the following year, you forfeit your ninth-round pick in the next draft. Again, some leagues require an automatic increase, in which case you might have to surrender your eighth-round (or lower) pick. Keeping a player is also referred to as *freezing* a player.

Auction Price Inflation

As you approach the 2014 auction, if you have a player you expect will produce $18 of value in 2014, and his salary—should you keep him—would only be $6, then he would be a good keeper. In general, every team will be keeping good bargains.

Suppose you must keep 10 players and the ones you choose have salaries that add up to $110. That $110 is deducted from your auction budget of $260, so you would go to the 2014 auction with $150 to spend. If we assume a 23-man roster requirement, you would need to buy 13 players.

When you make dollar values for 2014, you're going to follow the same process as usual. You identify the 276 best players for a 12-team league (or 345 for a 15-team league), and set all salaries such that they add up to a total of $3,120 (or $3,900), and the worst hitter and pitcher have a salary of $1.

But the keepers are not available at the auction. Suppose that, like you, everyone else kept $110 worth of salaries. That leaves 12 × $150 = $1,800 total money that can be spent at the auction.

But since everyone is keeping good bargains, the expected value of the kept players may be, for example, $145. This means that $145 × 12 = $1,740 of value is removed from the available player pool.

In a redraft auction, or first year of a keeper league, there is $3,120 to spend for $3,120 of value. But in this case there is $1,800 to spend for only $1,380 of value. This means that the auction prices will be inflated by 1,800/1,380 = 1.30. The average price will be 30% greater than the player's value.

League dynamics vary, but typically the inflation rate is a little higher for the mid- and upper-priced players, and a little lower for the less-expensive players. At the lowest levels there will be little, if any, inflation. (Even with 30% inflation a $1 player is still worth only $1.)

In most leagues you'll have enough advance notice of which players everyone is keeping to calculate the exact inflation rate. But in some you may not know until the auction who everyone is keeping. In that case, you'll need to do your best job estimating in advance. If you examine everyone's roster, some of their keepers will be obvious. Also, it never hurts to ask. If you send someone an email in January asking, "Who are you thinking of keeping?" sometimes people will tell you.

You should also split everything between hitters and pitchers. If the total inflation rate is 30%, it's quite possible the hitters will be 15–25% and the pitchers 35–45%, or vice versa. By knowing the expected inflation in advance, you will be able to prepare for the auction. Everything I've suggested in the auction strategy chapters still applies. Be fully prepared, use others' values to identify targets, plan your max bids in advance, etc. You will still mostly be looking to get discounts, or in some cases be willing to pay full price. It's just that the inflation factor will be added. If a $20 hitter will probably be inflated to a $26 price, then buying him for $23 is a nice discount.

I used 30% inflation as an example. In reality, it can typically be anywhere from 10% to 40%, occasionally even more. The nice thing is that you don't have to guess. You can either know exactly what it will be, or get a good estimate, prior to the auction. How to calculate the inflation rate before your auction is also discussed in chapter 6.

The inflation rate actually changes as each player is bought at an auction. If you expect 20% inflation and the first several players go for more than 20%, then the inflation rate has dropped. The ratio of remaining money to available value is closer. Some people will track the changing inflation rate by hand or even use software. It's not essential to do this, but keeping track can be helpful. The more the prices for the stars are inflated, the better the deals will be later on, and vice versa.

But you need to be careful about this. If you expect hitters to be inflated by 20%, and you pass on hitters being sold for less, then you may end up in a situation where inflation has increased later in the auction and you are forced to pay the full 20% or more. So make a target list and grab good buys as soon as they appear. Let your competition potentially have to overpay later on.

Snake Draft Inflation

When 2012 drafts took place, Mike Trout was not even guaranteed to spend most of the year in the major leagues. In many keeper leagues, he was already owned prior to 2012 because he was a top prospect. In other leagues, he was drafted in 2012, but not in round one. As it turned out, he was called up in 2012 and nearly won the MVP award. He cemented himself as a top first-round pick for 2013. Since all of his owners will be able to keep him at a bargain rate for 2013, this means there is one less first-round-worthy player available.

In any given league, there may be a few more situations like this. Perhaps three or more players who would be a first-round pick in a redraft league won't be available in your keeper league. There may be 12 teams with a first-round pick, but only eight first-round-caliber players available. And the same thing happens for round #2, round #3, etc. This is how inflation occurs for a draft league.

Since everyone has to forfeit a draft pick for each player they keep, eventually it will even out. If 12 teams must each keep ten players, that leaves 276 – 120 = 156 players available for 156 draft picks. So when you get to the lower rounds, you aren't losing much, if anything.

This is actually very similar to what happens in an auction league. But unlike with an auction, you don't need to calculate an inflation rate in order to determine how much to bid and what qualifies as a good discount. As with a normal draft, you will simply rank all non-kept players by their value, and then take whomever you think is the best choice when it's your turn. And you can still use my draft curve, as explained in chapter 9, to account for position differences.

Inflation typically does not apply to a dynasty league, because most players are kept each year, so those available to be drafted are mostly very-low-value players and prospects.

Paying for Future Potential

In the first year of its existence, a keeper-league auction or draft is similar to a redraft league, except that a premium is put on younger players who have a good chance to improve and turn into future stars. Even if a player may only be worth $5 for the upcoming season, if there's a reasonable chance he'll be worth $15 or $20 in a year or two, he's an attractive commodity.

How much you should be willing to spend depends on your league rules, how confident you are he'll get there, and if your goal is to win this year or rebuild for the future. For example, if you think it will take two more years, and your league requires a $4 salary increase each year you keep a player, buying him now for $10 means he'll cost you $18 by the time he's worth $20. That's not a great deal, especially since he may never even realize his potential.

As I've said in other chapters, you need to be prepared. Plan your bidding limits before the auction. You can always adjust on the fly, but for the most part you want to think things through in advance. When the young hotshot players with a lot of future upside are nominated, you don't want to have to make a split-second decision how much they're worth and realize later you made a mistake.

And don't go overboard loading up on prospects. Sure, there are some great prospects out there that should be owned. But often people will speculate on a young player who can't possibly help them for a few years when there are still many good current major leaguers available who would help them right now.

Deciding Your Keepers

When choosing whom to freeze, the obvious consideration is who will produce a lot more value than his salary or draft spot? And you can't go by what he produced last year, but rather what he's likely to produce in the upcoming year (and beyond).

For close calls, one thing to consider is the difference between the expected inflation rate for hitters and pitchers. If the pitchers are expected to have a higher rate, then it would be wise to keep a pitcher over a hitter, because it will cost you more of a premium to buy back the pitching talent.

Some conventional wisdom tells you to consider which positions are likely to have the most frozen players. For example, if a lot of shortstops will be kept, they will suggest you also freeze a shortstop. The logic is that shortstops will be scarce, and the bidding will be intense. I disagree with this. There will be fewer shortstops available, but just as many fewer teams who need a shortstop. So, worst case, you can still get a $1 shortstop at the end for $1, just as in a non-keeper auction. There is no scarcity.

And the same goes for categories. If more sluggers are kept than speedsters, there will be less power available in the auction, but also fewer teams that need power.

When considering signing someone to a long-term contract, not only do you need to guess how much this player will be worth long-term, but also how many other good options you're likely to have down the road.

Estimating the expected inflation rate is a critical factor in determining your keepers. Consider this example:

	Team A	Team B
Kept Salary	$ 45	$190
Expected Value	$ 95	$215

Team A has secured a $50 profit, as opposed to just $25 for Team B. But what will happen at the auction?

	Team A	Team B
$ to Spend	$215	$ 70
Acquired Value	$172	$ 56
Total Team Value	$267	$271

Using 20% inflation, it costs Team A so much to buy back their released talent that Team B ends up better off. Also, I've used 20% inflation for both teams—but since Team A needs to buy several high-value players and Team B does not—the actual rate for Team A might be higher than for Team B. In that case, Team A will be even worse off. Therefore, it's essential to calculate the expected inflation rate—or at least make your best estimate—before you make your final decision on your freeze list.

If the inflation rate is going to be very high, you may want to freeze as much sheer value as possible with any players who have a halfway decent price relative to value. For example:

	Cost	Value	Cost	Value
Frozen Player	$ 2	$ 8	$41	$40
Buy at Auction	$52	$40	$10	$ 8
Total:	$54	$48	$51	$48

In this example, if you freeze your $2 player who's worth $8 and release your $40 player who will cost you $41 to retain, it will cost you so much to buy back the $40 player—or a similar player—that you've spent $54 rather than $51 to reach $48 of value.

Who to Keep in Draft Leagues?

You follow a similar procedure for a draft league in that you try to identify your best bargains. If you have to forfeit a 12th-round pick to freeze someone who would probably be a sixth-round pick, he's a good keeper.

But as with an auction, you must also consider the cost to repurchase a higher-value player. If Miguel Cabrera was your #1 pick in 2013, and you think he'll be one of the top-three most valuable players in all of baseball for 2014, then you may not want to release him, unless you already know that you will have a top-three first-round pick. If you get the fourth selection or worse, you would not be guaranteed to get him back or a similar value.

Overall, you need to try to figure out who is likely to be kept, and what that will mean for you. If you release your #1 or #2 pick, are you confident that you'll be able to draft someone with equal or better value?

And, if not, how much value do you think you'll lose? If you are concerned that by dropping your $35 #1 pick you might get stuck with a $32 replacement, that's a $3 loss.

If your alternative is to release an $18 player when you estimate you'll probably replace him with a $13 player, that's a $5 loss. In this case, you're better off keeping the $18 player.

When making your analysis, remember that due to differences of opinion, you're likely to get a better deal than you think in the middle and later rounds. Someone you think should have gone in round #7 might still be there for you in round #9 or later.

Who to Keep in Dynasty Leagues?

In dynasty leagues there is no cost to keep a player, so all the best players are kept. In some leagues you can keep everyone you want forever. And others do have a limit on how many you keep, but it's still a lot, and therefore you can keep the majority of good players and super prospects. Hence the name dynasty, because you can build a winning team and hang on to it more so than with a keeper league.

Hitting vs. Pitching Breakdown

You might start the first year of an auction keeper league planning to spend $180 on hitting and $80 on pitching. But for the next year, if you're freezing $80 of hitters and $40 of pitchers, then your plan for the auction would be to spend $100/$40. If the perceived bargains of your keeper hitters are better than pitchers, then you might want to shift a bit more to pitching to attain good balance, or vice versa.

Similarly, if the inflation rate is going to be much higher for hitters than for pitchers, or vice versa, you might want to alter the breakdown of how you spend to allow for that.

Contend or Rebuild?

Conventional wisdom states that keeper leagues tend to be cyclical. A team will trade great keepers for overpriced high-value players and will contend for a title, but the next year their list of strong keepers is depleted, so they won't contend and must rebuild. The following year they'll compete, but deplete their keepers and then have to rebuild again.

There is certainly truth to this, but I don't agree with the idea that you can't necessarily compete—or win—more than one year at a time.

If it's July and my team is 30 points out of first place, and I have little reason to expect things will get much better, then I have no problem giving up and trying to make trades that will help me for next year. In fact, to not do so would be foolish.

However, some people will enter the season already having decided that this will be a rebuilding year. It is an advantage to make this decision before your auction or draft, rather than waiting until July or later, because you can tailor your draft to go for young, promising players more than usual.

But I don't want to ever give up until it's absolutely a lost cause. During the off-season, if you're thinking that your team doesn't have a strong keeper list and perhaps should rebuild, the first thing you want to consider is exactly how much of a disadvantage you are at.

You can compare your keeper list to your league mates'—or estimate theirs if you don't know for sure yet. Perhaps you're locking in only $15 value and most everyone else is locking in $50. Being $35 behind everyone else is, in fact, a sizable disadvantage. Unless, perhaps, you're like Team B in the earlier example and everyone else is like Team A, in which case you'll come out of the auction on an equal footing, or perhaps even with an edge.

What if you're behind an average of $15? Or what if there are five teams with better keeper lists than yours, and their advantages on you are $15, $18, $22, $24, and $28?

This is a disadvantage, but one that can be overcome with a good auction and/or a little luck.

As I've explained in other chapters, I always feel that I gain a great edge at an auction or draft. If you have a superior strategy while others are overspending and wasting their money (or draft picks), you can make up that deficit. I would much rather take a shot at making up the deficit than to throw in the towel before the season has even begun.

If it doesn't work out and I am not competing by mid-year, then I can always make the decision to give up and dump a star or two for a good keeper or two. As I just said, this wouldn't be as effective as if I'd planned to rebuild before the auction, but I'd think it was worth a shot. There's a chance it would have worked out and I'd be competing for the title.

One unfortunate thing with a keeper league is that you never know for sure if the league will still be around the next year, or if you will definitely be in it again. Therefore, when in doubt, go for competing now rather than rebuilding.

If you are starting at a disadvantage, besides just trying to have a better auction than everyone else, you can consider gambling on an injury risk or two, provided the price is right. For example if I have Troy Tulowitzki projected for 450 at bats and a value of $28, and I can buy him at a price of $28 (plus reasonable inflation), then it's worth taking a chance. If he actually stays fairly healthy, he could get 550 at bats and produce $35. But if the price isn't reasonable, it's not worth doing.

If you do enter the auction having decided that this is a rebuilding year, besides looking for young hotshot prospects, it's also very helpful to buy a couple of studs. These will make ideal trading chips to pry away good keepers from contenders later in the year. Contenders will want stars, even if they're overpriced. You have to be careful how much you pay for the prospects, because if you pay too much you'll defeat the purpose. However, for the studs, you can pay whatever is necessary to get them. Since you don't care how bad your team is this year, you can afford to overspend and waste money at the auction. And if you already have a stud or two from the prior year, you can also freeze them, even if their salaries aren't good.

You can also speculate on setup men who might have a

chance of running into a closing job, and anyone else you can identify that for some reason has a chance of gaining significantly in value.

Trade Strategy

Chapter 11 discusses trade strategy in depth. For keeper leagues, there's also the phenomenon of the *dump trade*. This is when a non-contender trades a currently very valuable player to a contender for someone who has less current value but projects to be a great keeper. This helps the non-contender rebuild for next year, while the contender hopes the influx of present-day value will put him over the top to win the league.

In a redraft league, when you make a trade you typically want to be getting at least fair value. Since you're measuring all value in terms of the current season, it's easy to estimate if a trade is fair. For a dump trade, mathematicians can give you a complex method to evaluate the future value of a prospect compared to the other player's current value, but really, do we want to hear all that crap?

Even if you understand it, good luck trying to convince your prospective trading partner that his offer isn't fair because of some complex mathematical equation. So it simply comes down to a matter of what do you instinctively think is fair, and more important, what's the best offer you can get?

If you're good at negotiating, that will be helpful. Keep in mind that as the year evolves and the contenders are separated from the pretenders, all of the contenders will be talking to all of the pretenders, so there will be competition for trades.

When you give up a keeper for a star and think he'll put you over the top, the next day one of your rivals might do the same, and now you're not over the top anymore. So if you think this is a year you can win, try to make those trades before other contenders so that you get a jump on them.

Some leagues impose a salary cap on teams, which can limit the amount of dump trading. You can't accumulate too many stars or you'll be over the cap.

Dynasty leagues have no salaries, so there is less opportunity to trade a great prospect for a current star. There is still some opportunity, but not as much.

Winter Trading

Before you consider any off-season trades, start to plan your keeper list. As part of this effort, you'll need to make an early estimate of the inflation factor. If your league allows you to freeze seven players and you have eight great possibilities, there's no need to trade for more. In fact, you could try to trade two good ones for one even better.

If you have fewer than seven good ones, examine your opponents' rosters and see who has excess. Maybe you can trade one of yours for two of hers. Or maybe some of your opponents won't realize that their $40 value with a $40 salary is actually a great keeper because of the expected inflation rate, and they'll be willing to trade him.

If you do this during the winter, you may be able to beat everyone to the punch. Many of your league mates won't be thinking much about their teams until the spring.

Be sure to make an early projection of what you think your players will produce next year. You may love that your $4 pitcher was worth $15, but will he still produce $15 next year or will he regress? If he had a lucky BABIP and other factors suggest he's likely to regress to the $10 level—and your league rules require that you increase his salary to $7 if you keep him—then he may not be such a great keeper after all. But he might make attractive winter trade bait to someone who doesn't consider the regression.

Evaluating Minor Leaguers

In a redraft league, a minor leaguer is useless unless he has a chance to be called up and produce in the major leagues during the current season. But some keeper leagues—and especially dynasty leagues—make minor league players very relevant. Some have a reserve roster with as many as 17 or so spots, while others may have a separate reserve roster specifically for minor leaguers. This means you need to track and roster minor leaguers with good future potential. You may even need to consider college and high school players. A friend of mine once took a member of the Cuban national team in hopes that he would defect.

If your goal is to win now, you may want to select well-known prospects—even if you don't like them as much as some who are less well known—because when it comes to dangling them as trade bait, others in your league will value them more.

National Competitions

It's not feasible to set up keeper leagues to compete against people in other keeper leagues. Thus, in a keeper league you are always only competing against your own league mates; there are no large competitions where you compete against hundreds or thousands of others. One reason is that trading is an integral part of keeper leagues but is not allowed in most national competitions. Another reason is that a keeper league requires more than a one-year commitment.

About
the Author

Larry Schechter began playing fantasy baseball in 1992. In 2002, he won the CDM Sports national salary-cap challenge, defeating 7,500 other teams. In 2005, he beat 6,000 teams to become the first two-time champion ever.

These accomplishments earned Larry invitations to compete in the two most prestigious experts leagues: In 2003, he joined the *USA Today*-sponsored League of Alternative Baseball Reality (LABR), and in 2005, he was invited to play in Tout Wars. He also competed in the Fantasy Sports Trade Association (FSTA) experts league for four years. In all, through the 2013 season,

Larry has managed 22 teams in these leagues and has won nine league championships.

He has also been successful in fantasy football and basketball, currently ranking 14th on the National Fantasy Football Championship (NFFC) career winnings list at $110,700.

Aside from his fantasy sports activities, Larry is the founder and president of a successful financial services company. In 2003, he fulfilled a long-standing goal to perform stand-up comedy. From 2003-2010 he performed at many comedy clubs throughout the Northeast.

Larry lives in Upstate New York with his family. His wife, Joanne, an artist, puts up with his fantasy baseball obsession because it keeps him out of trouble. His son, Jared, age 15, also plays fantasy baseball and football. His daughter Talia, age 18, took an elective course in fantasy baseball in the fifth grade.

Although he is a die-hard Red Sox fan, Larry says that he'll buy a Yankee in a second if it'll help his fantasy team.

You can follow Larry on Twitter @LarrySchechter
www.winningfantasybaseballthebook.com